Trade Unions and Politics

Trade Unions and Politics

A comparative introduction

Andrew J. Taylor

St. Martin's Press   New York

First published in the United States of America in 1989

332.2

Printed in Hong Kong

TL3t

Library of Congress Cataloging-in-Publication Data
Taylor, Andrew, 1954–
    Trade unions and politics : a cooperative introduction ; Andrew J.
Taylor.
        p.   cm.
    Bibliography: p.
    Includes index.
    ISBN 0-312-03172-6
    1. Trade-unions – Political activity.   I. Title.
HD8031.T39   1989
322'.2—dc19   89–5930
                                                                    CIP

KP

For Helena Jayne

Contents

List of Figures and Tables

Figure

Tables

Preface

The purpose of this book is to analyse and compare the role of
trade unions as political actors in liberal-democratic industrial
states: in particular, the United States, Britain, West Germany,
Sweden and Japan. As such, it is not concerned with formal
political institutions (for example, parties, parliaments, executives) so it assumes the reader will have some familiarity with the
political institutions of the societies examined, although institutional
detail has been included where necessary.

The comparative method has both advantages and disadvantages.
The obvious advantage is breadth of study, which permits generalisations across political systems, enabling us to examine how the
same phenomenon is treated in different political systems and
contexts; this approach, however, sacrifices the detail of the
specialised study. My experience of teaching comparative government and politics has caused me to be profoundly sceptical about
its scientific possibilities and suspicious of grand theoretical
frameworks – which often obscure more than they explain, and
sometimes become an end in themselves – but the study of politics
is essentially comparative. I have, therefore, striven to avoid
presenting a potted country-by-country study in favour of a
thematic approach, though most chapters analyse their subject
matter according to country. Such a structure, though complex,
allows the reader to follow the unions' political role in a particular
system, or to pursue a theme across national boundaries. Only the
reader can judge if the book achieves this.

Why write a comparative book on trade unions? The first reason
is that comparative politics has in recent years shifted away from

systemic comparison to sub-system comparison; virtually every political institution has been analysed comparatively but unions remain relatively understudied. There is a vast amount of material on individual states but few attempts to pull this material together in a digestible and convenient form. The second reason is that during the last decade or so unions have enjoyed a very bad press, being blamed for virtually every economic and political ill afflicting the industrial body politic. This might have made for good journalistic copy or political sloganeering but it is poor analysis. Unions are not perfect but they are certainly not the fount of all evil, they are the product of the society in which they are situated, and this book tries to place them in their context.

The central arguments of this book are that unions are inevitably *political*, whether they or politicians like it; that within capitalist industrial states they are relatively *powerless*; and that unions are primarily *reactive* and *defensive* in their political behaviour. As the international post-war economic boom collapsed in the 1970s unions were increasingly seen, to a greater or lesser degree, as a 'problem' about which something 'had to be done'. The purpose of this book is not to apportion blame or responsibility but to show how unions fit into the politics of liberal-democratic capitalism, and what their position is in the structure of political power. Authors, I believe, should always make their biases clear at the very outset; these are mine: unions meet a deep-seated need for collective protection from the operation of the market and, despite their faults and imperfections, unions remain a bulwark of democratic freedoms. No dictatorship of left or right can tolerate free, independent trade unions.

The central concern of comparative politics is the state. This book draws on the experience of five: the United Kingdom, the United States, the Federal Republic of Germany, Sweden and Japan. These five were selected because they represent a sample amenable to comparative analysis and represent a variety of liberal-democratic industrial political systems. The United Kingdom was chosen because of the long history of union political activism in the first industrial state, and because the UK is so often cited as an example of the consequences of excessive trade union power. The United States offers an opportunity to examine unions in a political culture hostile to collective action, but whose fragmented political system enables a well-organised group to achieve political influence. Sweden is interesting because of the ideological and political dominance of Social Democracy in which the unions are allocated a defined position within a corporatist political system. West Germany represents a case mid-way between the USA, the UK and Sweden. Here, an established union movement with a long history of political activism was destroyed and remade and accorded a legitimate role as a social partner in the increasingly conservative new German political system. Finally, Japan. In some ways Japan represents an obvious contrast to the other systems, but in other ways it exemplifies the subordination common to unions in the politics of the advanced capitalist industrial states. There is also considerable ignorance and mis-understanding about Japanese trade unions and industrial relations in the West; perhaps this book will enhance understanding of this complex, perplexing, yet fascinating, political system.

The organisation of the book is straightforward. It is a truism that the present is an extension of the past so Chapter 1 presents a brief overview of the political development of the five union movements in the twentieth century. This is examined through their growth as pressure groups, as electoral actors, and the evolution of their relationship with the state. Each of these is treated in greater detail in subsequent chapters. Chapter 2 explores the relationship between structure, ideology and political be-haviour. It presents basic data on composition and the degree of centralisation in each union movement. The distribution of power in the unions, the nature of union government and internal union politics are considered as external behaviour is, in part, produced by internal politics. This leads to a discussion of the role of national union centres as labour's political spokesgroup. Finally, Chapter 2 examines the impact of voluntarism on union political behaviour and attitudes. Chapter 3 examines the party–union relationship. In particular, why unions attach themselves to a party, the variety of structural, ideological and personal connec-tions and the role played by unions in making party policy. Chapter 4 continues the party-political theme through, first, the unions' role in recruiting the parliamentary elite and the degree of influence enjoyed by the unions over 'their' parliamentary repre-sentatives. This is then widened into an analysis of the voting behaviour of trade union members and, in particular, the impact of partisan dealignment. Chapter 5 considers the unions as interest groups, using variations of corporatism to analyse the different degrees of closeness enjoyed by union movements with their respective states. Chapter 5 concludes by analysing the breakdown of union–government relations in the 1970s. Chapter 6 is concerned with the rise of white-collar trade unionism, public sector trade unionism and the political management of the unions in the 1990s. Chapter 6 critically examines the 'new working class's' supposed consequences for 'traditional' unions as political actors: just how 'different' is the new working class? These chapters are the heart of the book and are concerned essentially with the politics of the 1970s and 1980s. Chapter 7 presents the book's conclusions and offers an analysis of the position of trade unions in the power structure of liberal capitalist industrial states, concluding that the *image* of union power cultivated in the media and by politicians has disguised their basic *powerlessness*.

In the late 1960s and 1970s unions were the target of polemics and a convenient scapegoat for the economic problems of the advanced capitalist economies caused by the destabilisation of the international economic balance created in the 1940s. Subsequent developments and continued economic instability have demonstrated that unions had little responsibility for events; though they are still universally regarded as a problem, it is now possible to begin a reassessment of their role in the political economy. This book is intended to be one small contribution to that process.

ANDREW J. TAYLOR

Acknowledgements

This has been the most difficult book I have ever written, but this has not detracted from my enjoyment of the task. The difficulties have been eased and the enjoyment enhanced by my colleagues at Huddersfield. The research was excellently supported by the Library Staff at Huddersfield Polytechnic and help was provided by the Centre for Japanese Studies library (University of Sheffield). The London Embassies of the United States, Sweden, Japan and the Federal Republic of Germany provided much useful information from their own resources or were able to suggest individuals and organisations to contact, as did the TUC. It would take too long to thank the many individual trade unions in Britain, the USA, Sweden, West Germany and Japan who replied to my requests for information, but without their help the book would have been significantly poorer. Professor Watanuki (Sophia University) provided much useful information on Japanese unions. Steven Kennedy of Macmillan was a patient and encouraging editor. This book draws on my experience teaching my course, 'The Politics of the Advanced Industrial States', and I should like to acknowledge the contribution of my students at Huddersfield who have taken the course since its inception in 1981. I should also like to express my gratitude to my father who over the years has punctured my neat theories about unions and politics.

The author and publishers would like to acknowledge with thanks the International Labour Office for permission to reproduce extracts from *The Yearbook of Labour Statistics 1986*. Copyright © 1986, International Labour Organisation, Geneva.

Every effort has been made to trace all the copyright-holders, but if any have been inadvertently overlooked the publishers will be pleased to make the necessary arrangement at the first opportunity.

Finally, my wife Dawn helped in the writing of this book in many more ways than she knows.

ANDREW J. TAYLOR

List of Abbreviations and Acronyms

ABF	Workers' Educational Association (Sweden)
ACAS	Advisory, Conciliation and Arbritation Service (UK)
ADB	General Federation of Civil Servants (FRG)
ADGB	General German Confederation of Trade Unions
AEU	Amalgamated Engineering Union
AfA	General Federation of Free Employees (FRG)
AFGE	American Federation of Government Employees
AFL	American Federation of Labor
AFSCME	American Federation of State, County and Municipal Employees
AFT	American Federation of Teachers
AMP	Associate Membership Program (US)
AMS	National Labour Market Board (Sweden)
APEX	Professional Executive and Computer Staff (UK)
ASTMS	Association of Scientific, Technical and Managerial Staffs (UK)

BDA	Federation of German Employers' Associations
BDI	Federation of German Industry
CBI	Confederation of British Industry
CDU	Christian Democratic Union (FRG)
CGD	Christian Trade Union Federation (FRG)
Churitsuroren	Federation of Independent Unions of Japan
CIO	Committee (now Congress) of Industrial Organisations (US)
CLP	Constituency Labour Party
CND	Council for National Defense (US)
COHSE	Confederation of Health Service Employees (UK)
COPE	Committee on Political Education (US)
COWPS	Committee on Wages and Prices (US)
CPSA	Civil and Public Servants' Association
CSU	Civil Service Union (UK)
CWA	Communication Workers of America
DAG	Salaried Employees' Union (FRG)
DBB	Civil Service Federation (FRG)
DGB	German Workers' Federation
DNC	Democratic National Committee (US)
Domei	Japan Confederation of Labour
DSP	Democratic Socialist Party (Japan)
ETU, now EETPU	Electrical Trades Union
FDP	Free Democratic Party
FOS	Modified Labour Market Model of Spring 1987 (Sweden)
FPD	Federal Postal Division (US)
FRG	Federal Republic of West Germany
GCE	Federation of Christian Trade Unions (FRG)

GCHQ	Government Communications Headquarters
GDBG	Federation of German Civil Servants
GDP	Gross Domestic Product
GEDAG	Federation of German Salaried Staffs
GMBATU	General Municipal and Boilermakers Allied Trade Unions
HSC	Health and Safety Commission (UK)
ISTC	Steelworkers (UK)
JSP	Japan Socialist Party
Keidanren	Federation of Economic Organisations (Japan)
Koenkai	Personal support organisations (Japan)
Komeito	Clean Government Party (Japan)
Komuin Kyoto	Joint Struggle Council of Government Workers' Unions (Japan)
Korokon	Roundtable Conference for Public Corporations and National Enterprises Labour Problems (Japan)
Korokyo	Council of Public Corporation and National Enterprise Workers' Unions (Japan)
LAC	Labor Advisory Council (US)
LDP	Liberal Democratic Party (Japan)
LKAB	State mining corporation (Sweden)
LLPE	Labor's League for Political Education (UK)
LMSA	Labor-Management Services Administration (US)
LO	Landorganisationen i Sverige, Swedish Trade Union Confederation
LPSL	Local Public Service Law (Japan)
LRC	Labour Representation Committee (UK)
MSC	Manpower Services Commission (UK)

MITI	Ministry of International Trade and Industry (Japan)
NAGE	National Association of Government Employees (US)
NALC	National Association of Letter Carriers (US)
NALGO	National Association of Local Government Officers (UK)
NAM	National Association of Manufacturers (US)
NATGA	National Air Traffic Controllers' Association (US)
NEA	National Education Association (US)
NEC	National Executive Committee, of the Labour Party (UK)
NEDC	National Economic Development Council (UK)
NFFE	National Federation of Federal Employees (US)
NGA	National Graphical Association (UK)
NHS	National Health Service (UK)
Nikkeiren	Federation of Employers' Associations (Japan)
NIRA	National Industry Recovery Act (US)
NLRA	National Labor Relations Act (US)
NLRB	National Labor Relations Board (US)
NPA	National Personnel Authority (Japan)
NPSL	National Public Service Law (Japan)
NTEU	National Treasury Employees' Union (US)
NUM	National Union of Mineworkers (UK)
NUPE	National Union of Public Employees (UK)
NUR	National Union of Railwaymen (UK)
NUT	National Union of Teachers (UK)
NUS	National Union of Seamen (UK)
NWLB	National War Labor Board (US)
OECD	Organisation for Economic Cooperation and Development
OTV	Public Service and Transport Union (FRG)

PAC	Political Action Committee (US)
PATCO	Professional Air Traffic Controllers' Association (US)
PC	Personnel Commission (Japan)
PCNELR	Public Corporation and National Enterprise Labour Relations Law (Japan)
PCNELRC	Public Corporation and National Enterprises Labour Relations Commission (Japan)
PED	Public Employees' Division (US)
PLP	Parliamentary Labour Party (UK)
RCN	Royal College of Nurses
Rengo	Confederation of Public Sector Trade Unions (Japan)
SACO	Sveriges Akademikers Centralorganisationen (Sweden)
SACO–SR	SACO after its merger with the Civil Service Federation (Sweden)
SAF	Svenska Arbetsforeningen, Swedish Employers' Federation
Sanbetsu-Kaigi	Congress of Industrial Labour Organisations (Japan)
Sanrokon	Industry and Labour Roundtable Conference (Japan)
SAP	Svenska Arbeter Partei, Social Democratic Party (Sweden)
SCAP	Supreme Command Allied Powers (Japan)
SCPS	Society of Civil and Public Servants (UK)
SDP	Social Democratic Party (FRG)
Shinsanbetsu	National Federation of Industrial Organisations
Shunto	Spring Labor Offensive (Japan)
SLD	State/Local Division (US)
Sodomei	Japan Labour Federation
SOGAT 82	Society of Graphical and Allied Trades (19)82
Sohyo	General Council of Trade Unions of Japan

TASS	Technical and Supervisory Staffs (UK)
TCO	Tjanstemannens centralorganisationen, Central organisation of salaried workers (Sweden)
TGWU	Transport and General Workers' Union (UK)
TUC	Trades Union Congress (UK)
TUCC	Trade Union Coordinating Committee (UK)
TUFL	Trade Unions for Labour
TULV, now TUFL	Trade Unions for a Labour Victory (UK)
UAW	United Auto Workers
UCW	Union of Communication Workers (UK)
UK	United Kingdom
UMWA	United Mineworkers of America
UPBP	Union Privilege Benefit Programs (US)
US	United States
USDAW	Union of Shop, Distributive and Allied Workers
WCL	War Committee of Labor (US)
Zenmin Rokyo	Japan Private Sector Trade Union Council
Zenro (later Domei)	Japan Confederation of Labour

1

Historical Background and Political Development

The Inevitability of Politics

Trade unions are organisations founded by working people to protect and enhance their working conditions through collective action, notably *collective bargaining* (unions representing the interests of working people to their employers with whom they enter into agreements on their behalf), and *political action* (unions acting as an interest group and/or as an ally of a political party competing for government office so as to influence public policy). Though the antecedents of trade unionism have been traced back to the medieval craft guild, modern trade unionism is a consequence of industrialisation in the late eighteenth and early nineteenth century as a response to the inequalities of social, political and economic power of the emerging industrial society. The ideology of industrial capitalism held that all individuals were politically and economically equal and that labour–management relations should therefore be conducted on an individual basis. In the real world, however, the market's operation meant that the individual worker was at a profound disadvantage when compared to the employer who enjoyed far greater resources with which to impose a 'bargain' on the workforce. The only solution open to the worker was to organise and, thereby, amplify the individual worker's power to the point at which workers could realistically hope to challenge the employer. Trade unions are not alien to the market economy: they were created by it, and out of the workers' everyday experience of its operation.

Unions and their members quickly found that they could not

1

confine their activities to the immediate workplace: workplace issues had an inherent tendency to become political issues. There were two reasons for this. First, unions were regarded by the economic and political elites as a threat, possibly a revoluntionary threat, to the status quo. Unions were inevitably drawn into politics both to convince these elites that they were legitimate organisations and to secure the removal of legal restrictions on their activities. Second, though unions were founded to defend pay and conditions these could not be divorced from wider considerations such as living conditions; also the individual at work could not be protected solely by collective bargaining. The surest way to secure permanent concessions on, for example, safety regulations and hours of work was to persuade government to pass legislation to compel general adherence. As unions expanded and the problems of industrial society multiplied then what constituted the members' interests expanded to embrace the full range of public policy and not simply 'economic' issues. Unions were thus from their inception political organisations and their original purpose – the collective defence of the individual – remains as valid as ever.

The involvement of unions in party politics reflects the growing electoral importance of industrial workers and the emergence of class politics. All the movements examined developed a connection with a party to complement and supplement collective bargaining activities. The connection with a party reflects union perception of their subordinate position in society, but also the conviction that liberal democracy and party competition offers a means whereby that subordination might be modified. Participation in party and electoral politics demonstrates the unions' desire for involvement in the status quo.

In all five political systems a broadly similar path of development was followed: initially unions were suppressed, there then followed grudging acceptance and later, a greater or lesser degree of integration. This developmental process was prompted by the need to win the cooperation of unions in wartime, resolve economic crisis, or act as a counterbalance to the economic and political power of employers. The state has, therefore, played a crucial role in the political development of trade unions – in some, law was instrumental in overcoming obstacles to union growth, in others elites believed governability would be enhanced by union involvement. In all five political systems the purpose of union political activity is to influence the state.

The Political Development of British Trade Unions

Government has always suspected unions, so from their earliest days they have sought to persuade governments that unions were part of society, not its enemy. Throughout the last century unions strove to secure access to the political process; by the end of the century unions had become significant political actors with their own lobby, the *Trade Union Congress* (TUC) (founded in 1868), considerable electoral experience (sixty trade unionists served as MPs between 1874 and 1910), and several were interested in creating their own party.

Party politics has long been central to British unions. Union political attitudes and behaviour were a complex and contradictory amalgam of sectional–occupational and class consciousness, but its rationale was to remedy the defects of collective bargaining. Legislation offered permanence and general applicability, so circumventing the employers' economic power, but the unions were (and for good reasons) ambivalent towards the law. They welcomed legal intervention which extended their rights and immunities, but resented attempts to restrict and control their activities.

In the nineteenth century unions looked to the Liberal Party, but by the 1890s many in the unions claimed that this strategy was obsolete because of the Liberals' unresponsiveness in the face of renewed employer hostility. The solution was, they argued, independent political action; to equate this, however, with socialism was more controversial. The 1899 TUC decision to found the *Labour Representation Committee* (LRC) was a *refinement*, not a significant departure from past practice. The LRC, which became the Labour Party in 1906, was a defensive reaction designed to boost union political influence by creating a reliable parliamentary platform. In return, Labour secured finance, organisation and (potentially) an electoral base.

There was, however, a tension between those who saw the party as primarily a union institution and those who envisaged a wider destiny. The historic compromise of the 1918 Constitution reconciled both: the unions secured a majority of votes at Conference, whilst Clause 4 (the socialist objective) provided a focal point for all factions. The union relationship with the Labour Party is ambiguous. Though the unions were responsible for its emergence, and Labour has regarded itself as the unions' political expression, each has their own role in the polity as party and interest group.

In the 1914–18 war the TUC was accepted as the authoritative representative of the industrial workforce, reflected in the creation of the Ministry of Labour, membership rocketed from 4.1m (1913) to 8.3m (1919), and union demands radicalised. In the 1918 General Election the Labour Party's parliamentary representation increased from 39 to 59, polling 2.4m votes (22.7 per cent of the votes cast); it was clear Labour would supplant the Liberals as the opposition to the Conservatives. The necessities of war which compelled government to court the unions were, however, transient. Industrially, between 1919 and 1927, the movement was in permanent crisis: membership fell by 3m and a series of defeats culminated in the disastrous General Strike (May 1926). The relationship with Labour in government was equally troubled: the minority governments (1924, 1929–31), determined to show their fitness to govern, refused to make any special concessions to the unions, revealing with startling clarity the recurrent divergence between the unions and the Labour government.

The General Strike's defeat provided an opportunity to formulate a new political strategy. Under Walter Citrine (TUC General Secretary) and Ernest Bevin (TGWU General Secretary), the TUC sought an accommodation with the State and Capital, whilst simultaneously promoting Labour. The TUC acknowledged that Party responsiveness in government could not be guaranteed, whilst Labour recognised that the unions had separate interests. This strategy had two elements: first, extending the TUC's role as labour's spokesgroup irrespective of which party was in government; this was conceded by the Conservative dominated governments of the 1930s. Second, responding to Labour's defeat in the 1931 General Election by asserting themselves in the process of reforming the party's electoral appeal. Recognising the consequences of organisational, ideological and political divergence, the TUC and the Labour Party agreed a joint programme to avoid a disaster on the lines of 1931. The policy consensus thus formulated was realised by the 1945–51 Labour governments.

By the end of the decade recovery was underway: TUC membership passed 4m in 1937 (the level of 1927) and in the 1935 General Election Labour polled 37.8 per cent of the vote. If, however, an election had been held in, say, 1940 it is unlikely that Labour would have won; the 1939–45 war was vital for Labour's 1945 victory and the rise of union political influence. The unions' importance was symbolised by Bevin's appointment in 1940 as Minister of Labour, the most powerful figure in the Coalition after Churchill, responsible for organising the war effort. Without union cooperation total war could not be fought; in return for cooperation Bevin was determined to make the unions a permanent influence on government.

Plans for post-war reconstruction (the 1942 Beveridge Report on social services and the 1944 White Paper, *Full Employment*) agreed by the Coalition bore the stamp of the unions, or had their interests in mind. Mass unemployment made the unions into firm supporters of government intervention to secure full employment. By 1944, the TUC was confident that their influence would be maintained in peacetime; the Coalition's declarations indicated that whoever was in government would consult the unions and follow policies broadly in their interests. This remained the elites' governing style until the late 1960s when, after two decades of relative economic decline, government aspired to transform both the unions and their political role.

The Political Development of American Unions

The *American Federation of Labor* (AFL) was formed in 1886. Despite this and rapid industrialisation, unionisation proceeded slowly because of, first, the nature of the labour market. In eastern urban areas, for example, immigration undercut union organisation, whilst westwards expansion ensured a volatile labour market. The AFL, therefore, concentrated on craft workers who were easier to organise than the shifting, amorphous and unskilled masses who were seen as competitors. Not only did this give the AFL an unpleasant racist tinge, it also limited its recruitment. Second, the law hindered union growth. The process of gradual legal acceptance failed to appreciate the ingenuity of American lawyers. The Sherman Act (1890), for example, was a populist anti-big business measure never intended to apply to unions but it was ruthlessly applied to trade unionism.

Many employers clung tenaciously to a fundamentalist capitalism which regarded unions as enemies to be crushed. The *National Association of Manufacturers* (NAM) was established to secure 'the right to manage', individual employers used legal action, blacklists, and company vigilantes, refusing to recognise unions even when a majority of employees were members, and often making employment conditional on renouncing union membership ('the yellow-dog contract'). If these measures failed they could rely on the National Guard or Federal troops. No liberal–democratic political system can rival the United States' sometimes vicious repression of unionism.

Union growth is a twentieth-century phenomenon in which politics played a significant role. The 1914–18 war not only increased membership but gave labour its first significant access to government through the *War Committee of Labor* (WCL) and representation on the *Council for National Defense,* (CND) Labour's new status seemed confirmed by President Wilson's address to the 1917 AFL convention, the first President to address a labour convention, but with the war's end labour's prestige and influence declined. Similar factors explain the 1941–5 growth spurt where, in return for cooperation, Federal government encouraged unionisation and collective bargaining and labour was represented on the tripartite *National War Labor Board* (NWLB). Again, peace brought a diminution of labour's influence, though on nothing like the scale after 1919. By far the most significant growth period is 1931–7; for the first time labour enjoyed a sympathetic political climate and growth was largely dependant on it.

The contemporary labour movement was forged by President Franklin Roosevelt's New Deal. Politically, Roosevelt looked to labour as a countervailing force to a hostile business community and in 1936 unions entered electoral politics in an officially partisan role for the first time. The *Norris–La Guardia Act* (1932) made a number of important changes to the unions' legal position, but of greater importance was section 7(a) of the *National Industrial Recovery Act* (NIRA) (1933), which extended recognition and protection to the right to join a union and bargain collectively. In 1935 the Supreme Court struck down NIRA but Congress passed the even more favourable *National Labor Relations Act* (NLRA)

(1935) – the Wagner Act – which expanded section 7(a) of NIRA into the Federal promotion of collective bargaining, good industrial relations and established the *National Labor Relations Board* (NLRB) to police the system. One year after Roosevelt's crushing victory in the 1936 election the Supreme Court upheld NLRA which, together with subsequent amendments, remains at the heart of the labour relations system.

Up to the 1930s the AFL was officially non-partisan, though it leaned towards the Democrats from 1906 in reaction to the NAM's Republicanism. Between 1906 and 1922 AFL electoral activity was hesitant for though it preferred Democrats it could not publicly endorse the party because of its minority status and because many union members voted Republican; nonetheless by 1912 the AFL supported the Democrats in Presidential elections. Its electoral activity was organised by the Labor Representation Committee, re-named the *Non-Partisan Campaign Committee* in 1920. In 1924, however, faced by a choice between pro-business Republican and Democratic candidates the AFL endorsed Senator La Follette Jr, the Progress Party Candidate, who polled 17 per cent of the vote. This was the AFL's first endorsement as an organisation. In the 1928 the Presidential election it did not endorse the Democrat so whilst the AFL was pro-Democrat it was not yet part of the Democratic coalition. The 1928 election was significant, however, since for the first time ethnic minorities and wage earners switched to the Democrats.

In the light of labour's role in the 1936 elections it is noteworthy that in 1932 the AFL as an organisation maintained a benign neutrality towards the Democrats. A major contribution to this change was the entry into politics of the *Committee* (later *Congress*) *of Industrial Organisations* (CIO), originally an internal AFL organisation, led by John L. Lewis of the Mineworkers. The CIO organised unskilled workers (many from ethnic minorities) in the new mass production industries traditionally ignored by the AFL unions. The CIO found a political champion in Roosevelt, though Roosevelt's pro-labour attitude was not anti-business. The motivation behind his legislation (especially the NLRA) was to boost the workers' consumption via collective bargaining, and to compel business to behave in its own and the country's best interest by cooperating with labour. The New Deal did, nevertheless, establish a powerful bond between organised labour and the Democrats but only after the break with the business community in 1935 did Roosevelt assiduously cultivate the unions.

In 1936 CIO unions formed *Labor's Non-Partisan League* to organise support for the Democrats, but in US labour politics things are seldom as they seem. In 1935 the AFL and CIO split over various doctrinal and personal quarrels, the Non-Partisan Labor League was branded by AFL loyalists as 'communist dominated', whilst in 1940 Lewis (a Republican) refused to endorse Roosevelt, making a nationwide radio broadcast attacking him. He was ignored. In the 1940 and 1944 elections the AFL remained aloof, though union leaders made it plain where their sympathies lay, and labour's Democratic connection was sealed by the CIO's *Political Action Committee* (PAC) (1943) set up in reaction to the 1943 Smith–Connally Act, which curbed the right to strike. PAC gave labour both a nationwide and local campaigning ability and, for the first time, a major say in policy and candidate selection.

Beginning with the Smith–Connally Act and culminating with the 1947 Taft–Hartley Act, which *inter alia* balanced the Wagner Act's unfair management practices with unfair labour practices, opinion shifted against the unions. Much of the unrest of this period was believed to be communist inspired (communists were prominent in several CIO unions) and unions came under massive pressure to purge themselves, which they did in November 1946. The Truman Presidency was therefore crucial for the political development of the American unions. The Taft–Hartley Act was passed by a Republican-dominated Congress against the veto of President Truman. The Act revealed the political weakness of organised labour, the ease with which Taft–Hartley passed Congress came as a great shock to the AFL, which formed *Labor's League for Political Education* (LLPE), similar to the CIO's PAC. Politically there was now little difference between the two and both campaigned for the Democrats in the 1948 elections.

Though the AFL was always the larger, union political influence was undoubtedly weakened by the AFL–CIO split, but despite their antipathy they cooperated in the war effort and converged politically. The death of Philip Murray (CIO President) and William Green (AFL President) in 1952, enabled their replacements, Walter Reuther (Auto Workers–CIO) and George Meany (Plumbers–AFL) to begin merger negotiations, which was achieved in 1955. One of the first fruits was the creation of the *Committee on Political Education* (COPE) from the LLPE and PAC. Labour now had a united voice, symbolised by George Meany, and what was regarded as the best lobbying machine in Washington. However, visibility and organisation did not guarantee political influence.

The Political Development of Swedish Unions

From the 1870s unions were closely entwined with the *Social Democratic Party* (Svenska Arbeter Partei – SAP), founded in 1889. In the 1890s the SAP actively promoted unionisation, helping to form the *Landorganisationen i Sverige* (Swedish Trade Union Confederation – LO) in 1898. The LO did not affiliate to the SAP: the original LO constitution did stipulate this, but it was abandoned after union protest.

As in Britian, nineteenth-century Swedish politics were dominated by the franchise question as industrialisation created a working class demanding a role in the political process. The SAP, though originally marxist, quickly abandoned revolution in favour of organising powerful unions and securing the vote to provide a base peacefully to transform Sweden. This strategy – revolutionary ends by reformist means – together with a willingness to work with other parties, characterised the labour movement's development. Rapid union growth, however, encouraged a belief that industrial action could force political change, resulting in general strikes (1902 and 1909) in support of electoral reform (male suffrage was conceded in 1907). The LO did not recover from the 1909 defeat until the 1920s and this forced the LO further down the parliamentary path.

The SAP's political development was deeply influenced by its relationship with the unions, and vice-versa. Union stress on economic issues and the need to win the vote encouraged the SAP to see the unions as the only counterweight to the power of the ruling class. From this developed a common ideology and strategy based on the winning of political power through elections and using it to better the position of the working class.

The first thirty years of this century were ones of deep class bitterness as the ruling elites strove against democratisation, and

the *Svenska Arbetsforeningen* (Swedish Employers' Federation –
SAF, founded in 1902) struggled to impose 'freedom of labour'
and 'the right to manage' on the LO. In resisting, the LO and SAP
were pulled closer together. Electoral reform quadrupled SAP
representation in the Riksdag (Parliament) and by 1914 the unions
were small but securely established. The strains of the 1914–18
war resulted in SAP members entering government for the first
time (1917), where they used their position and wartime unrest to
secure universal suffrage and the eight hour day. The 1920s were,
however, years of retreat because of recession. Unemployment
increased vulnerability to SAF attack; ideologically SAP had no
response to recession, and electoral gains were halted by lack of
support in the rural areas. The movement's political fortunes
revived after 1928: SAP policy changed to using public spending to
boost demand to achieve full employment and it secured an
electoral pact with the Agrarian Party. This gave the SAP office in
1932, and in 1936 they formed their first majority government,
remaining in office until 1976.

The LO's role in sustaining the SAP was vital, and this
sustenance was not only electoral. Constant industrial strife,
disliked by many Swedes, led to the creation of the *National
Labour Court* (1928) to supervise legally binding collective
agreements, a development bitterly opposed by the LO. However,
industrial strife affected the SAP's electoral popularity so the LO
was persuaded to accept the Act and use it to improve its image.
After 1932 the LO used its authority to forbid individual union
actions which might threaten the government's employment
policies or its survival. Between 1920 and 1932 Sweden had nine
governments, and the LO's behaviour and the SAP's policies
secured political stability.

Despite the SAF's anti-LO stance and suspicion of Social
Democracy an accommodation was reached. The first was the
December Compromise (1906) which established managerial
supremacy but recognised the LO's legitimacy in collective
bargaining. Constant industrial unrest was costly, whilst successive
franchise reforms pointed to the ultimate political supremacy of
the working class. These provided the stimuli for compromise and
the 1928 Act laid the foundation. Initially both the LO and SAF
regarded it as a gross infringement of their rights but they also
recognised the public frustration which provoked it. They there-

fore accepted it fearing the alternative: state regulation. The final stimulus were the Adalen disturbances (1931) when troops shot five striking timber workers, symbolising the futility of confrontational labour politics. After 1932 the LO and SAF, prodded by the Social Democratic government, moved towards an accord and negotiations began in 1936 for the *Basic Agreement* signed at Saltsjobaden in 1938 which encapsulated the spirit of compromise and provided a major foundation for Swedish political stability.

The 1930s saw the beginning of a separation of economic from political power, something fundamental to the 'Swedish Model'. SAP–LO hegemony was not based on nationalising industry but on the use of state power won in free competitive elections to counterbalance private economic power. In this way SAP government sought to satisfy the basic interests of workers and employers within a national consensus of full employment and high profits. Social Democratic dominance was secured and a consensus between labour and capital was reached, but the movement's dominance should not be overstated. Between 1932 and 1976 the SAP often depended on the support of minority parties in the Riksdag, for six years there was a wartime coalition, and for three years the SAP and the opposition parties had equal numbers of MPs. Beneath the surface, as the 1970s showed, lurked many of the old instabilities.

The Political Development of German Unions

The authoritarianism of German politics before and after 1871 meant that trade unionism and socialism were regarded with great hostility. The working class movement was, however, fragmented: the prominence of Social Democracy fuelled the formation of non-political, liberal and christian unions. As industrialisation accelerated Bismark attempted to eradicate autonomous working class politics by 'state socialism'; though not directed explicitly at the unions they nevertheless suffered. Repression and state socialism, however, failed to wean the working class from Social Democracy. In 1878 the *Sozialdemokratische Partei Deutschlands* (SPD) polled 444 000 votes (7.6 per cent) and in 1890 1.41m (20 per cent); the anti-socialist laws not only failed but were counter-productive and repeal of the anti-socialist laws led to an upsurge in industrial action and the formation of the *General Commission* as a national centre. Unions began to concentrate: by the 1890s 60 per cent of members were concentrated in five federations (metal working, construction, transport, wood, and textiles). After recession in the 1890s growth continued between 1907 and 1913 membership of the *Free Trade Unions* grew by 652 000, total membership by 1 273 000, and collective bargaining expanded. In 1907 there were 5324 agreements covering 11 550 enterprises employing 900 000; by 1913 this had increased to 2m workers. There were major strikes in, for example, textiles (1903–4), mining (1905) and construction (1910). These developments indicate the growing confidence and stability of the unions: between 1900–14 the number of full-time union officers rose from 269 to 2867 whilst the General Commission in Berlin employed 34 paid officials.

In the 1880s the SPD had been the dominant partner but by the 1890s the balance between the party and unions was shifting. The SPD's electoral growth owed much to the Free Trade Unions' efforts who after 1890 increased their electoral role. By 1906 the Free Trade Unions had five times the membership of the party but had not expanded into large scale manufacturing industry. Union leaders believed this could be achieved by cooperating with the employers and the state, and gradually they distanced themselves from the marxist SPD to attract non-SPD members into union membership. This had serious implications for the SPD.

Friedrich Ebert, appointed party secretary in 1906, was determined to maintain the union link and increase the SPD's electoral attractiveness by promoting reformism. This involved conflict with those who adhered to revolution and opposed working within the existing political system. Unions, slowly winning employer acceptance, argued that political militancy would invite state retaliation, and scare away potential voters and members. Furthermore, unions resisted any suggestion their activities be subordinated to the party. Before the Mannheim Congress (1906) the SPD and Free Trade Union leaders united to crush the radicals achieved by extending to the unions parity in decisions affecting the working class. Elite opinion remained hostile: the SPD's electoral advance in 1912 (polling 34.8 per cent of the vote compared to 29.0 per cent in 1907) and the strikes of that year were seen as proof positive of working class 'revolutionary' intent.

In 1914 a labour truce was declared but the old conflicts soon re-emerged. The ruling elites were forced to concede full organising rights (1916) and consult the unions as well as employers; the war also promoted inter-federation cooperation. The General Commission continued to support the war despite growing war weariness to avoid repression and to claim a place in the post-war reconstruction process. As Germany collapsed further concessions were made, culminating in the establishment of parliamentary democracy in 1918.

Collapse brought the SPD into government for the first time; major gains were made but Germany, afflicted by massive economic and political turmoil, entered the extended crisis of the Weimar Republic. Attempts to reconcile management and unions failed but Article 165 of the Constitution established a Federal Economic Council with employer and employee representation. This had the power to vet economic and social legislation but it never had parity with the Reichstag, and by the end of the 1920s had degenerated into a talking-shop. The unions strove to make the Republic and parliamentary democracy work, and whilst they and the SPD were committed to social change as a long-term goal they did not pursue this for fear of jeopardising the Republic, failing to affect significantly the development of post-Imperial Germany. Conservative elements regrouped and emerged into Weimar politics and the party system fragmented: in 1919 the SPD polled 45.5 per cent of the vote, in 1933 only 18.3 per cent; the Communists polled 2.1 per cent in 1920 and 12.3 per cent in 1933; whilst the Nazis vote rose from 6.5 per cent in 1924 to 43.9 per cent in 1930.

The Weimar unions fragmented on ideological, occupational and confessional lines. The *General German Confederation of Trade Unions* (ADGB) – the pre-1914 Free Unions – was the largest. Individual unions retained their autonomy with the ADGB acting as their political representative. Officially non-partisan, it enjoyed close links with the SPD. The *General Federation of Civil Servants* (ADB) was a pro-SPD–ADGB white-collar federation; the *General Federation of Free Employees* (AfA) organised white-collar workers and civil servants hostile to socialism and was deeply suspicious of the ADGB. Despite their mutual hostilities the ADGB, AfA and ADB did co-operate industrially after 1923 whilst maintaining their political autonomy. The second major group was the *Federation of Christian Trade*

Unions (GCE), the *Federation of German Salaried Staffs* (GEDAG) and the *Federation of German Civil Servants* (GDBG) who cooperated in the *German Workers' Federation* (DGB). This was politically non-partisan and promoted class collaboration. The communists wielded considerable influence inside many unions, and after 1924 began to build their own. The communists were expelled from the ADGB which they branded (as they did the SPD) 'social fascist'.

This fragmented union movement was in no position to resist the Nazis. Fearing civil war and a conservative reaction it did nothing, surrendering the political initiative to the bitterest foe of trade unionism. After the seizure of power the unions and the SPD were dissolved and the long nightmare of National Socialism began.

The Political Development of Japanese Unions

Before 1945 unions were of little significance in Japanese politics. Industrialisation, though necessary for the regime's nationalist aspirations, encouraged the break-up of traditional social bonds and the early unions were suppressed by the *Public Police Act* (1900). However, as industry grew, so did the working class and its discontents, trends accelerated by the 1914–18 war. Unrest led to the formation of the *Trade Union League* (in 1920 it had 100 000 members) and, after 1917, a communist party. The rise of mass politics was reflected in demands for the vote: in 1890 1.13 per cent of the population had the vote, and though the franchise was extended (1902–1920) it remained based on property qualifications. In 1928 the vote was given to all men over the age of 25, the high point of relative liberalism known as Taisho Democracy. *Sodomei* (Japan Labour Federation) was founded in 1921 with 100 000 members in 300 unions; by 1931 it embraced 818 unions, and in 1936 1000 unions and 420 000 members.

Unions were small and fragmented, based on the enterprise not the industry and the union movement was dominated by the seamen and railway workers. Private manufacturing, especially big industry, was largely unorganised. In 1936 there were about 6.5m industrial workers; of these, 3m were in enterprises employing five or less workers. Two-fifths of industrial workers in large-scale industry were young girls from rural areas employed in textiles, living in factory dormitories under a paternalist regime, an environment profoundly inimicable to unionisation. This liberal interlude was ended by economic crisis. The state responded with repression: in 1932 alone 8000 people were arrested on 'suspicion of being communists'. Fragmented unions were incapable of resisting the rise of militarism, many union members supporting the goals of Japanese nationalism. Nevertheless, the foundation of post-war labour–management relations were laid in the inter-war years. Three factors were especially significant: the company centred ideology, labour flexibility, and government's willingness to leave labour market policy to employers. Such a system created a division between those who worked for the largest companies which could afford the lifetime employment system and the vastly larger number employed in smaller enterprises. Unions were based on the individual enterprise, a structure which inhibited the development of industrial or national general unions. By the 1920s half of the unionised workforce were members of enterprise unions and whilst the lifetime employment system was not universal it was a significant development.

So by the 1930s a union movement existed, albeit a modest one. Union density was only about 6 per cent and there were a number of crucial imbalances – relatively few were members of industrial unions, only 10 per cent of workers were unionised in large companies, but the public sector was better organised (71 per cent compared to 25 per cent in private industry), and collective agreements were few. In 1936 there were a mere 121 collective agreements and of the 136 000 workers covered, 114 000 were seamen. Unions were also unstable, two-thirds of those in existence in 1923 had disappeared by 1929. In July 1940 all non-state sponsored unions, whatever their political loyalties, were dissolved and replaced by *Sangyo-Hokoku* (Service to the State through Industry).

On 22nd September 1945 the *Supreme Command Allied Powers* (SCAP) ordered the promotion of trade unionism. Three statutes were passed: the *Trade Union Law* (1945), the *Labour Relations Adjustment Act* (1946), and the *Labour Standards Law* (1947). These acts were modelled on US labour law and show the strong influence in SCAP of New Deal sentiments about the role of unions in the polity. There was an upsurge in unionisation as a result of the collapse of the Imperial regime, and of these statutes. In December 1945 there were 509 unions, by June 1949 this increased by 34 179 to 34 688, membership grew from 381 000 to 6 655 000, and density increased from 3.2 per cent to 55.8 per cent, though density fell back dramatically in the 1950s.

SCAP became increasingly ambivalent towards unions. Originally promoted as a buttress for liberal democracy, unions were increasingly perceived as a threat to liberal democracy. This was a period of massive labour unrest caused not only by post-war economic dislocation but by politically motivated strikes in which communists were prominent. SCAP acted decisively. In 1946 a demonstration of 70 000 union members was broken up by American tanks, a general strike called for February 1947 was banned and in July 1948 the collective bargaining and trade union rights of 1m public service workers were withdrawn. The SCAP-imposed Dodge Stabilisation Plan encouraged managerial assertiveness, the Socialists were forced out of the coalition government and in 1949–50 there was a purge of communists in the unions *(Sanbestu-Kaigi* – Congress of Industrial Labour Organisations was communist affiliated, Sodomei was social democratic). Inside the unions Democratisation Leagues were established and the movement split producing Sohyo (originally opposed to the left), a tendency which continued throughout the 1950s. The political exclusion of the unions and their party-political allies was completed by the emergence of the *Liberal Democratic Party* (LDP) in 1955 from the unification of several parties and party factions.

Once managerial authority was established a modified enterprise union system and lifetime employment was promoted to contain working class demands. Recognising their weakness the unions began to cooperate industrially in *Shunto* (the Spring Labor Offensive) after 1955, though politically they remained divided. Whilst the employers and their allies seemed triumphant, reality was more complex. The post-war unrest convinced them of the need for consensus, especially in the economically critical very large export oriented corporations. The public sector remained characterised by a high level of political and industrial militancy. The industrial–political system which emerged accomplished this, but the economic crisis of the 1970s revealed the recurrent tensions in the Japanese political economy obscured by these developments.

Conclusions

During the course of this century unions became prominent, and in some cases significant, elements in liberal-democratic politics. For British and American unions it was the demands of total war and the growing electoral power of organised labour which secured access to the political process, in Sweden the political dominance of Social Democracy led to their integration, whilst in the case of Germany and Japan it was dictatorship, defeat in war, and the imposition of liberal democracy which (in the former) prompted the recreation of a once powerful union movement, and in the latter created a modern labour movement. By 1950, unions were prominent political actors in all five systems.

Prominence, however, was not equivalent to power. In Japan unions, though vocal, were marginal participants in the policy process, in the United States the high point of union influence also marked the beginning a long decline. In both Britain and West Germany unions speedily found there were limits on union political influence, and in Sweden unions accepted a national consensus which compelled them significantly to modify their policies. This common experience raises important questions about the unions' subordinate position in the political process.

Political strategies originally intended to expand union influence became mechanisms for circumscribing influence. Participation in electoral politics and the policy process was for limited purposes and was defensive. Forging links with a party and the state to benefit their members meant union involvement in a political exchange whereby government concessions were granted in return for union concessions. This became a norm to which unions excluded from the political process aspired. Brokerage made unions into *de facto* supporters of the status quo, whatever their complaints about specific policies. This is not to deny that unions gained nothing from participation; the gains made were, however, fragile. Nowhere were unions able to entrench themselves in the policy process so as to prevent, when the recession of the mid-1970s occurred, major assaults on what they considered to be their vital interests and, in some political sysems, the rolling back of union influence in the political system.

2

Structure, Politics and Ideology

Chapter 2 examines, first, the organisation and structure of the union movements in the five countries considered, and explores the relationship between structure and political influence. Second, what is the nature of union government and, in particular, the extent of oligarchy? Third, what is the role of the national centres in their respective political systems. Finally, is there a union ideology which underpins political behaviour? This chapter's hypothesis is that a centralised union movement composed of few industrial unions with a collectivist ethos enjoying a high density of membership will be more influential than a decentralised movement with many unions and a low density of membership.[1] This hypothesis can be expressed diagramatically (see Figure 2.1 and Table 2.1).

Figure 2.1

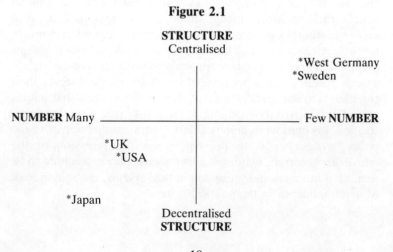

STRUCTURE
Centralised

*West Germany
*Sweden

NUMBER Many ————————————— Few **NUMBER**

*UK
*USA

*Japan

Decentralised
STRUCTURE

18

Table 2.1 *Political influence, ranking by characteristics*

Fewest unions	Most centralised	Most political influence
West Germany	Sweden	Sweden
Sweden	West Germany	West Germany
USA	USA	USA
UK	UK	UK
Japan	Japan	Japan

Trade Union Structure and Political Influence

Traditionally unions are analysed according to the types of workers they recruit (for example blue-collar–white-collar, or skilled–unskilled–semi-skilled), or according to whether they recruit all workers in a single industry (industrial unions) or across industrial boundaries (general unions). Such classifications tell us little about their political influence, and some unions movements do not fit these neat categories at all.

Of the five systems, Japan undoubtedly has the most complicated structure. In 1983 there were 12 520 000 union members out of a workforce of 57m (a density of 29.7 per cent) organised in 74 486 unions. This is the consequence of *enterprise unionism*, whereby each enterprise has its own union organising blue- and white-collar workers, though they do cooperate. These are not *branches* or company unions, but independent unions in their own right. Membership is commonest in large private companies and the public sector, 56.5 per cent of union members are employed in companies with 1000 plus employees and the millions who work in the myriad of small companies which supply them are seldom union members. The two largest unions are in the public sector and account for 10.2 per cent of membership. There are 720 craft unions with a mere 169 000 members, 1775 industrial unions with 682 000 members and 1501 with 259 000 members which do not fit any category. Sohyo (see p. 34), the dominant union centre, promotes industrial unions with little success but separate blue- and white-collar unions are rare, unionisation is confined to about 30 per cent of the workforce, is fragmented politically and is skewed towards the public sector.

Though the United States and the United Kingdom have far fewer unions there is a multiplicity of types (blue- and white-collar, manufacturing and service, and public and private sector) but there is a trend towards general unions. The twenty largest TUC unions account for 79.3 per cent of total UK union membership and 82.9 per cent of the TUC's members, which itself accounts for 95.7 per cent of total union membership. Density is about 40 per cent. The TUC has called frequently for the reduction of multi-unionism and the extension of industrial unionism but this is unrealistic. The tendency in both public and private sector is towards *super-unions* embracing blue- and white-collar unions from a variety of industries. Excluding Canadian members American unions have about 20m members, the bulk in AFL–CIO affiliated unions. After spectacular growth in the late 1930s, 1940s and early 1950s membership stagnated despite gains in the public sector, and density declined from 35 per cent (1954) to 19 per cent (1985). There are blue- and white-collar unions but no white-collar union centre. The twenty biggest AFL–CIO unions have 73.1 per cent of total AFL-CIO membership, and 34 per cent of the 92 affiliates have 100 000 plus members. The AFL-CIO has since its founding in 1955 promoted mergers, though it does not advocate any model.

In Sweden, membership and density are very high, but Sweden has separate blue- and white-collar federations. The largest is the LO with 24 industrial unions and a total membership of 2m embracing 90 per cent of blue-collar workers. The white collar *Tjanstemannens centralorganisationen* (TCO – Central Organisation of Salaried Workers) has a membership of 1.1m, covering some 75 per cent of the non-manual workers. The *Sveriges Akademikers Centralorganisationen* (SACO) founded in 1947 for graduates merged in 1974 with the Civil Service Federation to form *SACO–SR*. The occupational differences between the LO and TCO are blurring as industrial structures change and there is very little difference between the LO and TCO philosophies.

In West Germany, the union movement is dominated by the DGB and the DGB by IG Metall (a general manufacturing union) with one-third of the DGB's membership. All DGB unions are industrial unions and the DGB embraces 83 per cent of total union membership in the Federal Republic. There are several minor federations: the *Civil Service Federation* (DBB) 820 000 members, the *Salaried Employees' Union* (DAG) 480 000 members, and the *Christian Trade Union Federation* (CGD) 245 000 members. Of the DGB's unions three have 50 000 members or less, two have over 1m which together embrace 48 per cent of the DGB's total membership. Each DGB union has both blue- and white-collar members and, where appropriate, civil servants.

Union political ineffectiveness would thus seem to be maximised in Japan: multiple levels of organisation (enterprise, region, industry, and national) with authority concentrated at the lowest level. However, the system of company consultation and the annual wage bargaining round (Shunto) have given some unions, especially those in the very large, export oriented manufacturing companies, a voice in government. The image of tranquillity and cooperation in Japanese industrial politics should not disguise the fact that trustful labour–management relations were assiduously fostered by those involved. Economic difficulties in the 1970s and 1980s boosted the political influence of the unions, encouraging 'labour front unification'. Decentralisation is not, therefore, an insuperable obstacle.

The American labour market would appear to ensure decentralisation. However, there is a single union centre which has considerable authority in non-collective bargaining issues, especially politics. The situation in the UK is comparable, though the TUC has less authority than the AFL–CIO, a weakness with important political consequences. It was the inability of the TUC to impose 'order' in industrial relations which fuelled demands for the legislative reform of the unions. In the United States the AFL–CIO has never aspired to a role greater than that of coordinator and, in any case, the fragmentation of the collective bargaining and political systems and the industrial–political culture prevent it taking on such a role.

In Sweden and West Germany centralisation was both a response to major threats to the unions' existence and a means for securing participation in the political system. West German unions were moulded by the failure to resist the rise of Naziism, and destruction allowed a fresh start. The DGB's founders believed that a few centralised industrial unions would be more influential in collective bargaining and politics; as such, they were a buttress of the new democracy. DGB statutes were so drawn as to make it practically impossible for new unions to emerge, so inhibiting the movement's fragmentation. DGB influence over its affiliates is considerable but not total.

Faced by assaults from the SAF in the early years of this century centralisation became a matter of survival for the LO. The adoption of industrial unionism (1912), the modification of LO statutes (1935) and the 1941 constitution all increased the influence of the centre over the individual unions, a tendency increased by the growth of centralised wage bargaining under SAP governments. For political reasons the SAP encouraged the growth of centralisation in collective bargaining. Though independent the unions are aware of their collective strength and the LO emphasises inter-union cooperation at all levels for political and industrial purposes. There would thus seem to be a strong relationship between structure and political influence in that industrial unions offer the best prospect for political influence. But what factors determine union behaviour?

Union Government, Oligarchy and Political Behaviour

The Dilemmas of Union Government

The union movements examined are 'representative democracies', with elected officials, open and competitive elections, regular congresses to determine policy, with the membership as the ultimate source of authority and legitimacy. This does not prevent factionalism, corruption, anti-democratic practices, oligarchy and many other organisational maladies.[2] In common with all organisations, unions can be dominated easily by the organised minority and the professional leadership stratum who, by definition, are not 'representative' of the mass membership. However, union leaders must ultimately conform to the expectations of the membership; political involvement is particularly sensitive, union support for a political object in opposition to the views of the members can result in serious internal unrest and, ultimately, schism.[3] This can be seen in an extreme form in Japan where dissidents organise second unions, the main loser being Sohyo which is often accused of 'playing too much with politics in the way communists do, thus forgetting the well-being of rank-and-file members'.[4] It is a foolish union leader who fails to recognise that his power is only as great as the solidarity and support of the members.

The basic principle of union government is *membership primacy*.

The mass of the membership elect representatives or delegates to national conferences and conventions responsible for policy. National leaders and full-time officials are deemed to be the servants of the membership. The second principle is *assembly sovereignty*. The supreme policy-making body is a regular conference which determines policies put to it in the form of resolutions which, if adopted, can, theoretically, only be changed by conference. The third principle is *executive management*. Unions are too complex to be run according to mass democracy, they require a specialist bureaucratic stratum, the *de facto* union government, to direct their activities.

The tension between *democratic* and *executive* principles generates many problems. First, mass democracy is a myth. Participation, especially at the grassroots, is generally low and structures become controlled by a minority whose interests are not necessarily coterminous with the membership. Second, the complexity of a union's activities means that those intimate with them have a considerable advantage – the membership come to rely on, and defer to, their expertise. The danger as happened in some US unions, is that the leadership perceive the union to be their personal fief and the membership a threat.[5] Union government is about finding a balance between effectiveness and responsiveness; this is not easy and union leaders are frequently charged with being autocratic and ineffective.

1. Union government in centralised movements: Sweden and West Germany

Is oligarchy more likely in centralised movements? In West Germany considerable effort has, for obvious reasons, been made to make the unions democratic and effective. The DGB has three levels: *DGB-Circles* follow the structure of local government within which *District Councils* can be established to group all DGB members from all affiliated unions. At factory level workers have two organisations: the *Betriebsrat* (Works Council) and the *Vertrauensleutekörper* (shop stewards). Works Councils, established by law, represent *all workers, union members or not*, though in elections unions play an important role. Only union members can participate in shop steward elections and they are concerned solely with union matters; as such, they have no legal status. The nine DGB *Regions* correspond to the *Länder* (States) of the Federal Republic and act as regional coordinator and political lobbyist.

The Federal Congress meets every four years, composed of delegates from the affiliated unions. Members of the Executive Board, Executive Council and Auditing Committee, the regional presidents and three representatives from special groups (salaried staff, manual workers, civil servants, women and youth) attend as observers. Congress determines DGB policy and elects the Executive which is responsible for the DGB between congresses. It has 135 members: 26 from the Executive, the 9 regional presidents, and 100 union delegates and meets four times a year. The Executive Board monitors DGB activity and policy, it is also responsible for expulsions and new affiliates. The Federal Executive Board is composed of the presidents of the 17 affiliates, the DGB President, two vice-presidents and 6 elected officials. It functions via 9 departments with 22 sub-departments, meets monthly and is responsible for implementing policy, monitoring compliance with DGB statutes and policy, and promoting cooperation and coordination. The DGB also maintains a liaison office in the Federal Capital (Bonn) and at the Federal Legal Office in Kassel. The structure of individual affiliates follows this general pattern.

Membership sovereignty and executive management are regarded as vital for effective and responsible trade unionism supportive of liberal democracy. Pluralism, it is claimed, is enshrined by the unions who combine 'historical traditions, political orientation and intellectual leanings within the labour movement . . . The internal war of viewpoints within organised labour commits the movement to an autonomous and independent formation of opinion on the basis of mutual tolerance – a consensus that represents the common interests of working people'.[6]

Generally leaders have been responsive, but their autonomy is considerable. *Einheitgewerkschaft* (unitary trade unionism) and *Industriegewerkschaft* (industrial unionism) have increased the leadership's influence over the membership. West German union government is designed to boost central control whilst achieving a balance between democracy and oligarchy; this requires a highly skilled union leadership. The history of German unionism means that many union leaders tend not to recognise oligarchy as a 'problem', often projecting it as an advantage, conferring skill and knowledge and so promoting organisational effectiveness. In general, their members have agreed with them.

Swedish unions follow a common organisational model: at the workplace is the union club, section or a liaison officer. Above these are the branches which have been progressively merged so most are quite large organisations with their own full-time staff enabling workplace representatives to concentrate on basic union activity; but it also allows the tranfer of functions up the union hierarchy. Nationally unions have an executive and a larger union council elected by the congress; most meet every four years. Unions also have a specialised collective bargaining council made up of elected lay representatives to advise union leaders.

The LO's highest decision-maker is the Congress made up of 300 delegates (elected by the affiliates on the basis of their individual membership), the General Council and the Executive Council. The General Council, responsible for the LO between Congresses, meets only twice a year and is large: about 130 plus the Executive which is the real centre. Meeting fortnightly, it has 15 members elected by Congress plus the LO President (who acts as a general secretary), the Vice-President, Secretary and Negotiations Secretary. The remaining members are usually union presidents. LO activities are conducted through 11 departments: the Steering Committee (this services the Executive), and Redistribution Policy Department, Economic Policy, Labour Relations, Social Policy, Education, Information, International, Finance, Administration and Auditing. These employ about 250 people, and 200 work for the LO education service.

Centralisation has, at times, evoked a hostile response. The *LKAB Strike* (LKAB, the state mining corporation), for example, of December 1969–February 1970 involved 5000 ore miners striking against union bureaucracy, rather than the company. The miners were well paid but management and union were located in Stockholm, 1000km south of the Kiruna mines inside the Arctic Circle. Complaints about bureaucracy and centralisation were familiar but these came not from intellectuals berating alienation 'but from blue-collar workers who performed one of the toughest jobs in the country [who] declared they had lost confidence in the Social Democrat dominated labour movement'.[7] Swedish unions strive to take into account membership opinion; leaders nevertheless enjoy markedly different lifestyles, though salaries are relatively modest. One study concluded that 'the LO unions are increasingly governed *for* the members rather than *by* the members

... We have thus found relatively widespread feelings of power-lessness and distance from national union leaders among the rank-and-file members of the Metal Workers' Union.[8]

2. Union government in decentralised movements: the US, the UK, and Japan

Are decentralised movements less vulnerable to obligarchy? Evidence from the United States and Britain would suggest not. The AFL–CIO's senior figures, the President and Secretary-Treasurer, though elected by the bi-annual convention have traditionally enjoyed considerable autonomy. Between Conventions the AFL–CIO is managed by an Executive Council of 33 union secretaries usually representing the biggest unions, also elected by the Convention. The AFL–CIO also provides important services to its affiliates via its 11 Departments, each with their own director and staff; there are 9 industrial departments (Building, Food, Industrial Unions, Maritime Trades, Metal Trades, Professional Employees, Public Employees, Union Label and Services Department and the AFL–CIO Maritime Committee) which provide specialised services, including lobbying. The AFL–CIO also runs an electoral machine, COPE. The AFL–CIO has 50 state-central bodies and 731 local-central bodies. In 1980 it began to hold an annual series of regional conferences and related 'satellite' conferences in which senior AFL figures met local activists and members. Between 1980–5 35 satellite conferences were held in 29 states involving 20 000 participants.

Undoubtedly American unions have suffered from the Teamsters' unsavory reputation and the use of murder by United Mine Workers of America (UMWA) leaders to stop a reform movement. Media references to 'labor bosses' and the attempts of some leaders to live up to that image helps to convey the impression that unions are, in general corrupt and oligarchic. The Landrum–Griffin Act (1959) established the *Labor-Management Services Administration* (LMSA) in response to this to prevent the misues of union funds and provide advice, technical assistance and supervision for union elections.[9] American unions have responded to their poor image:

the labor movement must demonstrate that union representation is the best available means for working people to express their individuality on the job and their desire to control their own working lives, and that unions are democratic institutions controlled by their members and that we have not been sufficiently successful on either score.[10]

The basic organisational unit of British trade unions is the branch, usually geographical or workplace. Branch officials are elected by their fellow members and, increasingly, this is a full-time office. Branches commonly elect delegates to a national conference which may meet annually, but usually biennially. This is normally the highest policy-making body. Executive control is vested in a national executive elected by the members direct, by district organisations or from the national conference. Full-time union officers usually sit on these executives, recent legal changes laying down that any national officer with a vote must be directly elected by the membership. Regional or district structures are staffed by full-time officials more often directly responsible to the national level. At plant level shop stewards (full or part-time) manage everyday union activity; shop stewards are often organised into a shop stewards committee in a single factory and a combined committee in a multi-plant enterprise.

The basis of TUC organisation are Trades Councils composed of the representatives of trade unions within a given area. They vary enormously in effectiveness and are purely advisory with no policy-making functions which is the task of the individual unions. The TUC has 8 Regional Councils in England and 1 in Wales and Scotland which, in recent years, have become increasingly important.

The annual TUC Congress considers the work of the General Council, determines policy and elects the General Council. Decisions are taken on the basis of numbers affiliated by the TUC's members. Up to 1982 the General Council was created via a trade group system which over-represented the large manual and general unions; this was replaced by automatic representation by size: one seat for unions with 100 000 to 499 999 members, two seats for those with 500 000–749 000, three seats for those with 750 000–999 999, four seats for those with 1m–1 499 000, and five seats for those with 1.5m plus members. Eleven seats were to be filled by election from amongst unions with less than 100 000 members, plus six for women's representatives. These changes were crucial for they reduced the influence of the traditional blue-collar/ Labour-supporting unions in favour of white-collar/non-partisan unions. The 54 General Council members meet monthly, and are responsible for interpreting and implementing Congress decisions. In this, they have considerable latitude. The Chairman of the General Council is also TUC President and the post rotates annually to the most senior General Council member who has not held the post ('buggins' turn'); the General Secretary is appointed by Congress after nomination by affiliated unions, usually from within the TUC bureaucracy.

The General Council operates through sub-committees: Finance and General Purposes (the 'inner cabinet'), International, Education and Training, Social Insurance and Industrial Welfare, Employment Policy and Organisation, Economic, Equal Rights and Trade Union Education. There are 11 industry committees (Construction, Distribution and Food, Energy, Financial Services, Health Services, Hotel and Catering, Local Government, Printing, Steel, Textiles, and Transport), and 11 Joint Committees (for example, Public Services, Women, Race, and relations with the Labour Party). These committees are supported by the General Secretary and his full-time staff of 120. The TUC provides services to all affiliates via 7 departments: Education, Organisation and Industrial Relations, International, Social and Industrial Welfare, Economic, Press, and Publications and Finance.

Union leaders' claims to represent their members have been questioned in the light of evidence concerning ballot-rigging and defective democratic practices. The most blatant example of ballot-rigging was provided by the communist domination of the Electrical Trades Union (ETU, now EETPU) in the 1950s which culminated in a celebrated High Court trial. Recent examples are the ballots for the general secretary of the Transport and General Workers Union (TGWU) and the civil service union the Civil and Public Servants' Association (CPSA) (rerun after allegations of 'irregularities' were substantiated) and the failure of the National Union of Mineworkers (NUM) to ballot its members before the 1984–5 dispute.

This was used by the Conservative government to justify legislating on union elections. When elections for Engineering Union offices were held at branch meetings turn-outs ranged between 6–11 per cent; after 1972 and the introduction of postal ballots turnout increased to 22–50 per cent. The government contended that 'In the case of many unions the influence of the rank-and-file seems to be minimal and all too often it is evident that the policies which are being pursued do not reflect the views and interests of the member'. Though rejected by the TUC, this view was consistently supported by *union members* in opinion polls and General Elections. The legislation's intention ('giving the unions back to their members') assumed that membership involvement produced moderate trade unionism.[11] Militancy in the 1960s and early 1970s has been somewhat confusingly ascribed *both* to the diffusion of power away from national leaders *and* to the autocracy of militant union leaders. There is, however, no logical connection between moderation and involvement.

Enterprise unionism, majoritarian democracy and an egalitarian ethos inhibits the Japanese union leader. The 'ascendancy of the legislative organs over the executive councils and the predominance of collective decision making ... means that the scope of decisions left to the discretion of the Japanese leaders is relatively narrow. *Popular control takes precedence over administrative efficiency.*' A survey of union members confirmed a high level of membership involvement: 39.5 per cent always attended union meetings, 42 per cent did so sometimes and 13.9 per cent never attended.[12] This high level of attendance is due to the immediate relevance to the worker of union activity because of enterprise unionism.

Enterprise unionism exacerbates the separation of leaders from the group consciousness nurtured by the large companies: they are literally outsiders. Beyond this level, complex structures produce complex decision-making. Policy is determined by an annual congress supplemented by a special congress in February every year before the beginning of Shunto. This is composed of delegates from affiliated unions and representatives of the local trade union councils. Between congresses Sohyo is run by the Board of Councillors, supplemented by monthly conferences of affiliated union chairman. Decisions are implemented by the Board of Executives composed of the Sohyo President (chairman), 11 vice-presidents, the General Secretary, the Director of the Finance Bureau, 2 vice-general secretaries, and 17 executives. These, and the 15 auditors, are elected by the convention and serve full-time for two years. The Sohyo Secretariat has 12 sections: Finance, Planning, General Affairs, International Affairs, Politics, Mass Movement, Economy, Livelihood, Labour Policy, Women, Information and Press, and Joint Struggle. Executive members are responsible for a head office department. Industrial union federations form the *Private Enterprise Union Conference* (Zenmin Rokyo), the *Council of Public Corporation and National Enterprise Workers' Unions* (Korokyo) and the *Joint Struggle Council of Government Workers' Unions* (Komuin Kyoto). The basic organisational unit of Sohyo is the industry federation. There are also Regional Councils and District Councils; these are not directly affiliated to Sohyo but embrace all Sohyo affiliated organisations in a given area.

The result is a search for consensus between leaders and led, all the more essential given the fissiparousness of Japanese unions. Collective decision-making also disperses responsibility. Deep in the culture of Japanese unionism lurks a distrust of leaders, so great stress in placed in following correct procedures and protocols if a decision is to be regarded as fully legitimate. Membership insurgency does happen, particularly when a union leader is believed not to have followed 'due process' or to have pursued his instructions with insufficient vigour. [13]

Representational Politics

The Role of the National Centre

National centres have two roles: *internal movement coordination* (regulation of inter-union conflict, formulation and implementation of policies, and service provision), and *external political coordination* (representing the interests of their members as a pressure group). We are concerned here with the latter.

The representational function is complicated by multiple union centres, and union resistance to surrendering autonomy. Industrial unionism does not, however, automatically result in a single centre (Sweden and West Germany), and decentralised movements can generate a single national centre (Britain and the US). Centres have a close relationship with a party sympathetic to union needs; nevertheless, their spokesgroup role for the union movement, encompassing unions with a variety of ideologies and structures and their members' varying political loyalties, means they distance themselves from party-political identification. Union centres aspire to work with *all* governments. Centres formulate general policies and lobby governments for their implementation and they have offered, or been asked for, a political exchange (for example, pay restraint in return for full employment). The question is: can a centre deliver its support?

1. The Trades Union Congress
Established in 1868, the TUC's *Parliamentary Committee* put the movement's views to politicians. This role expanded vastly with the 1914–18 war, the reorganisation of the TUC (1918–21) and the creation of the General Council. The 1939–45 war and the growth of tripartite politics underpinned the General Council's political role, reaching its zenith with the Social Contract (1974–9) under which some perceived a shift in the TUC's role from representative to policy-maker. After 1979 this was sharply reversed by the Conservatives, though the TUC still aspires to its previous 'insider' role.[14]

Despite many *individual union* affiliations to the Labour Party, the TUC has no party-political affiliation. The only direct organisational link between the two is the *TUC–Labour Party Liaison Committee* which coordinates TUC and party policy-making. Labour is regarded by the TUC as the party most favourably disposed to its aims but the TUC frequently stresses its independence, claiming some of the unions' most significant gains in tripartite politics came under *Conservative* governments. The TUC embraces many trade unionists who do not, have not and will not vote Labour; to pursue a partisan line risks factionalism, and loss of the TUC's coveted 'sole representative' status.[15] The TUC can proceed only by consensus and the disaffiliation by the TUC of an offending union would entail grave consequences for its authority and representativeness as the expulsion of the EETPU in September 1988 demonstrated. The TUC cannot impose a policy, but relies on the authority given by a vote by Congress and the moral and group pressures to conform.

2. The Deutsche Gewerkschaftbund
The DGB is a confederation of autonomous unions whose purpose is to forge member unions into an effective collectivity to advance

the unions' 'social mission'. Rejecting a link with the SPD in 1949 was calculated to boost the DGB's influence with *non*-socialist parties and make union membership attractive to non-SPD supporters and non-unionised workers. In the new German democracy the DGB had a wider obligation: to support political pluralism; but non-partisanship does not entail political abstinence:

> They are not ... any more than all other representatives or interests are, politically neutral – politically abstinent – nor can they be ... simply because their efforts on behalf of the improvement of living and working conditions are political activity. This activity has to do with social, civil, economic, collective bargaining and educational policies with which the unions must concern themselves, and in connection with which the unions seek to gain improvements for all working people.[16]

The DGB must proceed by consensus; how could anything be imposed on IG Metall? The DGB's position can be pivotal because it articulates the 'general interest' enjoying authority as labour's authoritative spokesgroup. The DGB's influence is enhanced by three achievements: the unity of blue- and white-collar workers in industrial unions, the one-union/one industry principle, and unionisation and representation irrespective of partisanship.

3.   The AFL–CIO
Despite a formidable reputation, the AFL–CIO's effectiveness as labour's lobby has been questioned, reaching a nadir with the Reagan Administration. The AFL-CIO accepts that its effectiveness is likely to be maximised by participation in 'coalition politics' (lobbying Congress and Executive with other groups) as a response to both labour's decline and the reaction against 'big group' New Deal politics of which labour was a central element.[17]

A hostile economic and political climate, coupled with an awareness that the legislation promoted by labour in the 1930s may have worked to their long-term detriment, led to greater emphasis being placed on political action. On the eve of the 1986 mid-term Congressional elections the AFL–CIO President, Lane Kirkland, urged union members to vote for 'a Congress that will pass a good trade reform bill, that will protect the right of American workers to decent wages and working conditions and a healthy workplace, and one that will fight to save American jobs'.[18] The AFL–CIO is striving to change its image from that of a special (i.e. selfish) interest group to a public interest group by broadening its activities in the community and improving its relations with its members and the media.[19] The AFL-CIO cannot, because of fragmentation and the separation of powers, commit itself to a government or a policy and promise 'to deliver'; it can lobby Congress and influence electoral behaviour, but its influence is not based on intrinsic power or authority but on organisational competence.[20]

4. The LO and the TCO

Though the LO is the largest and most important federation, the corporatist nature of the political system and the changing occupational and industrial structure means that the TCO plays an important role. Cooperation with TCO was promoted by LO disquiet at TCO 'free-riding'. The LO's negotiations with the SAF were the means whereby 'the best possible results can be achieved on behalf of those groups which would find it hard to get their demands met on their own'. These negotiations were a 'hard fought and stubborn struggle . . . agreement has often been wrung from the employers by the threat of industrial action'. The LO 'reacted against having had to serve as a sort of battering-ram to clear the way on wages for other trade union centres'.[21]

Occupational change has narrowed the division between blue- and white-collar; as recession promoted restructuring more white-collar workers faced the same pressures as blue-collar ones, exacerbated by 'wage drift' and blue-collar unions seeking high pay for hard work as well as the objection of white-collar workers to the erosion of wage differentials.[22] The LO and TCO are fully aware of the need for cooperation: '[T]he common interest prompting the founding of the union organisations provide a natural foundation for cooperation between unions of manual and salaried workers. The co-operation which occurs in . . . social policy and bargaining is valuable and worth developing, both centrally and in the context of local union affairs.'[23]

5. Sohyo and the minor national centres

After Japan's defeat there were two union federations, *Sanbetsu Kaigi* (communist) and *Sodomei* (socialist); initially the former was dominant but the anti-communism of SCAP and the Japanese state led to their break-up and the formation of Sohyo in 1950. The bulk of Sodomei members joined Sohyo, but a minority refused and re-established Sodomei. *Shinsanbetsu* was part of the Mindo democratisation movement which opposed communism and rejected Sohyo as too centralised. Sanbetsu Kaigi, the communist union federation, weakened by anti-communism and defections to Sohyo, ceased to exist by 1958. Internal union conflict over the 1952 Peace Treaty prompted a number of unions to defect and join the remnants of Sodomei. This became known as *Zenro*, later *Domei*.

Sohyo (General Council of Trade Unions of Japan, 36 per cent of total union members) sees its role in terms of class struggle, creating a socialist society and has close links with the *Japan Socialist Party* (JSP); so close is the relationship that JSP is often portrayed as the political extension of Sohyo. Marxism's influence is important, providing many of the concepts and terminology used by Sohyo. Sohyo cannot be understood unless the importance of public sector workers (two-thirds of its members) is appreciated. These lack full union rights and their pay and conditions are determined by the government; economic action is an aspect of political struggle to achieve a socialist society. The relationship between the national centres is profoundly influenced by Sohyo's professed marxism and Domei's hostility to 'political' unionism.

Domei (Japan Confederation of Labour, 18 per cent of total union members) is a social-democratic federation which stresses collective bargaining and rejects class struggle in favour of the cooperative improvement of labour–management relations by involving unions in corporate and government decision making. Only when profit has been made can the struggle for its distribution begin. Similarly, Domei rejected Sohyo's intimacy with the JSP, stressing the inclusion of workers irrespective of their party loyalties. This, however, is nullified by Domei's role as the *Democratic Socialist Party*'s (DSP, formed in 1960 after a split in the JSP) patron.

Shinsanbetsu (National Federation of Industrial Organisations, 0.5 per cent of total union members) was formed in the early 1950s as an anti-communist/anti-socialist federation. It has abandoned industrial militancy and has no party-political connection but advocates unionism independent of management. It occupies a strategic place in the union movement as a bridge between Sohyo and Domei. *Churitsuroren* (Federation of Independent Unions of Japan, 11 per cent of total union membership) is a liaison committee rather than a centre, it has no party-political connections but has supported the Sohyo–JSP anti-war position and cooperates closely with Sohyo in Shunto. Churitsuroren secures the weight of Sohyo, whilst Sohyo gains access to a significant number of private sector workers. This fragmentation and the LDP's dominance limits Sohyo's representational function and the militancy of the public sector encouraged the private sector unions to distance themselves.[24] These centres account for about 66 per cent of total union membership, and some 4.8m trade unionists are outside these centres.

Sohyo has criticised 'Outdated doctrines or text-book ideas [which] checked the dynamic development of the movement. It frequently happened that, contrary to radical words and contexts, the movement itself was confined within old skins and invited distrust among [the] working masses.'[25] This was partly a response to the emergence of the industrial federations' sectoral role and the formation, in 1982, of *Zenmin Rokyo* (Japan Private Sector Trade Union Council) and later *Rengo* (Confederation of Public Sector Trade Unions) in November 1987. As a result of Rengo, Domei and Churitsuroren disbanded, Shinsanbetsu disbanded in the summer of 1988, and Sohyo's public sector unions will affiliate in 1990. Rengo represents a major simplification of the union movement, but the public–private cleavage remains important. The pressure for unification led Sohyo to modify its rhetoric and support unification. Zenmin Rokyo is a consequence of Sohyo's public sector predominance which 'has not only made it difficult to organise [a] powerful united movement involving unions in both sectors, but has also created a trend to increase ... the feeling of disunion'. Sohyo resolved, therefore, to 'do its best to reinforce mutual understanding and unify ideas among the affiliates and broaden unions in the private sector and enhance the function of the industrial organisations'.[26]

Union Ideology and Political Behaviour

Voluntarism and Union Politics

'Voluntarism', a vague and imprecise concept, asserts a union's autonomy, taking its own decisions and defining its interests with the minimum of external interference. Voluntarism, or *sub-group autonomy*, stems from the unions' contradictory position as both an opponent of, and a creation of, capitalist society. Unions are *defensive*, resisting external impediments to their activities and, whilst hostile to the power structure of capitalism, its liberal-democratic freedoms offer an opportunity to remedy the short-comings of collective bargaining. Voluntarism does not reject legal intervention absolutely, but experience dictates a preference for conducting affairs free from external intervention. Voluntarism is, therefore, a bulwark of independence.[27] How much autonomy should unions be allowed? Should they be allowed to pursue their interests at the expense of the community; if not, to what degree should they be regulated by the state? In all capitalist industrial states unions are voluntary organisations independent of the state, members are accorded control over their organisations and unions govern themselves under the law. All governments have, nonetheless, established a body of law to regulate their activities.

Trade union law has two aspects: first, to ensure that unions are properly conducted and that members' rights are secure; this is the *internal regulation* function. The second, the *external regulation* function, is politically contentious as it limits the scope of union action, delineating (for example) the procedures to be followed before a strike can be legal, the closed shop, arbitration and conciliation, restrictions on union membership for public servants or those in essential services, restrictions on picketing and solidarity strikes, and the control of union political activity. The difficulty lies in determining when *regulation* becomes *restriction*. Does legislation on, for example, picketing and sympathy strikes, whilst safeguarding individual and community rights, make effective industrial action impossible? Union political activity seeks to defend sub-group autonomy so the union–state relationship can be conceptualised as a constant struggle to create and recreate a balance between individual and collective rights. Because unions operate in an anti-voluntarist environment, they cannot avoid political involvement.

1. The United Kingdom
The state has traditionally remained aloof from industrial relations reflecting,

a belief that it is better in the long run for the law to interfere as little as possible in the settlement of questions arising between employers and workmen over pay and conditions of work. Parliament has long been committed to the view that the best means of settling such questions is voluntary collective bargaining and has equipped Governments in various ways to support, assist and promote collective bargaining.[28]

This depends on the organisation of union and employers into authoritative and representative bodies.

The TUC believed that the state's legitimate role was to complement and supplement collective bargaining and that governability was promoted by the TUC's presence within the political process. Collective bargaining was supplemented by creating a *countervailing political power* to the employer 'to enact a particular piece of legislation, *which will strengthen, or fill a gap in*, the scope of collective bargaining'. However, 'No state, however benevolent, can perform the function of trade unions in enabling workpeople themselves to decide how their interests can best be safeguarded. It is where trade unions are not competent, *and recognise they are not competent*, to perform a function, that they welcome the state playing a role, but ... this is ... the second best alternative'.[29] In effect, it was for *the unions* to determine the timing and scope of state intervention.

The prominence of the 'trade union problem' in the 1960s and 1970s challenged voluntarism and self-regulation as successive governments grappled with its consequences.[30] Union participation in policy-making, their claim to have created a fairer society and their legitimacy was successfully challenged and public opinion, reacting against the 'abuse of union power', approved intervention against a body perceived to be responsible for national economic and political decline.[31] This electorally popular appeal inspired successive tranches of union legislation. Sandwiched between recession and a hostile political environment the unions cited voluntarism in their defence. Legislation, they contended, was designed 'to prevent unions organising effectively, to limit their right to take action ... [the government] wants to meddle in their internal affairs ... to impose new limits on unions' political action'.[32] Three Conservative election victories and continued decline have, however, compelled a rethink of this absolutist commitment to voluntarism.

2. The United States
American labour similarly looks to legislation to augment collective bargaining:

> Unions are, first and foremost, organizations seeking to improve the lives of those they represent by improving their conditions of work . . . The labor movement also has sought to improve the conditions of life for all in our democratic society through political action and legislative efforts. Organized labor seeks, in sum, through collective bargaining, political participation and legislative activity to bring about a broader sharing in the riches of the nation.[33]

Voluntarism remains organised labour's aspiration, despite their reliance on law in the 1930s to promote unionisation. This produced a compromise permeating industrial relations – the NLRB, for example, argued that 'Long experience has taught us that when the parties fully understand their rights and obligations, they are more ready and able to adjust their differences voluntarily'.[34] Union dependence on legislative action and the juridification of industrial relations makes it peculiar that – American unions are sometimes dubbed 'non-political'. The AFL–CIO is political, it is a special interest with political goals, avoiding intervention in collective bargaining, but supporting legislation as a supplement to collective bargaining.[35]

The Reagan Administration demonstrated the vulnerability of labour's gains. The LMSA's *Co-operative Labor Management Programs* 'highlighted the agency's increased efforts to encourage and assist employers, employees and unions to undertake joint programs to improve productivity and enhance the quality of working life'. The Mines Safety Administration sought 'to reduce adversarial relations between labor and management over safety and health . . . to eliminate needless regulatory burdens, and . . . to encourage positive efforts by industry and labor to protect miners' safety and health'.[36] The shift of power to management prompted labour to protest that the Administration had abandoned the 'social contract', 'any time this country needed protecting it has called on its working class people . . . Now the shoe is on the other foot . . . America is the sum total of its citizens, and therefore the country has an obligation to its citizens'.[37] Labour's political task is to persuade 'the country' to recognise this obligation.

3. *Sweden*

Swedish employers and unions have since the 1930s agreed to avoid state involvement or intervention in their internal affairs: only when agreement cannot be reached do they take 'the political route'. Safeguarding collective economic and social interests necessitates, as the non-partisan TCO accepts, a relationship with government:

It would be absurd for TCO to make a principle of refraining from the promotion of salaried workers' opinions and demands on the grounds that the questions are actually or potentially controversial in terms of party politics. Party-political independence cannot impede TCO from expressing opinions on social questions of vital importance to salaried workers.[38]

The LO's aim is a social, political and economic democracy. Its constitution calls on unions to 'safeguard the interests of the workers in the labour market and in economic life', and through collective bargaining 'the trade union movement has, bit by bit, advanced the position of labour at the expense of capital'. However, 'Agreements of various kinds with employers cannot, of themselves, always suffice. Legislation and social reforms are essential if problems vital to workers are to be brought nearer solution'.[39]

Labour market self-regulation – conceded by the state after 1928 – entails a commitment to making the system work. This was, and is, symbolised by the *Basic Agreement* signed at Saltsjobaden in 1938 (to which government was *not* a party) in which the commitment to voluntarism was explicit. The costs of industrial conflict were regrettable, *but 'they cannot be regarded as sufficiently important to justify that the present freedom of collective bargaining be substituted by compulsory State control'*. So:

Nor from other points of view can the State be justified – apart from the sphere of social welfare legislation proper – in forcing upon Swedish employers and workers a regulation of working conditions, either in general or specific circumstances. So long as organisations on the labour market are also preared to take note of the general public interest involved in their activities, the measures reasonably called for in the interest of labour peace most naturally and appropriately rest with the organisations themselves.[40]

Economic problems in the 1970s and 1980s weakened the LO–
SAF relationship and forced government to take a higher profile in
the resolution of industrial conflict. The spirit of Saltsjobaden however remains, the labour movement's aspiration and motivation.

4.   The Federal Republic of Germany
In the Federal Republic there are obvious powerful historical
reasons for union support of voluntarism, and the DGB views
resisting any threat to the post-1945 political settlement as one of
its main responsibilities. Article 9(3) of the Basic Law guarantees
freedom of association, and unions are independent of government, party, religion, and employers. West German unionism is,
nevertheless, explicitly seeking to provide a corporate political
voice by 'informing the Bundestag, the Bundesrat, the state
legislatures, governmental authorities and the organs of the European Community of the unions' position on topical public issues
that involve worker interests [and] to disseminate union demands
in relation to the issues.[41]

West German industrial relations are highly juridified, but unions
are not specifically mentioned in the Basic Law and the Collective
Agreement Law draws no distinction between union and non-
union workers. Industrial relations law thereby provides a barrier
against voluntarism. Collective agreements are legally binding but
despite the prominence of law these agreements are negotiated
without overt government intervention: 'Workers must be guaranteed a fair wage. Special significance is therefore attached to tariff
[collective bargaining] autonomy and the free activity of trade
unions, as well as to employers' federations.' Responsible collective bargaining is the basis of cooperation between the social
partners and 'this means that the government has no right to intervene or to directly influence the outcome of the negotiations'.[42]
Labour market organisations stress that the peaceful resolution of
industrial conflict is a common interest. Both sides concede that
they have divergent and common interests, but the organisation
and weapons at their disposal (the strike and lockout) imposes a
peace obligation. Employers and unions 'are bound to find an
economically sensible compromise within their sphere of influence
as there is no one else to do it for them'.[43] This implies state
abstinence but at a time of recession and restructuring this does
not imply neutrality, neither has it banished industrial conflict.

5. *Japan*

The marginalisation of Japanese unions means that their politicial activity is directed at *gaining* access to the political process; however, their ideology and rhetoric is fiercely critical of that system. Political action is, according to Sohyo's *Fundamental Principles*, essential 'as not all labor activities can be confined to the economic sphere alone, but they must, of necessity, be extended to the political sphere'. Sohyo's *Basic Programme* is voluntarist:

> Trade unions should defeat all outside attempts to interfere with their internal affairs either by the government, employers or any other bodies. They should also be completely independent of, and free from, political parties. Under the existing circumstances, trade unions should not confine their activities to economic areas, but at the same time, trade unions should not be used as an instrument of struggle for political power.[44]

Article 28 of the Constitution guarantees workers the right to organise and bargain collectively; these basic rights are amplified by the *Trade Union Law* and the *Labour Relations Adjustment Law*. Trade union law regards unions as independent but the scope of the law restricts union activity; the only remedy is political, and would require a change of government.

Japanese unions welcomed democratisation, 'But formalistic democratization never succeeded in truly democratizing the mind and policy of the Japanese ruling class'. Unions, therefore, had to be permanently watchful because of the LDP who 'over more than a quarter of a century, have been pursuing anti-labor policies, in close partnership with giant corporation leaders, high officials of administration and judicature and with the majority of media leaders'.[45] Above the enterprise level unions (especially in the public sector) are perceived as sectional, giving union politics a distinctly adversarial twist. Sohyo, for example, seeks to 'protect and improve workers' living [standards] and rights, and to safeguard peace and democracy. What it has longed and acted for [is] to build a society in which workers are free and happy, and to realise [the] powerful unity of workers and trade unions to bring about such a society.' As the main obstacle is political ('the present corruptive dirty Liberal Democratic Party government'), the remedy is political.[46]

Sohyo's aim is 'to establish a coalition government on the principle to fight against the Liberal-Democratic Party, against monopolies, for the safeguarding of the peace Constitution, and protect the living [standards] of the entire people'.[47] Historically the main task of Japanese unions has been to defend themselves, which Sohyo maintains is still necessary, but with the growth of liberal democracy the unions aspired to a role comparable to that achieved by western unions. Sohyo must engage in a combined economic and political struggle:

> This posture of Sohyo is derived from *the general state of affairs prevailing in all advanced industrial countries as well as from the special Japanese situation.* The founding convention of Sohyo emphasized that given the reactionary nature of the Japanese employers and the conservative government, trade unions should act vigorously in the political arena if only to defend the economic life of the workers.[48]

Japanese unions are caught in the situation of seeking integration into a political process perceived to be hostile, facing a political and business elite which draws a distinction between public and private sector unions.

Centralisation, Fragmentation and Political Influence: Conclusions

Structure and Political Influence

Inferring behaviour from structure is hazardous but centralised industrial unions with a dominant national centre are more likely to be politically influential. However, traditional classification systems based on, for example, skill or breadth of recruitment reveal little of value about political influence and are of less and less utility as technology transforms the workforce. Exclusivist closed recruitment unions are dying, unions tend to multi-skilled embracing blue- and white-collar workers. Public sector unions are invariably amongst the largest and the public–private dimension is, by and large, the most important distinction. At first sight there would seem to be little common organisation in our five union movements but the general union predominates either in an industrial form (West Germany and Sweden), or in a conglomerate form (United States and United Kingdom), and in Japan the general union predominates beyond the enterprise in the form of the industrial federations of unions.

Political influence is not a crude function of size, numbers or membership density, important though these are. Influence depends on the degree of centralisation within each union and the degree of centralisation within the movement as a whole. This centralisation is not just organisational but ideological, and results in the dominance of the collective over the individual interest. The evidence indicates that political influence increases according to a movement's centralisation and density of membership – from Sweden, the most centralised and politically integrated, to Japan, the least. Industry based unions are few in number and so more easily coordinated and directed; they emerge usually as a result of trauma in which centralisation and a collectivist ethos are seen as essential for survival. Conglomerate general unions and enterprise unions are based on a historical legacy of organisational and ideological sectionalism but British and American unions have sought to modify this by merger or, in the case of Japan, by national coordination culminating in labour front unification.

Union Government and Behaviour

As organisations, unions have been subject to a barrage of criticism concerning their internal political processes. Any organisation, democratic or otherwise, is inevitably controlled by the leadership–bureaucratic stratum. Their activities are complex, so it is hardly surprising that professionals are pre-eminent and the membership passive. Politicians prefer to believe that the moderate minority are dominated and manipulated by the activist minority for political ends.

The political consequences of this are significant. 'Oligarchy' justifies altering internal union political processes and questioning the legitimacy and representativeness of union leaders. As the political behaviour of unions is determined by their internal politics, and when union behaviour is blamed for political and economic turbulence, it is not surprising that politicians see influencing internal union politics as a way of modifying external behaviour on more accommodating lines. A political system's needs vary: in West Germany and Sweden the political process originally required centralised unions, in the 1970s these were seen as something of an obstacle. In Britain, the unions were originally regarded as *insufficiently* centralised to engage in the sort of political exchange they and politicians desired. Up to 1979 efforts were made to augment the authority of leaders over their members; after 1979 the process was reversed, but both were motivated by a desire to alter union behaviour. In the United States a compromise worked out in the 1930s and 1940s was similarly subject to pressure in the 1980s from a government determined to deregulate the labour market. Though apparently decentralised to the point of fragmentation the Japanese enterprise union system, when coupled with company corporatism and Shunto, is surprisingly centralised, mainly because of the influence wielded by the enterprise unions in the export oriented corporate sector whose collective interests predominate. As a result of the economic crises of the 1970s, government, concerned to promote stability, sought to build on these characteristics whilst excluding the bulk of the union movement from influence.

Political Representation

The complexity of the industrial polity and the decline of classic parliamentary democracy made consultation with powerful societal interests essential. To be effective, this required the formation of a peak organisation to be consulted by government: the result was the emergence of the various national centres recognised by government as the authoritative representative of labour. However, both national centres and individual unions were, and are, in a difficult position.

This difficulty stems from the unions' contradictory position in the politics of capitalist liberal democracy, being both part of the status quo and an opponent of it. Unions began as outsiders seeking access to the industrial and political systems; their growth as organisations aided entry to the former but they also developed a close connection with a political party to aid their entry to the latter. Unions, therefore, strive to portray themselves as a societal interest but are often regarded as partisan, and this can reduce their influence.

National centres and many individual unions have intimate ties with a political party despite a universal proclamation of their party-political neutrality. This party is, or has been (except for Japan), a party of government. Their relationship is based on an exchange: organised labour's support for the party, in return for the party's support for the unions' legislative goals. However, as no union movement is politically monolithic and no party (with the exception of the SAP) is a governing party, the national centres maintain, or strive to maintain, contacts with the non-labour governing parties. To fullfil their representational task a commitment to non-partisanship is essential as its influence may be limited by too obvious a clash between the centre's interest group function and its partisanship. This is not, however, political neutrality.

Union Ideology and Political Behaviour

The contradictory position of unions in capitalist society explains the ideology of voluntarism. Remarkably, despite their varying structures and relationships with government, unions have a common ideology, indicating a common location in the power structure. Whilst the mix varies, the same elements are present: collective bargaining is supplemented by political activity, unions see themselves as the best determinants of what constitutes their interests, and regard state intervention in internal decision-making as hostile. Voluntarism is not a structured ideology but a rationalisation of union practise under capitalism.

Many of the political difficulties faced by unions stem from an ambivalent attitude to the law consequent on their subordinate position in the politics of capitalist society. Unions might prefer to win concessions through their own efforts via collective bargaining, but as unions can never achieve total coverage (of either members or employers) they inevitably operate from a position of relative powerlessness. To remedy this, unions exploit the political freedoms of liberal democracy, deploying their numbers and organisation in the political process to secure legal concessions to counterbalance this subordination. In this sense, legal intervention is sought and regarded as positive, whereas state intervention to remedy union activities serves the interest of the already powerful. State intervention in the unions' internal activities is, therefore, invariably resisted. Voluntarism is Janus-faced with respect to the state which is both sympathetic and hostile; from it stems the motor of the union–government relations as the unions seek concessions from the state which will not concede them without reciprocity. Striving to secure the maximum concessions from the state whilst seeking to concede the minimum to it is a recipe for instability.

The hypothesis set out at the beginning of this chapter is largely substantiated: Swedish and West German unions are the most influential, the Japanese the least, with the British and American unions coming somewhere between. Political influence is not a commodity possessed by nor an inevitable feature of, organisation; it is the product of relationships and is therefore *relative and changeable* as the balance of economic and political forces change in a political system. The one constant of this is that, as we shall see, unions remain relatively *powerless*.

3

Trade Unions and Political Parties

The Party–Union Relationship

The party–union relationship sprang from the political weakness of unions. As unions were outside the established power structure it was unlikely they would find allies amongst the established parties, though there were exceptions such as the alliance of some British unions with the Liberal Party in the late nineteenth century. As outsider groups they were drawn to outsider parties who made union concerns central to their appeal and who tended to be socialist. The link between unions and socialism (or in the case of American unions, with state intervention) was a reflection of the wish to restructure political and economic power in favour of outsider interests. In parliamentary democracies 'socialism' meant reformism not revolution, unions supported particular parties so as to influence them in government and secure concessions. Outsider parties welcomed union support, seeing in the unions a valuable source of finance, votes and organisation to support their electoral take-off. So the relationship was seen as mutually beneficial to two outsider groups striving for access to the political process.

The ideological range embraced by the party–union relationship is relatively narrow. The British, German, Swedish and Japanese relationship is founded on 'socialism', and in all (except the British) marxism has played a crucial role historically. Electoral politics and fear of exclusion from government prompted the abandonment of marxism in Sweden and Germany, and this is currently taking place in Japan. The socialist strain in American unions has

47

been submerged by other influences, notably the heterogeneity of the workforce and the hostility of the political system, though unions have sought, via the Democratic Party, reforms similar to those in the other states. The ideological relationship can be characterised as social democratic, defined as a reformist and non-marxist left-of-centre ideology which is sometimes only marginally different from moderate conservatism. Social democracy implies a degree of public control over private economic power but not the rejection of private property, a considerable degree of public provision of services such as health, education and welfare, a redistributive taxation system to promote social justice, and a political process based on the involvement of producer groups (especially employers and unions) with government to produce and sustain a national consensus. The political process itself remains based on group pluralism, parliamentarianism and electoral competition.

It has been suggested that the party–union relationship is profoundly influenced by the relationship at the time of its emergence. Put simply, if the unions were instrumental in founding the party then they will have proportionately more influence over it. In fact, this is borne out only by the British experience, where the Labour Party emerged from a decision of the TUC in 1899. In Sweden, the reverse applies. Here the SAP acted as a surrogate union federation until the founding of the LO. In Germany the pre-1933 relationship was akin to the British experience but in the remaking of the union movement and the party system after 1945 there was a conscious attempt at separation for electoral reasons, though links do remain. The Japanese party–union relationship is difficult to disentangle because mutual weakness and hostility from government forced cooperation, but after 1945 the JSP and Sohyo especially relied on each other, to the extent that the former came to be seen as an extension of the latter. In the USA the two-party system preceded the founding of the AFL and a majority of members supported the Republican Party. The AFL sought to avoid a partisan commitment (Republican or Democrat) and, as with so many aspects of modern American politics, the party–union relationship dates from the New Deal era. The Democrats and the unions were drawn to each other out of mutual self-interest but both brought to the relationship long established political traditions which makes their relationship an amalgam of British and West German practice: an intimate but arm's length relationship. In none can it be said the party is dominated by the unions, and in the cases of a close relationship (the UK and Japan), party and union leaders would agree that this has been a mixed blessing.

What, then, is the configuration of the current relationship? The development of the 'catch-all' party making a supra-class appeal was a significant development in the party–union relationship.[1] The party–union relationship is moulded by the party's need to create the broadest electoral base, and by the unions' desire to influence all governments irrespective of party. Influence implies power in the party's policy process and a capacity to deploy sanctions when confronted by an unsympathetic response. Vigorous and visible use of power may cost electoral support should the party be perceived as the unions' creature. Second, as subscribers to a democratic ethos union leaders are constrained to recognise the rights of others. Third, not every union member supports 'their' party, so partisanship might entail organisational costs. Finally, the dynamics of party competition force union leaders to accept that if the party is to form a government it must appeal to groups outside union ranks. Consequently, unions have remarkably few sanctions: to assert themselves would reduce the party's electability, whilst withdrawal would deny them a party-political vehicle, furthermore there is no guarantee that union members would obey an injunction not to support the party.

The party–union relationship is often falsely and crudely reduced to asking, 'who needs whom most?'. This ignores the fact that the relationship is *mutual*, an exchange between two oganisations with separate but overlapping interests which generates the tensions in their relationship. Generally, unions concede party predominance in the *electoral* sphere, whilst the party accepts union predominance in the *industrial* one. The two cannot, of course, be kept separate and the most successful party–union relationships are those with a clear division of responsibilities, or where a liaison capable of managing the tensions has been established.

The Structural and Organisational Relationship

The Federal Republic of Germany

In the Federal Republic the right to organise parties and unions is guaranteed by the Basic Law. Union political participation was a safeguard for democracy, but affiliation to the SPD on British lines was forsworn by the DGB. The DBG's founders insisted on party-political neutrality, even supporting some Christian Democratic Union (CDU) policies. Nonetheless, the SPD and DGB were political allies, 'I know I am among people who are most intimately bound up with us [the DGB]. A division between the [SDP] and the German trade unions is inconceivable. *We are the children of one mother.*'[2]

The DGB's political role is representation. As industrial unionism embraces a wide range of political beliefs it necessitates party-political independence but not political neutrality. The SPD's *Bad Godesburg Programme* (1959) which commited the party to reforming capitalism and the *volkspartei* (a 'people's' not 'class' party) model were crucial in the development of the party–union relationship. Hitherto there was no need for a 'workers'' organisation in the party as the SPD was, by definition, a workers' party but by 1967 there were calls for a 'workers' wing' indicating a decline in union influence. The DGB, however, remained committed to party-political neutrality:

> Since the political parties have developed into mass parties, there no longer has been a working people's party of the old style. This change placed increased responsibility on the trade unions to develop and pursue goals with, particularly, working people in mind. The unions are not seeking to become a substitute for a political party ... they must work out their own political conceptions for working people's liberation and attainment of equal status.[3]

The absence of institutional or organisational links does not mean the absence of all connections, or that these connections are weak or ineffective. The relationship is not one of one element dominating the other, the DGB never 'controlled party policy-making ... union officials never acted as a unified bloc within the party. It did mean, however, that the party in its decision making was well acquainted with union views.'[4] In government, however, acquaintance did not automatically result in responsiveness. The DGB and SPD elites agreed on the desirability of a close relationship but the consequence of DGB support for unpopular SPD *government* policies was internal union conflict and a mutual distancing, though the SPD remains the DGB's best party-political hope.

Sweden

Faced with employer intransigence the LO has not hesitated 'to take the political route', and, 'Here, in particular, the link between the LO and the [SAP] played an important part. Thanks to its contacts with the Party the LO has managed to achieve results in fields where it had proved impossible to make progress via agreements.'[5] The party-political relationship can be understood only in the context of an economic growth strategy

> intended to increase the total national product so that a 'zero-sum' type of conflict between capital and labour could be turned into a 'positive-sum' type of conflict: both parties could thereby profit from the increase in the total product, even if their relative shares were not substantially changed.[6]

The SAP and LO recognise that 'A strong and united labour movement is necessary in the light of the strength of its opponents. The LO and the SAP fight for the same goal but on different fronts.'[7]

Membership overlap is vital for unity. About 75 per cent of the SAP's members are collectively affiliated by their unions through their *arbetarkommun* (workers' branch); branches (not unions) can, after a majority vote, affiliate to the party, but only at local level. Fees are paid through the union, and any LO member opposed can contract out. The LO has 17 districts covering one or more counties, under which are 240 sections, one for each municipality; the SAP has a similar structure based on the *Social Democratic Clubs* and branches covering a single municipality, with SAP districts corresponding to administrative counties. Party and union organisation correspond, so LO–SAP cooperation is facilitated at all levels of the political system. Union members have seats on party decision-making bodies, but these are not allocated according to any precise formula, as in the British Labour Party – though, of course, they are party members. This overlap symbolises

> the natural feeling of belonging together for the purpose of safeguarding in the best possible way, the interests of the workers, [and] has resulted in a growing number of branches deciding in favour of collective affiliation, in spite of the efforts . . . being made by our opponents to try and drive a wedge between the two branches of the labour movement.[8]

Despite their close connection the SAP has never pursued 'class' politics at the expense of Swedish capitalism. This depends on a consensus between the LO and the SAP based on the former's willingness to accept the predominance of the SAP's electoral strategy which stresses the creation of a broad based electoral coalition. LO centralisation and the collectivist ethos of Swedish political culture has not prevented clashes between the LO's role in the *market* (defending the members' economic interests) and the *political system* (participating in corporatist politics). Union–government relations have often been difficult and the SAP's attempts to win and retain union support by boosting their role in the economy threatens the SAP's relationship with capitalism.[9] However, the LO recognises that the Social Democrats remain their best political ally in Swedish politics, so their political options remain limited.

The United Kingdom

It is often forgotten that the TUC and Labour are separate organisations. The TUC has no political fund and does not finance party politics; the only structural connection between the two is the *Liaison Committee* (composed of representatives from the TUC General Council and the Labour Party National Executive Committee), which has no autonomous decision-making power – its proposals must be approved by Congress, the Party Conference, and individual union conferences. A union may affiliate to the TUC but not to Labour, Congress decisions cannot bind the Party neither can Conference bind the TUC (though party affiliated unions are bound by its decisions just as TUC affiliates are bound by Congress) and no union leader can be both a member of the General Council and the NEC. Nevertheless,

> The Labour Party and the trade unions have grown together. You can't separate them. Most union members help to support the party through the political levy ... In return for that support, union members have a democratic voice at every level of policy-making: from their local union branch to the TUC-Labour Party Liaison Committee.[10]

The TUC has periodically asserted its independence because many unions and their members are not Labour partisans and the TUC *as an interest group* must attempt to influence all governments. Pronouncements on the relationship traditionally concentrate on two themes: the necessity of union political involvement, including party politics, and unity between the 'political' and 'industrial'. After 1979 a new theme was added: unity to promote Labour's electability.

The Labour Party is unique because of the national affiliation of the unions. At the 1984 Party Conference, for example, the unions provided 600 delegates compared to the 620 constituency delegates, they elected 10 members to the 30 strong National Executive Committed (NEC) (directly influencing the election of others) and their bloc vote determines party policy. The Chairman of the NEC (1985–6) was a member of GMBATU (see List of Abbreviations for these union acronyms), the Vice-Chairman a member of USDAW, the Treasurer of the NUS, The Trade Union Section of the NEC had members from COHSE, UCW, NUM, NGA, AEU, Textile Workers, TGWU, SOGAT 82, NUPE and NUR. Out of a total income of £4.5m (1985) union affiliation fees provided £3.5m (77 per cent) compared to £726,000 (16 per cent) from the CLPs; for the 1983 General Election the unions provided £2.1m of the £2.5m General Election fund. Of a total party membership of 6 200 159, the 44 unions affiliated 5 827 479 members (93.9 per cent), the 633 CLPs 313 099 (5.0 per cent), and the 9 socialist societies 59 581 (0.9 per cent). In the electoral college established in 1981 to elect the leader and deputy leader the unions have 40 per cent of the votes. Surely, this makes the Labour Party a union party quite unlike either the SAP or SDP?

The party–union relationship is complex and ambivalent. The unions and the party have their own interests; although the party began as a union offshoot, it is not the unions' political expression. Whilst union activity can be faciliated by party-political action the unions must remember the electoral interests of the party and that electoral success is essential if Labour is to defend the unions' interests. Conflict is therefore inevitable because of the unions' sectionalism and impatience with parliamentary politics and party frustration with the unions' conservatism and industrial behaviour which reflected badly on the party. Conflict could not be resolved by unions coercing the party or vice-versa.

Much of the Labour Party's history has been concerned with formulating mechanisms and policies to maximise cooperation, the most recent manifestations being the Liaison Committee (and the associated Social Contract) and *Trade Unions for Labour Victory* (TULV), founded in 1981, now called *Trade Unions for Labour* (TUFL). Originally created to coordinate opposition to the 1971 Industrial Relations Act, the Liaison Committee grew in import-ance and stature, becoming a policy-making body under the 1974–9 Labour government. After 1979 the Liaison Committee declined in importance but has since been revived.[11]

TULV was established by union leaders concerned at the decline of Labour partisanship amongst trade unionists. Active in the 1979 and 1983 elections its impact was limited by the political climate, but its existence testifies to union concern at the party's electoral viability. In 1985 TULV was merged with the *Trade Union Coordinating Committee* (TUCC) which coordinated the political fund ballot strategy. TUCC was explicitly independent of Labour, TUFL is overtly party oriented, establishing (for example) a Labour Victory Fund; the party General Secretary (a former union research officer and TULV secretary) and Treasurer also sit on TUFL.[12]

The unions' relationship with Labour is, therefore, paradoxical. They have enormous potential power, and party ethos derives much from the unions. This potential power has seldom been mobilised because of a desire not to damage the party's electoral image or provoke conflict with the constituency activists who, in the absence of a mass committed union membership, run the party. Essentially, the unions see themselves as the party's fulcrum whose task is to balance Labour's political equation, and structural connections do not necessarilly entail union tutelage of 'their' party.[13]

The United States of America

The political system's complexity makes it difficult to draw a clear distinction between the unions' pressure group role and their role as a Democratic Party supporter. American unionism is often described as, 'essentially trade conscious, rather than class con-scious', whose aims are expressed 'in terms mainly of higher wages, shorter hours, and better working conditions . . . regardless in general of political and social considerations, except in so far as these bear directly upon its own economic ends'.[14] This has been used to argue American unions are apolitical; this is ridiculous. To realise the *Gompers Doctrine* (unions should reward their friends and punish their enemies) would require a highly sophisticated political organisation, and a degree of unity and centralisation impossible for American unions to achieve. Organised labour regards the Democrats as 'friends', irrespective of what the Republicans do, and when the Democrats disappoint labour there is little evidence of 'punishment'.

The absence of a West European-type 'labour' party in the United States has not obviated the need for party-political links; indeed the industrial weakness of the unions propels them towards the Democrats. This strategy is limited by the separation of legislature from executive (so influence in one does not necessarily confer influence in the other), the coalitional nature of the Democratic Party means it contains elements suspicious of 'big labor' and, finally, the rise of new social movements has challenged labour's political influence. American labour leaders have consistently rejected both the idea of, and need for, a 'labour' party:

> If we attempted to take over the Democratic Party, why, we'd have to pay more attention to that than to the labor movement. And if we set up our own political party, we'd be telling this country that we're ready to run the Government, and I don't think we're ready – I don't think we're qualified to run the Government. I don't think General Motors should run the Government, and I don't think the AFL–CIO should run the Government.[15]

The Democratic Party's structure and rules, plus statutory restrictions on campaign financing, confine unions to supporting, not sponsoring, candidates. The dynamics of electoral politics make candidates reluctant to appear to be the tool of any special interest. Candidates will, nevertheless, be well aware of, and keen to secure, the resources that union endorsement brings, but organised labour is only one factor.

Congressional behaviour is not determined by party discipline but by many factors, one of which is the judgement of a congressman's performance made by special interest groups. Performance assessment by organised labour is represented by COPE ratings;

although there is no 'labour' party, there is a group of Congressmen who achieve high COPE ratings. The number securing a
rating of 80 per cent + pro-labour votes is a good measure of a
Congressman's sympathy for labour.

The number of Senators and Representatives scoring 80 per cent
+ peaked in 1975 and labour's most reliable allies were fewest in
1980 but there has since been a recovery.[16] The AFL–CIO's
report on the first session of the 99th Congress judged House
members on 17 key issues and Senators on 21, rating them 'Right'
or 'Wrong' according to the AFL–CIO's preference and calculat-
ing a cumulative percentage of 'Right'/'Wrong'. Out of a House
membership of 435, 150 (34.5 per cent) had 80 per cent +
cumulative 'Right' scores; in the Senate (100 members) 26 had an
80 per cent + rating, so out of a Congress with 535 members, 176
(32.8 per cent) can be regarded as 'labour's' party. The party
composition of this group is significant: all 26 Senators and 149 of
the House members were Democrats, the only Republican with an
80 per cent + COPE rating was Representative Renaldo of New
Jersey's 7th District.[17]

Important though the electoral–political role of the AFL–CIO
is, it is not directed at achieving a labour majority in Congress as
the Democratic Party contains elements hostile to labour and the
restricted geography of the labour movement (concentrated in the
North East) is a problem. Labour's party-political activities are an
extension of lobbying directed at achieving favourable legislation
(most likely from the Democrats).[18]

Japan

In the political systems considered here pro-labour parties all have
a prospect of entering government, except in Japan. Post-war
union militancy, business pressure to keep wages low, and the
growing hostility of the state inevitably led to the inter-penetration
of union and party. Militancy, however, provoked the break-up of
the existing union federations; indeed, Sohyo was originally
created to *avoid party-political dependence*. The turning point
came in 1955 with the remaking of the party system: the JSP
reunited, but more importantly the conservatives organised the
LDP with the explicit intention of creating a political and
economic hegemony. LDP hegemony was, of course, aided by the

economic boom filtering prosperity down to the working class after the restraint of the 1950s.[19]

Despite 'vexing internal problems and a period of open cleavage the JSP had, between 1949–1958, edged upward in each successive election, both as percentage of votes and a number of seats in the Diet . . . Some saw in these trends the approach of a Socialist era.' The absence of a mass electoral base, however, was a disastrous weakness, and the JSP's marxist rhetoric disguised the fact that a politically conscious working class was 'a mirage dimly seen on the horizon'; the result was union dominance of the JSP whose structure can be likened to an 'inverted pyramid'.[20] These tendencies had a major impact on the movement's structure, in 1954 leading to the formation of Zenro (later Domei) from Sohyo, and the defection of the DSP from the JSP in 1960. By the end of the 1950s the right had split away to form the DSP which caused the JSP to move leftwards. It lost more electoral support, becoming further reliant on Sohyo.

This over-reliance is characteristic of the Japanese party–union relationship. The basic criticism is that union prominence enervates the JSP. Sohyo's influence within the JSP is reflected in the number of unionists selected as JSP candidates and supported by their unions and who sit on official JSP bodies. The unions have been leading participants in the recurrent debates since the 1950s over the relative costs and benefits of party-political action. The unions, especially Sohyo, are pulled in two directions: the marxist tradition contrasts sharply with the collective bargaining function of trade unions and generates instability in the union movement. Party-political activism also promotes second unions, often established to oppose industrial action for 'political' purposes.

The JSP failure to expand from its union based electoral core has resulted in the fragmentation of the anti-LDP forces into DSP, *Komeito* (founded in 1964 to clean up government), and the JCP. The union base of the JSP remains narrow and dependent on public sector unions whose political and industrial militancy is grounded on legal restrictions which do not apply in the private sector. The JSP's loose and uncoordinated structure permits its dominance by the unions over whom the party has little control, yet the unions have never tried to impose a line on the party. To do so would shatter the JSP into its component factions.[21] This pattern is repeated with the DSP.

Union dominance and political militancy underpinned the defection of the DSP in 1960. The DSP has never achieved electoral breakthrough and has little effect on working class or union politics other than to buttress LDP dominance by fragmenting the opposition. Founded to occupy the middle ground between the LDP and JSP, the DSP's main ideological and policy commitment is democratic socialism: a welfare state and the integration of labour into the political process. Like the JSP, however, it is dependent on Domei for organisation, personnel and finance. It is traditionally regarded as right-wing and close to the LDP because of its origins and frequent denunciation of radicalism. Continued LDP dominance has led elements in JSP–Sohyo to advocate an anti-LDP alliance, though this never appeared except as parliamentary faction politics.

In 1969 the JCP had 38 seats in the Diet, more than in 1948 when it was seen as such a threat. The JCP retains considerable *individual* support in the unions, it has members in the Sohyo leadership and, despite recurrent conflict, they enjoy a common ideological heritage. The JCP is better organised, more flexible and better disciplined than the JSP and DSP and not dependent on the unions for a base, but it is small.

Japanese unions are extreme victims of a functional confusion common to all unions: to what extent are they 'party-political' or 'industrial' bodies? Of course, this is a false distinction but the debate over the balance between the two is ever-present. Political involvement is given an added twist by the marxist heritage which extends union activities into human liberation whereby unions, not the party, 'assume a certain responsibility for the souls of the workers'.[22]

Trade Unions and Party Policy-making

The Federal Republic of Germany

Ideology is important in the DGB–SPD relationship as 'German Social Democracy has always ... devoted special attention to theory and discussed their programs with a special intensity'.[23] Since 1949 the DGB has issued three *Basic Programmes* (1949, 1963, 1981), and four *Action Programmes* (1955, 1965, 1972, 1979) setting out medium-term goals and assessing the Basic Programme's realisation. The most important single document is, however, the

SPD's 1959 Programme. The labour movement's original post-war programme was radical. To avert the re-emergence of a conservative nationalism the DGB sought full participation at all levels of economic and political decision-making, a welfare state, extensive state planning to guarantee full employment and the socialisation of key industries. This depended on the SPD forming a government, but the election of the CDU (1949) established a conservative political environment.

DGB strategy was confounded by electoral defeat and the narrowly averted split of 1953 which its partisanship provoked. IG Metall persuaded the DGB to adopt an Action Programme (October 1954) stressing collective bargaining, not party politics. This reorientation was not generally accepted, partly because IG Metall's dominance was resented (it became known as 'IG Krawall' – IG Trouble) but also because the DGB failed significantly to influence CDU governments. The Bad Godesburg Programme was linked to DGB politics through the perennial conflict between *council democrats* (workers' control) and *social partners* (corporatists). The latter group were supporters of those in the SPD who advocated the abandoning of residual marxism in favour of Keynesianism as an alternative to the social market economy. The 1959 DGB congress began the process of reform which culminated in the 1963 Programme which followed the same lines as the SPD's Bad Godesburg programme.

The unions were divided by the SPD's entry into government. Greater consultation stilled many doubters but coalition government prevented the realisation of the DGB's key aim: the extension of codetermination. Problems of economic management also strained the relationship but the DGB did all it could to support the government, remaining tenaciously loyal:

> Only ... when the SPD had lost all bargaining power within the coalition and with the unions, and the party itself had become embroiled in a severe identity crises, did the unions distance themselves from the SPD. They did not want to get drawn into the downward spiral of the SPD and put further stress on the ability of their own organisations to integrate.[24]

Frustration and disappointment, however, did not lead to a leftwards swing by the unions.

The union impact on SPD policy comes through their factional role which is anti-left. SPD policy is determined by an 'inner cabinet' of about a dozen senior figures (when in government this is dominated by the SPD Chancellor) and the 39 member executive elected by the bi-annual congress. Congress, with 400 delegates, is the supreme authority, but usually approves the leadership's line.[25] Union influence is not only transmitted by personal relationships (which are usually very close) between union and party leaders but by the *Gewerkschaftsrat* (Union Council) and the *Arbeitsgemeinschaft fur Arbeitnehmerfagen* (AfA – Working Community for Workers' Issues). The Union Council was founded in 1967 by the SPD specifically to improve relations with the unions after the shift to the *volkspartei* model and concern over the possible adverse consequences of entry into government. Though deliberative, its composition means it cannot be ignored: on it sit the heads of all DGB unions who are SPD members, together with the heads of the white-collar DAG and DBB. AfA was set up in 1972 to supplement the Union Council. Its name suggests a rank and file body concerned with union members' interests; in fact, it was created by the SPD leadership to counter the growing power of the left-wing Jusos (the Young Socialists), AfA is especially important at *Land* level as it (like the Women's and Youth organisations) sends representatives and proposals to congress. Politically, the Union Council is more important than AfA, though neither has as much influence as the informal and personal contacts within the SPD–DGB elite. After 1982 the SPD proposed stronger links – suggesting, for example, preparing joint policies on the British model.

As the SPD is the only party openly courting the unions the DGB will continue to support it, but electoral dealignment and the opening to the Greens has worried the DGB. The SPD's anti-nuclear policy, for example, designed to woo the Greens, led Adolf Schmidt (leader of the energy workers and SPD deputy) to vote against the party and support the CDU–CSU Christian Social Union pro-nuclear policy in the Bundestag. State financing of political parties means that the DGB has little financial muscle to wield in the party. Individual unions do make contributions to the SPD and at lower levels specific payments have been made in support of union candidates but these have aroused controversy. However, these have been sporadic, are not DGB policy and are not comparable to sponsorship. Indirect support is of greater significance and includes a well subscribed workers' educational movement, recruitment of SPD members, a news service, over 50 union periodicals with a circulation of about 13m, bureaucratic services (direct mailing, posters, leaflets, petitions), and on rare occasions demonstrations and strikes.

Sweden

The closeness of the LO–SAP policy relationship is remarkable despite the absence of organisational links. Union influence at the national level of the SAP is weak, unions have no bloc votes, no guaranteed executive representation, and no offficial say in the election of the party leader.[26] Considerable hostility to collective affiliation is often voiced and contracting-out is widespread – about 65 per cent of the LO's members oppose collective affiliation (whilst supporting the party–union relationship) and affiliation votes are frequent. Frequent ballots, however, strengthen the party–union relationship and enable the case for and against to be debated openly, preventing ossification by keeping the party in close contact with the workforce. State subsidies mean that unions have no financial clout.

The *arbetarekommun* policy role is indirect but important. These are not delegatory bodies; union members attend and vote as individuals. They are important for the SAP in policy-making as they enable the party's message to penetrate to the grassroots and provide feedback, though the process is carefully guided by the party elite. There are also 500 SAP factory branches which discuss extensively policy proposals; the conclusions when communicated to the party's upper echelons are accorded great weight. In 1982, for example, the Metalworkers' Union involved 14 695 of its members in study circles (modelled on the SAP's system) to discuss political issues, mounting information drives in support of the party. Ultimately, policy is determined by the party congress which debates resolutions emanating from the movement's grass-roots. Once approved, however, there follows a *remiss* procedure in which policies are redebated at every level of the movement to achieve a durable consensus involving the maximum number of party members. The result of the *remiss* is subject to congress's approval.

There is, then, a complex consultation process to establish the workers' concerns and the results figure prominently in party policy despite the absence of unions as a party faction. An indirect relationship has a number of political advantages: the SAP penetrates directly to the factory floor – union members, and not just the activist stratum, have a say in party policy, affiliation votes periodically demonstrate the relevance of the SAP and party politics to union members in their everyday concerns, and finally, it partially preserves the SAP from the charge of being a union party.

Democratic socialism provides a common ideological heritage for the labour movement. Fourteen of the 24 LO unions have clauses in their constitutions committing them to socialism and, 'to establish that the trade union movement is to promote democratic socialism of the type represented by the Social Democratic Party'. There is no authoritative definition of socialism so 'the use of [socialism] would not help clarify the LO's orientation further'. Thus:

> The present constitution of the LO established that it as an organisation has a duty which goes beyond the boundaries of what may be considered to be the trade union sphere in the narrowest sense; that it shall not only defend the interests of its members in the workplace and on the labour market, but that it shall also defend those members' interests in the broader context of the community.[27]

For electoral (as well as ideological) reasons, the SAP refuses to be seen as the LO's party and there have been conflicts stemming from the dominance of the party's electoral strategy. Despite their supremacy the gap in terms of votes between the SAP and their opponents is narrow, and the party's main interest is in winning elections. This does not mean that the SAP shifts to the right; instead it modifies its policies to ensure electoral acceptance and extend the period of implementation. The SAP's strategy of *walfardstaten* involves the rejection of state socialism and socialisation of the means of production in favour of full employment sustained by private economic growth. Whatever programmes and policies have been adopted by the LO and SAP, this remains the core even when both realised the limits to reformism. Despite these strains the party–union relationship has been maintained out of a conviction that co-operation could maintain the welfare state and economic growth.[28]

Despite the consensual nature of Swedish politics considerable potential for polarisation exists in the historic compromise between capital and labour whereby capital accepted labour's political hegemony in return for accepting capital's economic hegemony. Any attempt by the LO or SAP, singly or together, to intervene in property rights reveals the limits of the compromise. Labour movement solidarity has been crucial at such times, blunting the attack of the movement's opponents, so helping to preserve SAP dominance even when the LO and SAP were in dispute.[29]

The United Kingdom

Affiliated unions have rarely asserted their power in the Labour Party and the chief characteristic of their role is reticence. Their influence in policy-making has been essentially negative, closing-off certain policy options.[30] Union bloc votes at the party Conference betrays the origins of the Labour Party. Antagonism to it lies not so much in its existence but in the consequences of an interconnected union and party leadership which excluded the CLPs. Resentment peaked in the 1950s with the alliance of the TGWU, the Miners and General & Municipal Workers who controlled conference against the left. The bloc vote destabilised after 1956 with the defection of the TGWU, and though a pro-leadership bloc vote was recreated after 1961 there were significant shifts between 1966–8. The autonomy of union general secretaries was circumscribed by the decentralisation of power in the unions and barriers between union and party activists were lowered by a common frustration over the performance of the Labour governments of the 1960s and 1970s.[31] The unions' role is generally conservative, being concerned with the party's electability.

Though organisationally separate and with different functions, they have complementary aims, but the number of trade unionists active in the party has fallen. Since 1964 there has been a steady decline in the number of trade unionists voting Labour despite continued growth in union membership; the number of union members collectively affiliated to the Labour Party by their unions *increased* by over 500 000 (8 per cent), but the percentage of TUC membership voting Labour fell by 1.9m (34 per cent). The level of union affiliation to Labour is largely an administrative decision, unions generally affiliating slightly less than their industrial membership. A comparison of the party affiliation with union membership of the ten largest party affiliated unions shows they, on average, affiliated 84 per cent of their industrial membership (Table 3.1): only one (the NUR) affiliated more than their TUC membership to the Party. The proportion of affiliated members will decline because of closer supervision of political contributions and the cost of affiliation on unions hit by recession. Both are striving to rebuild the party's grassroots organisation and contacts with the workforce.

Table 3.1   *TUC–Labour Party membership of ten largest party affiliated unions compared ('000), 1986*

	Membership affiliated to			TUC members affiliated to Labour (%)
Union	(a) Labour Party	(b) TUC	Difference	
TGWU	1250	1434	184	87
AEU	800	974	174	82
GMBATU	650	839	189	77
NUPE	600	663	63	90
USDAW	359	385	26	93
COHSE	200	212	12	94
UCATT	188	248	60	76
UCW	182	194	12	94
NUR	144	130	+14	110
EETPU	136	347	211	39

Source: Labour Party and *TUC Bulletin*, 5 (July 1986) p. 4.

In this context the party's commitment to socialism (Clause 4 of the 1918 Constitution) is important. Not all affiliated unions have a similar commitment in their constitutions but affiliation requires them to accept the Party's constitution, so in theory all affiliated unions are committed to socialism. Socialism, however, has become increasingly unpopular with union members and Labour voters, yet Clause 4 remains the party's essence and to remove it would be unthinkable, but the unions want an electable party.

The growing weakness of the party–union link, the undermining of two-party politics and the long established conventions of union access to all governments shook the TUC's political strategy. An electorally attractive Labour Party recognised as a party of government is central to the unions' conception of their role in the polity, and they are ill equipped to operate in any other mode. The desire to see the election of a Labour government led the unions to accept policies that were hitherto anathema, for example, on the role of the law in industrial relations and the need for a 'proto-incomes policy' (the National Economic Assessment) to underpin Labour's employment and economic policies.[32] Common aspirations facilitate cooperation, but cooperation is not always easy:

> It was the unions who spawned the Labour Party eighty years ago to achieve those objectives that lie beyond the promise of collective bargaining. The Union have watched the Labour Party grow up, like a parent watching its child – sometimes with admiration, sometimes with admonishment, sometimes with anticipation, and sometimes with astonishment.[33]

The point is that the unions have *watched* the party's development. Since 1900 both have insisted on their autonomy and, significantly, if any participant has enjoyed an edge it has been the party, whose supra-class national electoral strategy has been endorsed by the unions.[34]

The United States of Amercia

Labour's relationship with the Democrats is determined by the decline of party and the growth of a candidate centred electoral process.[35] This, the rise of new groups in the party and the unions' numerical decline meant that the unions' prominence before the controversies of the late 1960s and early 1970s disappeared. Unions nevertheless still have resources which made them significant in Democratic Party politics. Their disappointment with the Carter presidency and the 1980 election result forced them to overhaul their political arrangements away from the national level to grassroots candidate oriented action. The vital element was the *Committee on Political Education* (COPE).[36]

COPE exists at all levels of the political system. The state COPE makes endorsements (via representative conventions) for state-wide offices, such as governor or Senator. It also endorses the recommendations of Congressional District COPEs for the House of Representatives. Congressional District COPEs combine to plan and execute their activities statewide. Local Union COPEs engage in political education and provide delegates to City, County, or Congressional District COPEs. They operate via committees: Finance, Public Relations, a Screening Committee (this checks voting records, interviews candidates, recommends endorsements), Volunteers in Politics (manages the campaign), and the Registration and Precinct Organisation Committee (registers and maintains contact with voters). COPE's direct policy-making role is limited, but its indirect role in influencing the environment of candidate selection could be crucial. The modernisation of union political activities, for example, employing computers to match union membership and voter registrations to utilise direct mailing, makes COPE an influential and valuable ally.

Unions remain prominent at national level. In 1987, for example, there were 30 (8 per cent) individuals associated with unions on the 380 strong Democratic National Committee (DNC) and 5 (14 per cent) on the 35 member Executive. A *Labor Advisory Council* (LAC) was created in January 1982 with representatives from the 26 largest AFL–CIO affiliates to play an active role in fund raising and campaign strategy formulation. Currently the LAC is chaired jointly by the presidents of the Bricklayers and the Service Workers and the Communications Workers treasurer is secretary. The exchange of political intelligence was facilited by COPE representatives regularly attending DNC campaign targeting meetings, whilst the DNC sends representatives to the AFL–CIO's seven annual regional meetings. Labour is also represented on the party commission which draws up the rules for the primaries.

These changes were the inevitable consequence of a candidate centred electoral process and an adverse political climate which forced the unions out of 'smoke-filled' rooms:

[we] intend to stay active in every phase of the political life of this country. Our choice is not whether to be involved . . . we are involved . . .

Our choice is whether we will be among the victims or among the authors of events. Were it not for the labor movement, American politics would be taken over lock, stock and barrel, by the special interests hungry for money and power. Not just one party but both would be controlled by the bankers and oil barons and by the admen, lawyers, consultants and lobbyists who serve corporate greed. Our goal in politics is simply to elect people who share our committment to decent government – to policies that simply allow people to help themselves.[37]

The post-Meany AFL–CIO learnt the lesson that if labour was to be influential it must conform to the process and structures of the Democratic Party. They are also acutely aware of the dangers, as happened to Mondale, of a candidate being labelled as 'labor's'. The unions' purpose was not to control the party, this in any case is not possible, but to ensure that candidates paid due regard to union interests:

The labor movement influences the formation of the Democratic Party's national platform in the same way that other constituent groups do. Labor organizations testify and have input during the platform hearings in the year prior to [the] national Convention and *lobby for positions of importance to them in the same way as any other group does.*[38]

Japan

One of the main reasons why the JSP and DSP are electorally unpopular is their close relationship with Sohyo and Domei. Ideologically the main debate in the JSP has been over whether or not the JSP should be a supra-class party of a West European social democratic type. The JSP's minority status and reliance on Sohyo has inhibited the creation of a mass base, but an attempt to create such a base would most probably result in conflict between and within JSP–Sohyo and DSP–Domei. Both JSP–Sohyo and DSP–Domei have a similar relationship: in neither are unions affiliated on British lines, and influence over policy depends neither on personnel nor bloc votes but on the unions' role as a surrogate mass base and a mobiliser of votes.

Ideologically, DSP–Domei is closer to West European social democracy and is willing to work with the LDP but not with the JCP or the left factions in the JSP. It is devoutly anti-communist and rejects the JSP's tradition of class struggle in favour of a supra-class electoral strategy analogous to the catch-all model. This, however, contrasts strongly with its dependence on Domei, for those unions which split from Sohyo and the factions which left the JSP recognised the need for some form of party–union link but did not establish one different from the one they fled. The DSP represents Domei in the Diet, whilst Domei propagandises for the DSP but its small size makes it even less autonomous than the JSP, though it is less factionalised. The DSP's gradualist parliamentary socialism is not traditionally a major element in the Japanese left's political culture and is therefore unfamiliar to an electorate accustomed to the rhetorical clashing of opposed ideologies.

Forty years of exclusion led in the 1980s to a significant shift in Sohyo's role in the JSP; Sohyo became less concerned with 'correct' policy and more concerned with the organisation of an electorally viable anti-LDP coalition, paralleling attempts at inter-federation industrial cooperation. The basis was to be joint discussion on the regulation of electoral funds and the revision of the Public Office Election Law, this would be followed by broader discussions on policy. Sohyo intended to maintain its connections with the JSP and sought a more flexible relationship in the hope that this would modify the electorate's image of the JSP.[39] Sohyo's president was extremely critical of the JSP's conservatism in clinging to the party, complaining that it contained too many old men blocking the rise of new ideas and new blood. Consequently the party stagnated, losing electoral support.[40] In preparation for the 1982 elections Sohyo called for a recruiting and a grassroots organising campaign as well as a Y1000 per member levy to finance an election fund.[41] None of these measures had any perceptible effect on the movement's electoral fortunes, provoking a critical appraisal of the Sohyo–JSP link.

Sohyo's analysis identified five consequences of its relationship with the JSP. First, union dominance hindered the autonomous political development of the JSP into a mass party. Second, the absence of a mass party base meant that there was no countervailing force to the unions. Third, the inevitable consequence was that 'very frequently [the JSP] gives priority to trade union egoism instead of contributing to the growth of the party'. Fourth, despite the scale of its commitment Sohyo in fact did little to attract union members into party membership and participation. Finally, over-dependence meant there was an imminent danger of the JSP becoming Sohyo's electoral subsidiary, further reducing its attractiveness. From this, Sohyo drew four conclusions: first, and most obvious, the link with Sohyo weakened, not strengthened, the JSP. Second, party and union activity at the grassroots was virtually non-existent. Third, the guaranteed and uncritical support of Sohyo had made many of the parliamentary elite complacent. Finally, the JSP was too factionalised to be an effective policy-maker and political advocate.[42] The irony is that change could be brought about only by the massive *assertion* of Sohyo influence within the JSP, which might confirm for all time the electorate's view of JSP as a union party and split the JSP into pro- and anti-Sohyo factions, further fragmenting the anti-LDP opposition and perhaps depriving the unions of a voice in the Diet.

Unless the anti-LDP parties can cooperate, they are unlikely to challenge LDP dominance, but to challenge that dominance they need more effective organisation: 'Sohyo sincerely hopes that the opposition parties ... overcome their sectarianism, establish firm position [*sic*] to counter the fascist-like Nakasone Cabinet, extend ... cooperation and joint actions [*sic*]'.[43] This seems most likely to come from electoral success and less reliance on the unions, but without the unions they have little effective organisation. Sohyo's President Makieda, called for thorough self-criticism from Sohyo and the JSP, leading to an improvement in their electoral performance. Disinterestedness in union membership and socialism by the working class led Sohyo's General Secretary Tomizuka, to comment:

> In the light of our unfavourable result, some people say that the trade union movement is stagnating or the political influence of the bloc formed by the [JSP] and Sohyo is weakening. If the situation goes on like this, [the] employers' strategy to wreck [the] spring labor offensive will gather momentum, the Socialist Party–Sohyo block will be unable to apply a brake to a trend for its further decline, and it would allow the LDP to stay in power for years to enjoy despotic one-party rule.[44]

The continued decline revealed in the 1986 elections makes this comment even more apposite. The difficulty afflicting the party–union relationship is that recognising the weakness does not confer an ability to remedy the defects.

Parties and Unions: A Procrustean Relationship

The party–union relationship originates in the historical weakness of unions in collective bargaining and the electoral efforts of an 'out-group' (the industrial working class) to enter the political process. Union development as an interest group and the growth of labour sympathising parties to the point where they became governing parties promoted separation. The exception is Japan, but even here a more flexible relationship is sought precisely as a means of promoting the labour movement's political influence.

The emergence of corporatist politics and catch-all parties was the logical culmination of mass democratic politics, not a disjuncture in the development of the party–union relationship. Mass politics means that 'separate but interdependent' describes their relationship. Unions and parties in liberal democracies do have common interests, but they also have their own organisational imperatives: unions as interest groups, parties as electoral competitors for office. Significantly, many unions (even in Britain) and their central organisations insist on 'non-partisanship' so as to work with any government; too slavish an identification with a party might limit their influence. A political party dependent, and perceived to be dependent, on the unions is in danger of condemning itself to political marginalisation.

Unions look to political parties as a conduit for their influence and, in return, they provide important resources to the party. Consequently, they are concerned for the electability of 'their' party. Nevertheless, the most characteristic feature of the party–union relationship is the reticence of their participation, produced by an acceptance of the party's definition of its electoral interests by the unions. The catch-all party dare not rely on one socioeconomic interest or class, for to do so risks electoral defeat and exclusion from government, so its strives to construct a cross-class electoral strategy. For unions to impose a policy or programme risks promoting a negative electoral image, possibly resulting in the unions' preferred party exclusion from government. In Chapter 4 we shall consider the impact of this on political recruitment and voting behaviour.

4

The Decline of Working Class Politics?

Recruitment and Voting: Decline or Change?

In Chapter 3, we examined the organisational and ideological links between unions and parties. This relationship was seen as mutually beneficial but as parties and unions developed they generated separate interests whilst remaining interdependent. The change from 'outsider' to 'insider' led to changes in party social structure, whilst the decline of blue-collar industries and the rise of the public sector produced a more professional 'middle class' ethos. These developments converged to produce an activist stratum in the party whose concerns and attitudes were at variance with those of the traditional working class who became increasingly receptive to a right of centre political appeal. This has been described as 'the decline of working class politics' and this chapter examines the reasons for, and the consequences of, first, the declining presence of members of the working class in the elite of 'their' party and, second, the drift of working class voters from these parties.

First, in personnel terms there has been a decline in the selection and election of working class parliamentary representatives in Britain, Sweden, West Germany and Japan and, where the unions' party is a party of government, in the presence of trade unionists at cabinet level. In the United States the separation of powers and the absence of a separate labour party makes unions only one element competing for influence within the Democratic Party; nevertheless, a 'labour party' does exist in Congress, and American unions have striven to increase its size and influence. A common feature is, therefore, decline in union influence and presence in these parties due to the decline of traditional working class groups committed to party-political action, the rise of middle class activists and social movements who have challenged the position of the traditionally dominant groups.

The second aspect of decline is voting behaviour and partisan dealignment. In all the countries examined (except Sweden) union members have become increasingly less committed electorally to the party most closely identified with their interests. This is the result of both long-term socioeconomic change and short-term factors related to discontent among union members over party policy in and out of government. Unions can no longer take their members' electoral support for granted and justify their party-political loyalties, modifying their (and their party's) appeal to win back lost support.

Trade Unions and the Politics of Recruitment

The West German Social Democrats

Despite its democratic ethos the SPD's power structure places control over candidate selection in the hands of an elite composed of *Länder* functionaries and elected grassroots representatives; unions have little role in the SPD's recruitment procedures but organisational overlap results in considerable influence.[1] In the Bundestag (1983–6), 266 out of 520 deputies (51.2 per cent) were union members, of these 230 (86.5 per cent) were members of DGB unions. Of the 202 members of the SPD *fraktion* (parliamentary party), 196 (97 per cent) were members of the DGB. Table 4.1 shows the incidence of union membership in all Bundestag *fraktionen*; all but two DGB unions have parliamentary representation (Table 4.2).

Unions do not sponsor candidates, nor are 'union' candidates selected: aspirants must rise through the SPD, conforming to party expectations. Though the incidence of union membership in the Bundestag is very high, party loyalty is infinitely more important as a determinent of behaviour, 'union membership has become a hallmark of progressive political commitment and also a device to secure re-nomination... *Membership alone signifies at best an orientation not a policy priority*'.[2] The incidence of union member-

Table 4.1 *Trade union representatives in the Bundestag, 1983–6*

Party	Total MPs	MPs with Union Membership	MPs Union Affiliated to: (a) DGB	(b) Other Federations
CDU/CSU	255	52 (20.4)	21 (40.4)	31 (59.6)
SPD	202	196 (97.0)	193 (98.5)	3 (1.5)
FDP	35	3 (8.6)	1 (33.3)	2 (66.7)
Green	28	15 (53.6)	15 (100)	0 (0.0)
Totals	520	266 (51.2)	230 (86.5)	36 (13.5)

Source: *Datenbuch zur Gesichtes des Deutschen Bundestages 1980 bis 1984*, p. 280.

Table 4.2 *Bundestag Members by DGB union affiliation, 1983–6*

Union	Members	Union MPs %
Public Service	91	39.5
Education	42	18.2
Metalworkers	32	13.9
Paper Workers	18	7.9
Commercial Workers	13	5.6
Construction	10	4.3
Mining and Energy	7	3.0
Railways	7	3.0
Chemicals	2	0.8
Agriculture	2	0.8
Postal Workers	2	0.8
Art and Graphic	1	0.4
Plastics	1	0.4
Food Workers	1	0.4
Police Union	1	0.4
Total	230	100

Source: *Datenbuch zur Gesichtes des Deutschen Bundestages 1980 bis 1984*, p. 284.

ship has increased, but the number of union *officials* in the legislature has declined although the Schmidt cabinet (1976–7) contained five ministers who were former high union officers.

Union participation in recruitment is limited by the increasingly dominant white-collar public sector professionals politically to the left of the 'traditional' working class. A study of SPD branches in Mulheim (in the Ruhr) showed that members of the Metalworkers' and Mineworkers' unions were at a disadvantage in an increasingly socially mixed milieu. This increases the danger of the SPD's isolation from the blue-collar working class. There remains extensive support amongst the *industrial* working class for the SPD, but this is a declining socioeconomic group.[3]

Government was a mixed blessing for the SPD as it coincided with the rise of the New Left critical of the SPD's record and the displacement of the traditional blue-collar working class within the SPD. This produced both resentment and a decline in working class recruitment, the percentage of new party members who were working class fell from 55 per cent (1956–61) to 26 per cent (1974). This change in social composition confirming 'rather a sharp division between a mass public that is for the most part only peripherally involved in policy-making and a small political public of active and influential participants'.[4]

The Swedish Social Democrats

The SAP has never portrayed itself as a working class party, similarly the LO does not define working class interests solely in terms of union issues. The SAP has consistently polled about 70 per cent of the working class vote, but the proportion of parliamentary representatives from working class backgrounds has never been high. In 1912, 30 of the SAP's Riksdag deputies were ex-workers, by 1945 this had risen to 38, but by 1969 this had fallen to 12, reflecting the professionalism of politics, social mobility and the shift from blue- to white-collar occupations. Union *members* have, however, become an important element in the Riksdag: increasing from 11 in 1933 to 34 in 1969; many began as manual workers rising up the party and union hierarchy. Between 1917 and 1976, 81 individuals served as ministers in SAP governments, but only about one-third were of working class origin or began their careers as manual workers. Currently, about 60 members of the SAP in the Riksdag are members of LO unions but only one Cabinet member, Roine Carlsson (Defence Minister) is a former senior union official (president of the Paper Workers); the Deputy Minister of Social Affairs, Gertrud Sigurdsen, was formerly responsible for social policy at LO headquarters.

Sweden shows the fallacy of correlating political influence with the social composition of the governing elite.[5] The Riksdag is not socially representative; politics is essentially a male, middle class middle aged activity, both women and workers having been consistently under-represented. As the Cabinet is recruited from the majority party in the Riksdag it matches the social composition of the *parliamentary* elite, not the groups supporting those elites.[6] The elite have, however, pursued policies which have been in the general interest of both the working class and the nation as a whole.

Despite the absence of constitutional or organisational linkages between the SAP and LO, union influence is considerable. The LO is not entitled to representation on the party executive but is well represented on this and the smaller management committee. Thus, 'Important trade union representatives, and among them more often than not the Chairman of the LO, have always been members of the management committee *precisely because they are leading Social Democrats*. The LO leadership also holds regular talks with the Social Democratic Party leadership.'[7] Union centralisation and a common ideological heritage helped inter-organisational communication, generating an extensive and secure political base for the articulation and representation of working class interests irrespective of the social exclusivity of the governing elite. Thus, 'The changes in the social composition of the [SAP] elite ... does not point to an increasing "embourgeoisement" '.[8]

The British Labour Party

No trade union movement, with the exception of the Japanese, has so close a party-political relationship as the British; the legacy of the Labour Party's origins as a vehicle for *trade union* parliamentary representation; is symbolised by their committment to the sponsoring of MPs.

In the general elections of 1979 and 1983 there were 133 and 119 sponsored Labour MPs respectively, the 1979 figure being the highest in the party's history (Table 4.3). Sponsored MPs tend to be concentrated in Labour's safest seats in the old industrial heartlands whose decline has led some unions to bolster their representation by sponsoring MPs who have not worked in their industry. Trade union MPs, like all MPs, have been 'professionalised': they are younger and better educated than their predecessors. By 1985 only four of the ten National Union of Railwaymen

Table 4.3   *Trade union sponsored MPs in the Parliamentary Labour Party, 1983.*

Union	MPs	% Sponsored MPs
Transport & General Workers (TGWU)	25	21.0
Mineworkers (NUM)	15	12.6
Engineers (AEU)	13	10.9
General and Municipal (GMBATU)	11	9.2
Railwaymen (NUR)	11	9.2
Scientific, Technical & Managerial (ASTMS)	9	7.5
Technical & Supervisory Staff (TASS)	6	5.0
Public Employees (NUPE)	5	4.2
Professional, Computer & Executive (APEX)	4	3.3
Electricians (EETPU)	3	2.5
Communication Workers (NCU)	3	2.5
Health Service (COHSE)	3	2.5
Steelworkers (ISTC)	2	1.6
Print Workers (SOGAT)	2	1.6
Distributive Workers (USDAW)	2	1.6
Seamen (NUS)	1	0.8
Building Workers (UCATT)	1	0.8
Print Workers (NGA)	1	0.8
Postal Workers (UCW)	1	0.8
Others	1	0.8
Total	119	100

(NUR) MPs had direct work experience of the railway industry, while even in the NUM which (despite rule changes) only sponsors ex-miners, younger and better educated mineworkers have been selected. The MPs sponsored by the TGWU are socially and occupationally more typical of the generality of MPs. The occupations of the 24 TGWU MPs elected in 1983 were: trade union officers (4), teachers or lecturers (5), lawyers (3), civil servants (3), journalists (2), Labour Party officials (2), commerce and industry (2), manual workers (2), and scientists (1).

Sponsorship does not, of course, indicate the extent of *union* influence in the *Parlimentary Labour Party* (PLP). Sponsored MPs are not a cohesive group: the *Trade Union Group* is moribund, though some union groups (such as the Miners) are more active. These MPs are no longer a solid right-wing bloc in the PLP and they have a broader range of political interests than in the past. The post-war trend towards a more middle class white-collar parliamentary elite has slowed. Labour Cabinet ministers have entered adult life as members of the working class, rising via education and/or the labour movement to elite status. Of the Labour MPs elected in 1983 over half were the children of manual workers; there were 19 ex-miner MPs but 35 were the *children* of miners.[9]

Evidence gathered in the 1970s and 1980s confirmed 'the decline of working class politics' at Labour's grassroots.[10] A study of Sheffield, for example, came to conclusions similar to the Mulheim study cited earlier, and a survey of party Conference delegates found them to be 'Middle class, militant and male', and in the coalfield constituencies the influence of the NUM seemed to be on a downward spiral. Social change should not disguise the fact that the Party's electoral strategy has always devalued 'class', and sponsored MPs have accepted that their primary loyalty is to the party.[11]

Changes in political finance law under the 1984 Trade Union Act and the unions' political exclusion after 1979 led to a reassessment of the role and value of the sponsored MP.[12] Sponsored MPs were portrayed as a valuable asset, able to speak out on union concerns independently of an anti-union media and contributed to representative democracy in a House of Commons dominated by business interests.

The US Democratic Party

Party organisation in the United States is weak, especially at national level. The party–union rupture of the early 1970s associated with the *Commission on Party Structure and Delegate Selection* and the McGovern candidature of 1972, is of great significance. The 'new politics' of the 1960s led to 'a convention of middle-aged, white, upper income males', which was 'top heavy with liberals, reformers, and grassroots activists'. The rule changes deprived blue-collar workers of representation but 'If Six-Pack Joe and the machinists wife from Dayton preferred to stay at home, so be it: they had forfeited their right to representation'.[13]

The difficulty in selecting a Presidential candidate is, of course, that only one person can be nominated so selection depends on group bargaining. Inside the Democratic Party labour is a major group and the AFL–CIO's General Board has traditionally been 'consulted' on the party's candidate; consultation does not, however, necessarily entail influence. George Meany, then AFL–CIO

President, was hostile to the new politics and activists who were gaining influence in the party in the late 1960s, regarding them as out of touch with working people. They, in turn, were equally dismissive of 'ethnic, beer swilling slobs', though much of the conflict was largely symbolic and by 1973 the AFL–CIO was again participating.[14]

Union absence from Democratic politics was crucial for their influence as other groups filled the vacuum. The unions were divided over the new politics but all agreed that non-participation meant no influence over the nomination.[15] What role should the AFL–CIO play? Suggestions that they integrate with the Democrats threatened bi-partisanship; Democratic nominees were usually close on domestic issues, so had the AFL–CIO much to gain?: they might be committed to a candidate unpopular with some unions and party elements, or be committed to a loser. With no alternative but to support Carter in 1980 and faced by a Republican victory the AFL–CIO revised its political strategy.

The *Committee on Political Works* (1980) sought to increase union effectiveness in nominating a presidential candidate. Hitherto, the AFL–CIO had remained aloof, leaving the affiliates to support their preferences; once the primaries were completed and the leading candidate(s) were apparent the AFL–CIO and its affiliates swung behind a candidate before the party convention. Instead, the Committee advocated early endorsement by the AFL–CIO 'to enhance the chances of a *mainstream candidate* for the nomination *behind whom the AFL–CIO and its members could rally with enthusiasm*, both in the selection and general election process'.[16] To avoid factionalism an endorsement would be given only if affiliates representing over two-thirds of the AFL–CIO's membership as represented on the General Board approved. No union was to promote a 'bandwagon effect' by making its own endorsement before the General Board, and affiliates were to consult their members on who *they* wanted nominated. If there was no suitable candidate, the AFL–CIO would not endorse.

These procedures were used in the 1984 presidential election and enabled the AFL–CIO to mobilise early to influence the caucuses and primaries. Support for Mondale was based on a wide ranging consultation involving one-third of the affiliated membership. Mondale was endorsed by the General Board and Convention, all 94 AFL–CIO unions were committed to him. The AFL–

CIO's assessment concluded, 'it was labor's strong campaign and the votes of its members that revived Mondale's run for the nomination by helping him to carry key industrial states after a series of early setbacks . . . *Our campaign permitted him to go to the convention with the nomination sewed up.*'[17]

Rule changes, the continued decline in party cohesion, an anti-union climate and labour's disappointment with the Carter presidency inspired the overhaul of labour's creaking political machinery. This rethink was promoted by Meany's successor, Lane Kirkland, and his COPE director, John Perkins, who sought to recreate their relationship with the Democrats. The unions would engage in open party politics and not rely on backroom power broking, electing delegates in a coordinated manner and, to a large extent, they succeeded. Labour had to rebuild their connections with the party and electorate: 'Don't leave your base, but we have to get these so-called new collar voters and also to the Yuppies. We have got to get to them with a message that is both non-threatening and also at the same time inclusive, to include them in what we are doing. Our populist message can reach these people'.[18]

In February 1987 the AFL–CIO approved the procedures (based on 1984) to be used in the 1988 presidential election campaign. The aim was a pre-primary consensus over one candidate: all presidential hopefuls (Democrat and Republican) would be invited to speak to union members via video and in print; they would then be asked for more detailed responses which would be publicised. Not all Democrats welcomed this new style AFL–CIO. The Iowa state Democratic chairman, for example, criticised these procedures: 'I want to get out of the house of labor and across the street to the community hall . . . The method labor used to establish its agenda was poor from a perception point of view. Any time in a political party when one group tries to set itself up as the dominant force . . . that organisation is going to have a problem'.[19]

The JSP and DSP

Japanese parliamentary candidates emanate 'from a highly complicated power struggle between and among political factions within the unions. It has long been an established practice of Japanese labor unions to decide at their annual conventions which political

party or parties they will support'.[20] In Domei this is uncompli-
cated as all affiliated unions are committed to the DSP, so only
DSP supporters are nominted. Sohyo's size and breadth of its
affiliates' political allegiances makes its selection process more
complex. There are two major factions: the *Mainstream* faction
(the majority) who support the JSP, and the *Anti-Mainstream*
faction, supporters of the JCP who unsuccessfully seek to commit
Sohyo to communists as well as socialists. Despite declarations of
party-political independence Sohyo and Domei operate a system
of single party support; the marginalisation of Sohyo–JSP and
Domei–DSP in the Diet encouraged the former to advocate
cooperation between 'progressive parties' in the Diet in an
anti-LDP faction. The JSP convention of July 1986, for example,
advocated the unity of all centre-left pressure groups and parties
and the unification of the JSP, DSP and Komeito behind a basic
programme.[21]

Trade union candidates are of two types: organisation candidates who might be regarded as 'sponsored', and former union
officers or others who secure official endorsement. Parliamentary
representation reflects the structure of the union movement:
dominated by Sohyo and public sector unions providing the majority
of representatives (Table 4.4). In the 1980 elections, for example,
there were 90 successful union candidates compared to 93 in 1977
and 86 in 1974. Of these, 77 (85.5 per cent) were supported by
Sohyo affiliates, and 54 (58 per cent of total union candidates and
70 per cent of Sohyo candidates) were supported by public sector
unions. The most successful public sector unions were the
Teachers with 20 (26 in 1977, 19 in 1974), the Railway Workers 15
(13 in 1977, 15 in 1974), and the Postal Workers with 9 (8 in 1977,
7 in 1974). Compare this with the most successful private sector
unions: Chemical Workers (Sohyo) 4, Garrison Forces Labor
Union (Sohyo), and the Textile Workers (Domei) with 3. In the
elections to the Upper House (based on national and regional
constituencies) 12 union candidates were elected in the former and
10 in the latter. Sohyo had 8 and Domei 2 successes at national and
Sohyo 10 at regional level, Domei none. Two independents were
elected at national level. In the elections to the Lower House the
LDP, Komeito, the National Liberal Club, and the Social
Democratic Federation had no successful union-supported
candidates.[22] Of Sohyo's 135 candidates, 98 (72.5 per cent) were

Table 4.4 *Labour candidates and deputies elected to the Lower House of the Japanese Diet, 1980*

Federation	Candidates	Elected	Elected (%)
Sohyo			
Public sector	98	54	55.1
Private sector	37	23	62.2
Sub-total	135	77	57.0
Domei	15	10	66.6
Churitsuroren	2	1	50.0
Shinsanbetsu	–	–	–
Independents	11	2	18.1
Total	163	90	55.2

Source: K. Koshiro, 'Political Power of Labor Unions in the Diet', *Japan Labor Bulletin*, 20(1) (1981).

from public sector unions, 37 (27.4 per cent) were from the private sector: of the former 54 (55.1 per cent) were elected and of the latter, 23 (62.2 per cent). Of the 77 Sohyo Dietmen, 54 (70.1 per cent) were from public sector unions, 23 (29.85 per cent) were from the private sector.

Once elected, the unions retain a considerable interest in 'their' representatives. They have, after all, provided money and organisation for their election; but they do not control their behaviour. These representatives are party men, though their unions know full well that ties of sentiment and self-interest ensure their responsiveness. Factionalism dominates their behaviour, so 'While trade unionists within a party truly reflect party union ties, their presence is more the result of the party's accommodating the union ... than of the union's placement within the party as an outpost of influence'.[23]

Trade Unions and Voting Behaviour

West Germany

The DGB cannot urge its members to vote SPD without risk. In the 1953 elections (for example), after a series of industrial and political defeats, the DGB was persuaded by the SPD to call on its members to 'vote for a better Bundestag' (i.e., vote Social Democrat). This provoked a bitter attack from the CDU and threatened a split in the DGB as Christian trade unionists contemplated secession. Instead of campaigning, it issues *Wahlprufsteine* (election guide lines), setting out the DGB's basic policy positions and objectives and 'By comparing these ... against the platforms of the parties, the union voter is supposed to be able to decide which of them pursues policies most favourable to labour'.[24]

Blue-collar support for the SPD weakened as SPD Chancellors grappled with the post-1973 recession and the compromise of coalition politics. Out of government, party–union relations did not improve because of the development of cooperation with the Greens, many of whose policies were disliked by many unions.[25] The interests of the organised working class were challenged by factions such as the Jusos (the Young Socialists) who were unpopular with the SPD's blue-collar voters, and the unions became identified with the party's right wing in an attempt to retain these voters. Despite these problems the electoral links between the two are significant enough to warrant two derogatory terms: *verfilzung* (entaglement) and *rote Filzokratie* (the red rule of entanglement).

The main basis of SPD electoral support is the urban industrial working class, though there are significant regional (Bavarian workers, for example, are more conservative) and religious (working class catholics tend to vote for the CDU–CSU) variations. After the defeat and division of Germany many SPD areas were lost in the East and the influx of large numbers of anti-communist refugees and the importance of catholicism in south-western Germany complicated the SPD's electoral task. The 'people's party' concept and the Bad Godesburg Programme boosted the SPD's attractiveness: in 1953 the part polled 29 per cent of the vote, and in 1972 45.8 per cent. This electoral environment made it difficult for the DGB to openly ally with the SPD for fear of antagonising 'non-working class' voters without whom it could not win office. By 1969 the SPD was making inroads into the catholic working class, the rural areas, the middle and professional classes. These gains were reversed after 1976 as the SPD government suffered from left–right factionalism, the Greens, and unpopular government policies.

The SPD electorate is *more* working class than the population as a whole, SPD membership is *less* working class: it is increasingly a party of the better off and better educated. The decline of blue-collar manual workers, public sector employment, education and social mobility, the rise of new social movements unresponsive to traditional 'class' politics, all squeezed the SPD. In the 1983 elections 1.6m SPD voters defected to the CDU–CSU, and 700 000 to the Greens. Many were DGB members.[26]

The Bavaria state elections (October 1986) revealed a new set of problems for the SPD. Bavaria is dominated by the CSU (in the 1982 elections the CSU had 133 Landtag seats, the SPD 71) and had industrialised rapidly – 45 per cent of its industrial workers were employed in growth industries (electronics, data processing, chemicals, aerospace and cars). Bavaria is traditionally very conservative and in the elections the SPD produced its worst performance since 1949, losing votes to the Greens (who entered the Landtag for the first time). The SPD's disastrous performance in the January 1987 general election led to the resignation of Willi Brandt as party chairman in protest at continued decline. Of greater significance were the Hesse elections in April 1987. The SPD had governed 'red Hesse' since 1947, elections were not due until October 1987 but were brought forward because the SPD–Green coalition collapsed. Hesse is a major industrial area and the election was interpreted as a microcosm of current West German politics. The CDU was committed to continued economic growth and nuclear power, appealing to 'conservative' industrial workers who had traditionally supported the SPD but were concerned about the Red–Green coalition. The result was a major SPD defeat, where the CDU–FDP (Free Democratic Party) won 56 seats, the SPD–Greens 54

The rise of the Greens posed a major political problem for the SPD and DGB. Many industrial blue-collar workers are now regarded as being on the 'right', often opposed to Green policies on energy and economic growth which they regard as a threat to their jobs and living standards. Though white-collar workers support the SPD in greater numbers, their partisanship is brittle and many are also attracted to the Greens. Dealignment is not only the result of socioeconomic change but also the SPD's policies in government. These developments question the viability of the SPD as a *volkspartei* and like the Labour Party it is trying to refurbish its policies and image to increase its electability.

Sweden

Few labour parties enjoy the degree of working class and union partisanship secured by the SAP.[27] Yet, in 1976, reflecting a general shift to the right in the industrial democracies, the SAP lost office. Defeat in 1976 can be interpreted in two ways: a short-term reaction to specific SAP policies which did not represent a threat to the long-term vitality of social democracy. Alternatively, defeat could be interpreted as the consequence of long-term socio-economic change which has eroded the political ecology supporting the Social Democratic ascendancy.

Economic growth, the decline of homogenous working class communities, shrinking blue-collar employment, greater equality and a leftwards move of the bourgeoise parties all weakened the SAP's electoral base. However, its *potential* base remains very large and increasing with the growth of white-collar unionism, but SAP policies are not automatically attractive to these voters. The 1982 and 1985 elections demonstrated the SAP's continued ability to win elections but an interesting pattern was revealed. The SAP remains the largest party but only once (in 1968) has it won a majority of total votes and the fragmentation of the opposition is crucial for the SAP. Despite continued electoral dominance the SAP's margin of victory remains small – between 1960–85 it averaged 3.1 per cent. This, and the marginal voters in the SAP's electorate, points to a growing heterogeneity of support forcing the party to mould social democracy to specific *publics* rather than make a broad class appeal.[28]

The SAP's experience suggests that partisan dealignment can be restrained by penetrating the electorate; in this, the unions have a key role. The high density of membership and the inter-connection of party and union provides a strong base compared to non-SAP electorates (Table 4.5). The SAP's electorate and membership are dominated by manual workers who grew up in a Social Democratic occupational community, but they are a declining presence, a change disguised by the influx of white-collar workers socialised by their families' traditional SAP loyalty. Whilst 70 per cent of the SAP's members are collectively affiliated by their unions, however, 'It seems that a large majority of these ... *do not actually think of themselves as party members*'. SAP membership as a pro-portion of the electorate has been high since the 1940s, as without

Table 4.5 *Party preferences by socio-economic group, % of party electorate (1985)*

	Party							
	VPK	*SAP*	*CP*	*FP*	*MP*	*KDSP*	*M*	*Electorate (%)*
Industrial workers	18	29	11	8	7	12	11	18
Other Blue-collar	22	29	22	15	13	14	20	22
White-collar(a)	12	11	7	13	11	10	5	11
White-collar(b)	23	16	14	26	19	39	21	18
White-collar(c)	10	8	9	21	26	12	16	14
Self-employed	4	3	8	9	16	3	11	8
Farmers	0	1	26	2	3	8	2	4
Students	11	3	3	6	5	2	14	5

Notes: VPK: Left Communists, SAP: Social Democrats, C: Centre Party, FP: Liberal Party, MP: Moderate Party, KDS: Christian Democrats, M: Green Party, White collar: (a) lower paid, (b) medium paid, (c) higher paid.

Source: *The Swedish Institute.*

such collective membership membership would have stagnated.[29]

Attracting votes has three main elements: the pre-election policy consultation process, 'information drives' by the LO inside the workplace, and the long-term political education process. Annually 30–50 000 SAP members attend courses for activists, whilst 20–60 000 attend study circles, many of which are run by the *arbetarekommun*, or by the Workers' Educational Association (ABF). The SAP has considerable access to the media: 'the Swedish press shows a clear bourgeoise bias, non-socialist papers accounting for about three-fourths of circulation. Only ... one-fifth of total circulation is affiliated to the [SAP], which has consistently won the votes of more than 40% of the electorate'. State support has been especially important at local level and all parties have benefited, but there are 21 daily labour newspapers and the LO is the only federation with its own papers. It owns *Aftonbladet* (a Stockholm evening paper, circulation 500 000) and is part-owner of a number of local papers, the biggest (100 000 circulation) being *Arbetet* published in Malmö. All unions have their own journals which devote considerable space to political affairs. Though the SAP has experienced dealignment, its ability to transmit its message down to the grassroots has sustained Social Democratic voting.[30]

The United Kingdom

The classic study of voting behaviour in Britain stressed the connection between class, union and party: those factors which inclined people to join trade unions (occupational community, political socialisation, market situation, and so on) inclined them to vote Labour. This study also warned that the unpopularity of trade unions might transfer to the Labour Party, leading to a significant loss of support.[31]

The erosion of Labour voting amongst trade unionists is part of a wider process of class dealignment beginning in 1951 when Labour polled its highest ever percentage of votes cast. The 1970s were crucial, accelerating this process despite predictions that Labour had yet to come into its full post-war electoral legacy. The two elections of 1974 did not see the withdrawal of loyalty but it became more conditional and the electorate more instrumental. Dealignment was also influenced by the electorate's perception of Labour's leftwards drift, the unpopularity of the unions, and the ebbing of support for central tenets of the party's philosophy.[32]

Short-term political discontent meshed with long-run electoral change in the 1979 General Election. The heaviest desertions from Labour were young non-manuals and skilled workers (Table 4.6). The 1979 election showed once again Labour's tendency when in government to antagonise its most loyal supporters, and industrial relations lost Labour the election. The election also demonstrated one further problem. In the 1960s partisanship helped obscure discontent over policies but after 1970 policy became increasingly important in determining electoral choice. Many of Labour's policies were deeply disliked not only by the electorate but by its own supporters, and in 1983 Labour polled its worst result since 1918 after four years of economic decline. Labour's electorate is increasingly complex, reflecting socioeconomic change, and can be sub-divided not only in terms of status but also in terms of production sector and region, with voters having competing interests.[33] Labour lost because of its policies and the 'Winter of Discontent': three issues central to the outcome – unemployment, prices, and industrial relations – centred on the role of the unions.

In the 1983 election there was a further swing from Labour amongst the working class, though a Conservative lead amongst skilled workers was cancelled by Labour's lead amongst the

Table 4.6 *The trade union electorate, % change, 1974–87*

| | October | | | | Net difference |
	1974	1979	1983	1987	1974–87
Trade Unionists					
Conservative	27	33	31	29	+ 2
Labour	55	51	29	43	−12
Liberal–Alliance	16	13	20	25	+ 9
ABC1 (Upper/MC)					
Conservative	56	59	55	54	+ 2
Labour	19	24	16	13	− 6
Liberal–Alliance	21	15	28	30	+ 9
C2s (Skilled Manual)					
Conservative	26	41	40	42	+16
Labour	49	41	32	35	−14
Liberal–Alliance	20	15	26	21	+ 1
DE (Semi/Unskilled)					
Conservative	22	34	33	31	+ 9
Labour	57	49	41	46	−11
Liberal–Alliance	16	13	24	20	+ 4

Note: Excludes minor party votes.

unemployed. Labour underwent a major retreat as the party of the working class becoming the representative of a *fragment* of the working class. Labour won a minority of manual workers and trade unionists: those employed in private industry, owning cars and their houses were far more favourable to the Conservatives. Class, whilst still the basic determinant of voting, is being over-layed by a complex of cross-cutting cleavages. Recent research points to the effect of *production cleavages and sub-cleavages* in the working class: union–non-union, public–private, manufacturing–service, blue-collar–white-collar, and so on. Manual workers were heavily represented in state industries and manufacturing, which were heavily unionised, and here employ-ment has declined fastest whilst the growth in aggregate union membership has not led to an increase in Labour voting. *The Economist* recommended any 'aspiring Labour member of parlia-ment . . . [to] find a decaying city centre with high unemployment, an ageing population and an air of despair'.[34]

Union response to defeat in 1983 was more circumspect than in

1979 as a result of a general awareness that a Conservative government and mass unemployment did not automatically result in Labour victory. The unions conceded that the electoral behaviour of their members was increasingly instrumental, and the Party's refurbished image was formulated with the 'new working class' in mind, a class no longer responsive to traditional cues. In the aftermath of electoral defeat and the miners' strike (1984–5) the unions helped stabilise the party (via Trade Unions For Labour), supporting the leadership's efforts to mould an electorally attractive party.[35]

Labour's poor showing in by-elections and Conservative strength in opinion polls led some unions (such as the Engineers and Electricians) to hint, as the 1987 election approached, that they might talk to the Alliance and speculated on reducing their commitment should Labour sustain its third defeat. Others, such as the TGWU, called on Labour to concentrate on issues such as unemployment and the welfare state to maximise support, since failure to do so would result in the defection of further union voters. In the 1987 General Election Labour increased its vote on 1983 by a mere 3.3 per cent.

During the past 20 years, the number of trade unionists voting Labour has declined dramatically. There has been a significant divergence between union membership and Labour voting: between 1964 and 1983 the number of trade unionists voting Labour fell by 1.9m (34 per cent), union affiliations to Labour increased by 0.5m (8 per cent), whilst TUC membership rose by 2.1m (34 per cent). Despite their commitment the unions are seemingly fighting a losing battle against long-run electoral trends.

The United States

Republican strategists speculate frequently about the transfer of working class voters from the Democrats. In 1969, for example, the AFL–CIO held exploratory talks with the Republicans and when, in July 1972, the Teamsters voted to endorse Nixon he described this as potentially one of the most significant decisions of twentieth-century American politics.[36] However, the expected realignment never materialised.

The Democrats have polled a majority of union members in every Presidential election since 1952, with the exception of 1972 (Table 4.7a and b). Republicans recognise their inability to win

Table 4.7a *Working class electoral behaviour, %, 1952–84*

	1952		1956		1960		1964		1968*	
	Dem	Rep	Dem	Rep	Dem	Rep	Dem	Rep	Dem	Rep
Blue-collar	55	45	50	50	60	40	71	29	50	35
Union Household	61	39	57	43	65	35	73	27	56	29
National Vote	44	55	42	57	50	50	61	38	43	43

	1972		1976		1980*		1984	
	Dem	Rep	Dem	Rep	Dem	Rep	Dem	Rep
Blue-collar	43	57	58	41	46	47	46	53
Union Household	46	54	63	36	48	43	53	45
National Vote	38	61	50	48	41	51	41	59

Table 4.7b *Working class electoral behaviour, Democratic lead, %, 1952–84*

	1952	1956	1960	1964	1968*	1972	1976	1980*	1984
Blue-collar	10	–	20	42	15	−14	17	− 1	− 7
Union Household	22	14	30	30	27	− 8	27	5	5
National Lead	−11	−15	0.2	0.2	−0.7	−23	− 2	−10	−18

Notes:
* = excludes independent, – = Republican lead. All minor parties–candidates are excluded.

Sources: *National Journal*, 12 (1 November 1980) and the AFL–CIO

union as opposed to *working class* voters: 'Some workers just can't pull that Republican lever. It's almost a religious kind of emotional thing.'[37] In the 1970s and 1980s there was a shift of working class votes from the Democrats but election results and poll data show the continuation of a 'natural' Democratic majority, though this became more difficult to mobilise as workers ceased to be the beneficiaries of New Deal policies.[38] In the 1984 Presidential elections the Republicans appealed explicitly to these voters and Reagan was *personally* very popular with working class Democrats, though again this did not translate into realignment.[39]

In 1982 the AFL–CIO's counterattack began using COPE and

labour's *Political Action Committees* (PACs). COPE reports on issues and candidates, publicises voting records, organises voter registration, and mobilises the union vote. The 1947 Taft–Hartley Act and campaign finance legislation forbid the use of union funds for electoral activity, and unions must form PACs supported by voluntary subscriptions. PACs are not new but their importance increased dramatically after 1974. Each PAC cannot contribute more than $5,000 to any one candidate's primary or subsequent election campaign but there are no restrictions on what can be spent on *issue politics*. In the 1984 elections there were 350 labour PACs but only 60, based on the biggest unions, participated widely (Table 4.8). Substantial though this effort is it is outshone by business. In 1974 there were 89 corporate and 201 labour PACs (15 per cent and 35 per cent of total PACs) and by 1986 the number of business PACs increased to 1744 (42 per cent) and labour to 384 (9 per cent). The AFL–CIO estimates that in the 1984 elections Republican PACs outspent Democratic PACs by 8:1, while labour PACs were outspent by business PACs by 4:1. One right-wing group, the National Conservative PAC collected $20m in 1983–4. Not suprisingly, calls have been made to curb PAC spending.

COPE's ability to mobilise labour behind Mondale in 1984 was reflected in his vote. Union members supported Mondale over

Table 4.8 *Top ten money spending labour PACs, 1983–4*

Union PAC	Amount ($m)
National Education Association PAC	2 177 756
UAW Voluntary Community Action Program	2 131 847
Active Ballot Club (United Food Workers)	1 933 898
Machinists' Non-Partisan Political League	1 865 697
Seafarers' Political Activity Donation	1 669 279
Committee on Letter Carriers' Political Education	1 600 890
CWA–COPE Political Contributions Committee	1 584 840
Transportation Political Education League	1 564 127
PEOPLE (AFSCME)	1 442 006
Sheet Metal Workers' Political Action League	1 233 667
Total	17 204 007
Total Labour PAC Spending	47 544 022

Source: Federal Election Commission, *FEC Final Report For' 84 Elections* (1 December 1985) pp. 13–14.

Reagan by 61 per cent to 39 per cent; this was repeated throughout all regions, age groups (except for the under-35s) and occupational categories (except for transport and service workers). In the Congressional elections AFL–CIO members voted 72 per cent to 28 per cent for union endorsed Senate candidates and 69 per cent to 31 per cent for House candidates. Union leaders recognised that Reagan's popularity ensured he would win, but they welcomed COPE's new style.[40] Despite this, American unions, like their British counterparts, face a hostile environment. No matter how effective COPE is until the long-term decline of union membership is halted, it will be mobilising a shrinking section of the electorate.

Japan

Japanese electioneering owes more to patron–clientalism than class loyalty. Apart from the media, parties utilise *koenkai* (personal support organisations), campaign postcards, and personal solicitation of votes. Koenkai are least effective in the case of the JSP and DSP. Electoral law forbids 'canvassing' but the 'solicitation of votes' by personal acquaintances is permitted and the JSP does well out of personal contacts: 'It is characteristic of the LDP that it relies not so much on mass communication or the media as on direct and personal contact with personal support organisations. *This indicates clearly that the LDP has more means of penetrating to the grassroots than others.*'[41]

The inevitable consequence of the unions' dominance of the JSP and DSP electoral organisation is that they tend to ignore non-union members (Table 4.9). The opposition parties *could* generate greater popular support – a study of local politics in Musashino, for example, demonstrated the JSP's ability to create a progressive coalition in stark contrast to national fragmentation. The hostility of the political environment 'where the ruling party has carried out a vast campaign of bribery and mystification to secure rural votes, and where the traditional fragmenting operations of the ruling class ideology are still effective' has to be appreciated. So, '[J]ust as Sohyo fails to extend its cover to any but "permanent workers", so the JSP fails to attract much support from the poorest and most discriminated against in Japanese society'.[42]

A union recommendation *does* influence behaviour: up to 50 per

Table 4.9   *Social network involvement by occupational category,* %

	Koenkai member	Neighbourhood contacts	Neighbourhood political discussion	Member of trade assoc.	Union member
White-collar	17.6	55.5	25.1	–	51.4
Service Ind.	15.8	54.8	16.8	–	20.0
Blue-collar	16.6	70.8	31.8	–	42.7
Merchants–					
Manufacturers	22.0	75.5	41.0	57.0	–
Farmers	18.3	97.5	42.9	34.0	–

Source: J. Watanuki, *Social Structure and Voting Behaviour in Japan* (Tokyo: Sophia Institute of International Relations, 1980) Table 9, p. 32.

cent of members in a public sector union, and 30 per cent in a private sector union admit that union recommendations influence their voting. Nomination by big public sector unions with nation-wide membership (for example, the Telecommunication Workers, the Railway Workers, and Post Workers) virtually guarantees election. The same also applies to nomination by some private sector unions such as the Automobile, Electrical, Textile, Ship-building, and Steel unions. Union recommendation is no formality; only when this has been given are unions permitted to raise and spend money on campaigning.

The dependence of the JSP and DSP on the unions has not made them immune from partisan dealignment. Class politics emerged in the 1920s but failed to influence partisanship significantly; electoral politics were dominated by two conservative parties and industrial workers were in a minority. In the 1950s a steady growth in conservative support was followed by the growth of leftism as the industrial working class expanded. Nevertheless, there remained a large conservative working class, and the 1960s were a decade of stagnation for the JSP and their situation worsened with the political and economic uncertainties in the 1970s.[43]

Voting by social category is what one would expect in an industrial democracy and the connection between union membership and voting is clear (Table 4.10). Blue- and white-collar workers have similar patterns of class identification and party support, and there is a distinct cleavage between the unionised and non-unionised. Studies of voting behaviour note that '[U]rban, mobile, unionized wage earners in large enterprises are simply far more likely to vote for one of the opposition parties than are the rural, stationary, non-unionised, self-employed engaged in small-scale agricultural and commercial enterprises'.[44] The union connection is vital as 'union ties ... are the counter networks which lend support to the JSP, JCP or DSP candidates ... *neighbourhood or trade networks are overwhelmingly under the influence of LDP candidates*, though all other parties utilise those networks, too, whenever possible'.[45]

Table 4.10 *Voting by occupation and union category, %*

		Right	Centre	Left
Unionised:	White-collar	20.0	20.0	20.0
	Blue-collar	19.4	16.1	64.5
Non-unionised:	White-collar	49.7	16.6	41.7
	Blue-collar	42.6	14.7	42.7

Source: J. Watanuki, *Social Structure and Voting Behaviour in Japan* (Tokyo: Sophia Institute of International Relations, 1980) Table 6, p. 29.

The 1986 general election indicated that class voting had entered serious decline. The JSP lost 27 seats (from 112 to 85) in the Lower House of the Diet; it was now smaller than the LDP faction of ex-Prime Minister Tanaka. Electoral decline can be closely related to the changing structure of Japanese industry and the decline of unionisation from 34.5 per cent (1970) to 28.9 per cent (1985); what remains is factionalised. Sohyo–JSP remains larger than Domei–DSP, but 60 per cent of Sohyo's members are in the public sector compared to 7 per cent of Domei's and the JSP's union base is eroding. Union opposition to the LDP's privatisation of the railways, for example, has lost the unions 10 000 members to second unions opposed to industrial action for political ends. Also, as many Japanese depend on rail transport, disruption caused not only hostility to the unions but, by extension, to the JSP. This decline has led to a reassessment of the party link. Masashi Ishibashi (then JSP chairman) had been striving to persuade the movement to abandon its marxism but failed to stem the loss of votes with the LDP taking, for example, five seats in the Tokyo area from the JSP. Continued economic growth has benefitted the LDP, but many JSP policies are increasingly unpopular with the electorate, especially the young. Some JSP strategists are now advocating for the separation of union and party to promote the growth of a social democratic catch-all party, though the signs are not propitious.

Party Politics: A Poisoned Chalice

As a remedy for market weakness party politics has an irresistible logic for trade unions. Workers are, after all, in a majority, having more votes than capitalists and, thereby, significant gains have been made. Party involvement, however, also entails costs. Further, we ought to remind ourselves of the complexity of political attitudes, for as V. O. Key noted 'Whether a labor vote exists that can be delivered by labor leaders is in a way a nonsense question'. He continued:

> The influence of labor leaders over their members probably differs enormously with time and circumstances and in each instance is so intermingled with other influences as to be beyond measurement... Union members, like the rest of us, manage to get along with a multiplicity of loyalties... Membership of a union does not mean that a person is invariably governed in voting by his interest as a union member. Moreover labor leaders compete with others for the vote of union members.[46]

A majority of the working class seldom vote consistently for their party. Labour parties recognise this, defining themselves as catch-all, not class parties, striving to govern in the national interest. Over-dependence on a class base or sectional interest can and does lead to the loss of electoral support – and, ultimately, political marginalisation, hence the appeal beyond their union or class base. All recognise the need for parliamentary representation and party-political action for both propagandist and policy purposes. In only one political system (the United States) do legislators have any autonomous power because of the separation of powers and weak party discipline. However, these same factors make it impossible for organised labour to deploy sanctions against legislators as labour is only one voice. Close identification with a party, then, does not necessarily give unions influence with that party when it forms a government as the party invariably claims a wider destiny. In Sweden, West Germany and the United Kingdom unions have highly visible connections (though in the case of the first two organisationally weak connections) with their respective party. In all three, however, proximity – be it organisational, ideological and/or personal – does not confer automatic influence. The danger of not pursuing this strategy is shown in the case of Japan where the party–union relationship is close but this reduces the party's attractiveness to non-trade union voters, and the JSP has been excluded from government since the 1940s.

Party politicians are seldom altruists. Unions can provide electoral organisation, finance, and manpower in addition to direct access to a large number of potential voters. In their early years these parties saw the organised working class and union support as a major precondition for electoral take-off. Once they become governing parties the connection can seem to be markedly less advantageous for both. When union wage demands came to be accepted as the main cause of domestic inflation these parties, except the Japanese, urged restraint: corporatist bargains were offered, hints concerning the consequences of failure and emotional appeals to a shared historical legacy were made. In every case there has been a sharp decline of 'working class' politics. Union members and manual workers are both less partisan in their electoral support for 'labour' parties, and less visible as an element in party social composition as a result of social, technological and ideological change. In some cases, notably the United States, West Germany and the United Kingdom, this has promoted conflict between the 'new' and 'old' groups in the party. Partisan dealignment, social change and internal party conflict have combined to undermine the electability of union supporting parties who suffered from the growing unpopularity of trade unions as the economies of the industrial states worsened.

Despite these problems, however, in no instance has the party–union link snapped. The general relationship was perhaps best described by Jack Jones (General Secretary of the TGWU in the 1970s) who was asked at a time of deep crisis between the unions and a Labour government if he ever thought of abandoning the party, replied 'Divorce never, murder often'.

5

The Rise and Fall of Corporatism

The Union–Government Relationship

Why did unions and government become so involved after 1945? The basic reason was the unemployment and recession of the inter-war years, together with the Second World War and its consequences. Unions were determined to secure a political settlement conceding them enhanced economic and political rights to prevent a repetition of the inter-war years. However, there was an acute awareness of the long-term dangers of this settlement. The inflationary consequences of full employment were regarded as politically corrosive as those of mass unemployment; an increased role for government raised doubts about the viability of political pluralism and concern was expressed about the dependence of governments on electorally unaccountable interest groups. Full employment would increase the power of trade unions, perhaps to the point where they exercised a veto power. The result would be a crisis of governability: governments would cease to govern, managing a complex group-based political process in which consensus became an end in itself, creating a deadlocked political system incapable of effective decision-making for fear of offending a major interest.[1]

Collective bargaining could not be left to bargainers but the complexity of the industrial polity meant that a successful anti-inflation policy would have to combine technical effectiveness and political acceptability; the former is largely dependent on the latter as an unacceptable policy cannot be effective. Union involvement in the political process would promote legitimacy and government authority by projecting an image of openness and responsiveness and, thereby, agreement (or at least acquiescence) from those deemed capable of frustrating a policy, or ultimately a government. During the 1970s these aspirations were elevated by politcal science into a general theory of government–*corporatism*.[2]

Corporatism is a pattern of government–group relations in liberal-democratic, industrialised polities where economic interest groups (recognised as authoritative and representative by government) participate in the policy process. Participation has three dimensions: unions *represent* their members within that process, they *bargain* with government on the contours of policy, and finally, they participate in *implementing* policy. Such a generalised concept cannot be applied universally, even though all the political systems considered have conceded a degree of participation to unions, not all are corporatist.

The political systems considered can be divided into three sub-categories. *Integration* is where unions (typically via their central organisations) are accorded the status of governing institutions. In return, they are expected to reconcile sectional demands with a national policy consensus agreed between government and groups. Sweden most closely approximates this model. *Inclusion* is where unions achieve a representational status, are consulted frequently by government but are excluded from effective decision-making. These unions strive for integration and though this may be achieved sporadically it is never institutionalised. This is the situation in West Germany and the United Kingdom. *Marginalisation* refers to the situation where unions achieve representational status but are confined to the periphery of the political process. This can result either from a deliberate act by the governing elites (as in Japan and, increasingly, in Britain), the unions' own organisational defects (such as excessive fragmentation), or the dispersal of and separation of government power, as in the United States.

Nowhere are unions excluded from participation but they remain subordinate as the state's prime task is maintaining the conditions necessary for continued capital accumulation. Whatever prominence unions achieve, the interests of capital predominate, as became apparent in the 1970s.

The Evolution of the Union–Government Relationship

Sweden: The Roots of Integration

Sweden's success in overcoming recession in the 1930s and 1970s has been ascribed to the willingness of groups to recognise a superior national interest and modify their sectional behaviour to achieve long-term gains. This is 'the Swedish Model': interest groups articulate opinion, define problems, contribute to policy formulation, and participate in implementation. This requires a political culture which stresses cooperation, group characteristics such as inclusive membership and centralisation, and government non-intervention (a crucial incentive for cooperation has been threats of state intervention).

This system dates from the 1930s and it is easy to assume the 'naturalness' of the Swedish Model, forgetting that it came at the end of a period of deep political and industrial turmoil. The legacy of bitter conflict and a perception by employers and unions of Sweden's vulnerability in the aftermath of the 1929–31 economic crisis was crucial, as was the victory of the Social Democrats. The Social Democratic government encouraged centralised union decision-making and wage bargaining with the SAF (which was anxious to avoid state regulation) and the Basic Agreement was their response to domestic and international pressures. The SAP's victory in 1936 and the war-time coalition helped the institutionalisation of this, and union access was secured at every level of the political process.

By the 1950s the Swedish Model of centralised wage negotiation coupled with an active labour market policy was taking shape. The Rehn–Meidner Model (Gosta Rehn and Rudolf Meidner were Social Democrat economists) formulated in the early 1950s was designed to secure full employment, low inflation, economic growth and economic efficiency. Integral to the concept was a wage policy which stressed equal pay for equal work irrespective of the industry's or firm's profitability. Wage solidarity would both restrain inter-union competition and compel industry to be efficient and profitable; any worker made redundant (for example) as a result of this policy would be retrained by the state for employment in industries short of labour.[3]

This system was dependent on centralised collective bargaining dominated by the LO and SAF whose negotiations determined the overall wage increase in the private manufacturing sector, enabling government to operate a 'hands-off' policy. The Swedish Model depended on a powerful spirit of cooperation based on the LO–SAF conflict of 1900–30, a high degree of organisational coverage, and an expanding international economy able to absorb Swedish exports. By the end of the 1960s these factors were fading as the structure of both labour market and the international economy changed.

The Politics of Inclusion: The Federal Republic and the United Kingdom

1. The Federal Republic
In reaction to their pre-war experience, German trade unionists wanted a few strong industrial unions as a protection for democracy; the British allowed the creation of a zonal secretariat which organised a conference at Bielefeld (March 1946). The conference approved the industrial union principle and their inclusion in one federation and in April 1947 the unions in the British Zone organised the embryonic DGB under Hans Bockler. By 1948, the unions in the American and French Zones were included, and the DGB was founded in 1949. The new unions were motivated by the need to secure a high degree of solidarity, whilst promoting the virtues of compromise, tolerance and non-partisanship so as to blend the various ideological strands of the working class into a single movement. One main purpose of this was to make the unions into the key force in the new Germany.[4]

The DGB's original aim of remaking the German political economy by democracy, public ownership and economic planning foundered on the realities of Cold War politics and the conservative victory in 1949. However, there is a strand in German political culture which accords a legitimate political role to interests. As the Federal Republic would be a liberal democracy, this would mean conceding a prominent role to the nascent unions in the political system. The establishment of a conservative political system between 1949–53 compelled the DGB to accept what was, in terms of its original aims, a limited role. As the Federal Republic developed the DGB was accorded a prominent role in politics, a role enhanced by the national consensus on the overriding need for economic regeneration in the 1950s and 1960s.

The DGB's position in the politics of the Federal Republic is a complex amalgam of tradition, a reaction to the disasters of the 1930s, a compromise with the social market ideology which placed the interests of business first, and an appreciation of West Germany's dependence on the international economy. Union leaders are accepted as participants in elite politics, but are seldom accorded equal weight with the employers. The DGB argues:

> There is no strict borderline that separate governmental and political matters . . . from economic and civic affairs. The unions are, like numerous other associations and organisations participants in a process of national opinion forming, which takes place through a consensus of individual and group interests.[5]

2.   The United Kingdom

Union–government relations have gone through a number of phases: 1870–1916 when unions were established as participants in the political and industrial systems; 1916–28 when a residual belief in direct action was abandoned in favour of accommodation with the state; and 1928–45 when this was achieved. The war and the 1945–51 Labour government established an increasingly unstable pattern of union–government relations which survived until the mid-1970s irrespective of which party was in government.[6]

In the first period the unions faced and overcame a number of legal threats and had, by the early years of the century, established themselves as organisations and were looking to increase their political role both electorally and as interest groups. This coincided with an upsurge in industrial unrest which confronted the political elites with a situation that the nineteenth-century political system (based on parties and elections) could not resolve, a situation exacerbated by the consequences of war. By the end of the 1930s the TUC was recognised as the authoritative spokesgroup for labour, was consulted on policy issues, with representation on many government bodies. This sytem emerged in a piecemeal fashion in an attempt to improve governability and avoid systemic crises; it was only with the appointment of Ernest Bevin as Minister of Labour in 1940 that a determined effort was made to entrench the unions within the state.

The post-war Labour government's attempts to institutionalise this failed largely because of a lack of union centralisation and the absence of an overarching national consensus, as in Sweden or Germany. As the experience of the war receded government–union relations settled down to one where unions were allocated a consultative position in a tripartite policy process in which they exercised a degree of veto power over certain policies. They nonetheless remained on the periphery of decision-making and as Britain's economic difficulties multiplied their participation was regarded as increasingly dysfunctional to the political system's operation.

Both British and German unions, despite a very different pattern of development, generated a *state fixation* from which they expected to make gains and which was used by the state in an attempt to secure union acquiescence in policies which were not always in the immediate interests of union members. In both cases the unions were confined to the margins of effective decision-making.

The Politics of Marginalisation: Japan and the United States

1. Japan

There are parallels between Germany and Japan. The original intention of SCAP was to encourage unionisation and political participation as a counter to the militaristic and nationalistic elements in Japanese society. Once again, the exigencies of Cold War politics produced a change resulting in a rollback of union influence in the early post-war years, but here the parallels end. Whereas German unions had played a pivotal role in politics since the end of the nineteenth century, Japanese unions were weak in every sense and a mass union movement emerged only after 1945. Japanese unions had no tradition of working with a state which had consistently sought their eradication. Japanese politics had no tradition of group politics or consultation (except with big business), whilst explosive growth, industrial unrest, marxist rhetoric and the visibility of communists after 1945 made unions appear a destabilising factor.[7]

The unions' inability to penetrate the policy process was not simply because of LDP dominance; in other conservative de-nominated political systems unions have become influential. The legal disabilities of the public sector unions (the largest section of the union movement) and the fact that the state as their employer sought to restrain their wages produced a militancy which made cooperation difficult. Second, Sohyo's use of marxist terminology convinced the LDP that the unions were anti-system. Third, the emergence of Shunto (the Spring Labor Offensive) in 1955 made business and government resist union incorporation, whilst the disruption it sometimes caused made unions unpopular. The LDP calculated it had little to gain from cooperation. Fourth, even if the LDP had been disposed to cooperate the political and organisational fragmentation of the unions would have made this difficult and time consuming. Fifth, by contrast, business was well organised and there was a long tradition of government–business interpenetration. Both the *Federation of Economic Organisations* (Keidanren), the spokesgroup for large enterprises in the public and private sectors, and the *Federation of Employers' Associations* (Nikkeiren) handled labour affairs, maintaining a close liaison with government. Sixth, in the 1950s and 1960s an abundance of labour not only weakened the unions but obviated the need for government intervention in the labour market (except in the public sector). The privatisation of key policy areas (such as manpower and incomes policy) which in other systems aided union access to the policy process, hindered access in Japan. It was only with growing economic instability in the 1970s that this 'non'-relationship with government began to change as the elites encouraged recognisably corporatist politics.

2. The United States

The US political system is neither politically nor ideologically suited to tripartite politics, though such structures existed in wartime. First, tripartism is not easy to promote in a federal system with multiple levels of government and a separation of powers. Second, though the example of West Germany shows that federalism can be overcome, there is in the US a powerful belief in *laisser-faire* and 'small government'. Both unions and employers have historically been suspicious of state involvement, and as the modern state emerged only in the 1930s with the New Deal, pro-business and anti-government sentiments were deeply entrenched in the political culture.[8]

Depression, mass unemployment, industrial militancy and then the demands of war laid the foundation of the government–union relationship. The rapid growth of unionisation in the new mass production industries led by the CIO and the increasingly partisan electoral role of the unions was accompanied by increased Federal legal and economic intervention under the New Deal which raised the stature and influence of the unions. The AFL and CIO believed the war, in which there was a growth in tripartism, would consolidate their position, but from 1943 a reaction against the unions set in culminating in the Taft–Hartley Act (1947). The result was a tacit compromise between business, labour and Federal government on the role of unions in the political economy.

Industrially the compromise expressed itself in the growth of the legally binding contract negotiated by large companies and unions at national level. These were wide ranging, covering issues (such as pensions and health care) which were more usually embraced by the welfare state, not just wages and conditions. Politically it took the form of accepting the unions as participants in the various aspects (electoral, legislative and bureaucratic) of the political process. Union leaders were incorporated into a relationship with business and politicians designed to stabilise the compromise worked out in the 1940s. Of course, much of the participation was symbolic but the fragmentation of the political system enabled the unions to achieve an unrivalled reputation as a lobbyist in Congress and become a major actor within the Democratic Party. The role of the state – in effect Federal government – was to guarantee and stabilise the system by making legislative concessions and administering the system of labour law through the National Labor Relations Board (NLRB). In the United States, then, the collective bargaining contract, union political involvement, and the system of labour law encapsulated a tripartite consensus which lacked tripartite institutions and enjoyed the support of both Republican and Democratic administrations.

Lacking a significant degree of institutionalisation, however, this settlement was vulnerable to political change as the economy's structure changed and as the US's world economic dominance declined. In the 1970s this happened: as industry faced increasing competition from abroad, employers ceased to value the stability provided by the established system, whilst social change reduced the influence of the unions in the party system. Beginning with the Carter presidency and accelerating under the two Reagan administrations the unions were forced onto the defensive.

Though beginning from very different starting points and in a very different institutional context, both the American and Japanese unions found themselves to be peripheral to the political process. In Japan, marginalisation was their normal situation and it was economic crisis which prompted a change of attitude, whilst in America it was the onset of economic crisis which demonstrated the actual position of the unions in politics.

Trade Union Participation in Policy-making

Before considering the unions' role in the policy process it is necessary to consider the main targets of group activity and what factors make a group influential.[9]

The Levels of Group Activity

Group activity is directed at the executive–bureaucracy and the legislature. Public opinion is a target but it is notoriously difficult to mobilise public opinion on union issues and in many countries opinion is hostile. As an aid to influencing parliament and the bureaucracy unions do organise demonstrations and campaigns, but these can be counterproductive.

The most visible group forum are legislatures, responsible for debating and approving legislation. Links with political parties ensure that unions have a voice in parliament, likewise specialist investigative committees and legislation scrutiny committees allow the transmission of union views. However, party government and executive dominance means that the parliamentary aspect of the policy process is largely symbolic. The exception is the US Congress. Only in rare circumstances (for example, coalition, minority government, a massive rebellion of government supporters) does party discipline weaken or collapse.

Interest groups devote the bulk of their resources to securing influence within the bureaucracy, the source of most legislation. Unions use their specialist knowledge and their claim to be a major societal interest worthy of consultation to become participants in policy-making. Civil servants and politicans see cooperation as an opportunity to improve the quality of policy and governance.

The Determinants of Influence

Organisational characteristics are important, but are not the sole determinants of influence. As a major interest group, unions can claim consultative rights, but they are not the only group that can legitimately make such a claim. Governments consult a wide range of interests, not only to diversify their sources of advice but also to avoid over-dependence on a group or groups. The complexity of the industrial polity means that policy tends to be a compromise between the wishes of government and groups. Groups find it very difficult to deflect a government determined to pursue a particular policy, so they tend to concentrate on influencing the details of legislation. Frequent attacks on the policies of an elected government might lead to a diminution of access.

Influence depends on providing government with a resource it values. This could be specialist advice – no civil service has a monopoly of wisdom, and consultation might reveal unforeseen problems which could cripple a policy and ease implementation by familiarising those affected with the policy's intentions. Finally, the political value of consultation in promoting political legitimacy should not be underestimated. It is not easy for groups to rail against a policy if government can show that they have been extensively consulted.

Consultation and participation does not, however, mean that a group will influence policy significantly. In market economies business and business interests are the dominant influence, often without overt political activity. Visibility and access are not measures of influence.

Integration in the Policy Process: Sweden

The institutionalisation of the union–government relationship means the unions have little need to 'lobby' government as they are present as an integral part of the policy process at every level. In 1982, for example, the LO was represented on 291 public bodies of all types and on 78 labour market organisations.[10]

Although the Ministry of Labour was originally established to help solve labour unrest and promote harmonious industrial relations, it is now unimportant as a channel for union influence. Its responsibilities – notably the labour market (employment service, training and job creation), occupational health and safety, and equality – are important to the unions, but exclude other policy areas of equal importance. Unions utilise more important aspects of the policy process: enquiry commissions, *remiss* procedures, and administrative boards. Commissions, composed of both experts and group representatives, allow direct input into the policy process. They are established frequently to consider a policy problem and set out solutions and, unlike similar bodies in other political systems, they are not a substitute for action; their purpose is to find agreed, workable solutions. Group representatives attempt 'even though they are formally independent of instructions from their particular association, to achieve compromise decisions based on the various group viewpoints represented on the commission'.[11]

The *remiss* procedure occurs after the production of a report and is crucial to the Swedish policy process. It, and its recommendations, are 'sent for the written comments of government agencies, special-interest organizations, and other relevant bodies. The Cabinet, taking due account of these comments, uses the reports as the cornerstone of its own recommendations to Parliament, which assume the form of a government bill.'[12] The unions spend a considerable amount of time formulating their *remiss* responses. After 1945 the political importance of the *remiss* procedure grew as government became more dependent on group involvement and as the issues dealt with by the policy process grew in complexity. No government would proceed with a bill if the results of the *remiss* procedure were negative; this means that the formal legislative process in the Riksdag represents the *end of the policy process*. This is because, first, all the important debates take place before a bill goes before the Riksdag, and second, voting in parliament is dominated by party discipline, and the SAP dominates both the Riksdag and government. The parliamentary process is largely formal, though the unions have members in the Riksdag.

The 14 central ministries are responsible for policy formulation, but implementation is by autonomous administrative boards composed of government and group representatives. The LO and the TCO are represented on about 30 (for example, the National Board of Education, the National Board of Occupational Safety, the National Board for Consumer Policies and the National Tax Board) but the most important is the *National Labour Market*

Board (AMS) responsible for implementing manpower, training and employment policy. Cabinet and Parliament have delegated a considerable amount of autonomy to the AMS; at national, regional and local level it has a decisive influence over the shape of labour market policies and labour market organisations (employers and unions) have a majority on the AMS. In 1984–85 of the AMS's 13 members, 9 were from the 'social partners'; LO 3, SAF 3, TCO 2, and SACO–SR 1. This, it is argued, allows policy to be formulated by those with the greatest knowledge and who are most directly affected. Policy is therefore not only consensual but can adapt rapidly to changing circumstances.

Sweden's political process is often referred to as *Organisations Sverige* (Organisational Sweden) and the groups as *Kravmaskiner* (demand machines) with a veto over parliament. The emergence in the 1950s, for example, of *Harpsund Democracy* (consultations between SAP politicians, civil servants and group representatives at the Prime Minister's weekend residence) demonstrated the importance of groups in post-war politics. It was abandoned after charges that it was a threat to democracy and accountability, though the 'spirit of Harpsund' still dominates the policy process. Whatever the dangers, the participants stress the system's ability to promote consensus and effective policies, and the political process depends on group involvement. After 1945, as a consequence of SAP hegemony, parliament's decline, and the pressure for consensus unions shifted from being 'sectional' to 'public', but integration is not cost-free and has promoted public debate about the demise of pluralism and parliamentary democracy. Swedes are acutely conscious of the dangers of becoming a corporate state.

The Inclusion of Unions in the Policy Process

The Federal Republic

Post-war democratisation and the corporatist tradition of German politics meant that interest groups would have an important role to play and the DGB was organised, in part, to be an effective interest group. Industrial unionism, centralisation and non-partisanship, for example, were organisational characteristics designed to improve the DGB's influence over government. The implications of this for pressure group politics and the influence of the DGB in the policy process are clear. It offers the opportunity of building up a 'patron–client' relationship, in which union influence is at its most direct during the preparatory phase of legislation. In this sense, the Federal Ministry of Labour is labour's 'spokesgroup' but the DGB's policy concerns extend beyond its confines. Union participation in the policy process is sanctioned and legitimised by the Social Partner ethos which allots unions a role in all areas of policy. [13]

The Bundestag's role as a policy-making forum in West Germany is limited despite coalition politics, as party discipline is strong and coalitions have proved durable. Legislative committees, however, do have some importance. Bundestag standing committees' places are allocated proportionately so encouraging bi-partisanship, they operate in closed session and take evidence. These committees are a major target for DGB lobbying as they can affect the details of legislation. Some committees are closely tied to their 'parent' ministry, whilst others (for example, Labour and Social Affairs) are more open to group influence. In coalition governments, these committees sometimes wield considerable influence. SPD members of standing committees invariably support the DGB's position but they often find allies in the CDU–FDP members. This 'pro-labour, bi-partisan' majority often present reports acceptable to the DGB, though this does not mean acceptance by government. Nevertheless, such reports could be used by non-SPD Chancellors to balance anti-union elements amongst their supporters. Bundestag members are also active in *fraktion* working parties *(Arbeitsgemeinschaften)* which take evidence from interest groups. The SPD *Arbeitsgemeinschaften* allow compromises to be formulated and a united parliamentary front presented.

Though all interest groups strive to make their voice heard in the Bundestag, it is inevitable that in a parliamentary system with strong party discipline effective decision-making resides in the executive. The DGB's most effective lobbying activity is within the ministries. As a major interest group the DGB can secure access up to and including the Federal Chancellor, though its relationship will vary from ministry to ministry, the strongest being with the Ministry of Labour. The welcome given to the DGB was, of course, warmer under SPD governments but, as the SPD could not afford to snub the employers conservative governments cannot ignore the unions. Policy-making is dominated by the higher political and administrative echelons of the Federal government, which includes group representatives. Party government promotes coordination but there is a strong tendency in West German government for 'departmental clientalism', in which ministries become identified with a group. This, and a rigid definition of responsibilities makes the policy process often partisan and complicated. This increases the importance of the Chancellor's coordinating role, so access to him is important for interest groups, and the unions enjoyed a close relationship with Schmidt. Obviously they lacked this influence with Kohl.[14]

There are limits on union–government integration. There is no doubt that the social market ideology and the conservative cast of most governments after 1949 elevated business interests and discouraged the unions from seeking integration. Social market theorists recognised that unions would have to be given a place in the political and industrial systems, but for internal political reasons many unions were reluctant to be drawn too deeply into the state's embrace. Functional representation (including concerted action in 1966–77, discussed in the final section of this chapter) and *mitbestimmung* (codetermination), created a *dual representation system* which helped unions reconcile the sometimes contradictory demands of the industrial and political systems with their role as social partners, but it did generate membership hostility.[15] Despite these problems and the hostile environment of the 1980s the DGB retains a strong commitment to working within the political structures of the Federal Republic and places great value on its status as a social partner.

The United Kingdom

In Britain the party which controls the House of Commons forms the government and the strength of party discipline means that the Cabinet controls the legislative process. The tradition of sponsoring MPs and the Labour Party's close links with the unions means that the unions have ample opportunity to air their views in the House of Commons. Also, the system of specialist committees (established in 1979 to both monitor and investigate departments and policy) which produce reports to which the government must respond provide an opportunity for access. These committees strive to produce agreed reports, even though places are allocated in proportion to a party's strength so the governing party has a majority. Government is not obliged to act on their reports.[16]

As in Sweden and West Germany, this means the 'real' decision-making process is in the bureaucracy. This, and the system's continuity means that major interest groups have built up a considerable range of contacts with ministries, and a characteristic feature of British government in this century has been the cultivation of these links by the civil service. From the 1920s, for example, it became established practice to consult the TUC on proposed legislation. In 1979, for example, the TUC calculated that members of the General Council sat on 67 governmental or outside related bodies; a second estimate was that General Council members sat on 107 committees.[17] The established practice of consulting interested parties on the details of legislation means that groups such as the unions can, under certain circumstances, be very influential by bringing to bear their specialist knowledge. From the civil servants' point of view there are obvious advantages in being able to consult with a single peak organisation (the TUC) recognised as the authoritative representative of union opinion. However, two points should be borne in mind. First, the social origins of senior civil servants are not those of trade unionists, and it is inevitable that civil servants feel 'more at home' with those from a similar social background. Second, the secrecy of British government enables selectivity to be practised in consultation. Consultative status is accorded a group in return for it agreeing to abide by 'the rules of the game'; this not only preserves confidentiality but entails working through 'established channels'.

The Ministry of Labour (founded in 1918, now the Department of Employment) was originally established as a channel for union influence. It had a clear conception of its role: promoting good industrial relations by helping capital and labour solve their problems and dissuading governments from legislative intervention. This changed when civil servants and politicians came to see this system as a contribution to economic decline. From the late 1960s, the ministry saw its task as reforming the unions, so losing its 'non-political' image in the eyes of the unions. This process accelerated in the early 1970s with the hiving off of functions to autonomous agencies (with union representation) such as the

Manpower Services Commission (MSC), the *Health and Safety Commission* (HSC), and its conciliation work to the *Advisory, Conciliation and Arbitration Service* (ACAS). This was encouraged by the unions so as to distance these functions from political interference.

Both the Labour and Conservative parties contain strong corporatist elements.[18] The British state tried to enmesh the unions in a cooperative framework, but did not give the unions a significant degree of influence inside Whitehall. Tripartite structures such as the *National Economic Development Council* (NEDC, founded in 1962) were concerned with 'educating' the unions in their economic responsibilities, or latterly the MSC with implementation. In neither instance was executive power achieved. The problem was: how far could government surrender its sovereignty to an unelected interest group, and how far could unions and the TUC guarantee membership compliance with any bargain? The historical tradition of 'weak' corporatism means that post-war politics has been concerned with constantly recreating the union–government relationship without jeopardising the unions' desire for autonomy or government legitimacy.[19] Neither could persuade the other to surrender sovereignty. The state's granting of representative status to the unions reflected an increased concern over their behaviour. However, the unions consistently refused to concede the state a corresponding role. Government–union relations have been based on independent voluntary cooperation, not compulsion. This flexible, uncodified relationship was part of a wider constitutional tradition of consulting major interests as an aid to good government.[20]

The Conservative government elected in 1979 saw tripartism in general, and union involvement in particular, as a major contribution to political and economic decline. In the early years of the Thatcher government great stress was laid on reducing the influence of interest groups in Whitehall, on the grounds that it was government's job to govern; groups could be consulted, but they enjoyed no special rights: the veto power was in the hands of the electorate. The new Conservative government had little knowledge of individual union leaders and reacted strongly against the tradition of 'beer and sandwiches at No. 10' as a response to industrial relations problems. The scale of the change can be seen from the fact that when the MSC was created unions and

employers enjoyed equal representation on the Commission
(three each) whereas the government proposed that employers
should have six members and the unions three on the Training
Commission set up in 1988 to replace the MSC. The Training
Commission (and all union representation) was abolished in
September 1988 after the TUC voted to oppose the government's
training scheme.

Constitutional tradition and bureaucratic conservatism means
that the unions and the TUC are still consulted and represented on
many official bodies, but events since 1979 suggest that in Britain
the unions are moving from inclusion to our last category, marginalisation. This could probably be halted only by the election of a
Labour government.

The Marginalisation of Unions in the Policy Process

Japan

As a parliamentary system in which the government reflects the
composition of the Diet the LDP's political dominance after 1955
means that parliament is of little importance in the policy process.
However, the JSP (with its many union members) and the other
opposition parties retain a considerable presence in the Diet, and
can exploit parliamentary procedure to disrupt government business, and the committee system also offers opportunities for
influence.

Under the constitution, business not transacted in one session of
the Diet cannot be carried over to the next. Opposition parties
can, if the end of the session is nearing, delay legislation to secure
concessions or embarrass the government by walking out, daring it
to use its majority to force legislation through and risking the
charge of authoritarianism. Standing and specialist committees
which investigate bills or specific issues are an obvious target for
groups. Membership is allocated according to party strength, so
although the LDP is the largest single party non-LDP members
might be in a majority. Only if the opposition could act in concert
would it be possible to block legislation, and the LDP was usually
able to exploit differences within the opposition. The LDP now
controls all the standing committees. Hearings have provided an

opportunity to embarrass government and win concessions on legislative details, but their impact has been reduced by the tendency of ex-civil servants who enter the Diet to gravitate to the committee closest to their former ministry. As they are pro-business and conservative the executive, bureaucracy and legislature are drawn together further excluding the influence of an 'outsider' like the unions.[21]

Politically it made sense to discriminate against the public sector, institutionalise Shunto and give the economically vital private sector unions vicarious participation in economic decision-making via *company corporatism* in the major manufacturing corporations. A policy process dominated by the LDP, bureaucracy and business was difficult to penetrate. The unions' impact has been limited to 'an occasional political compromise ... Only on rare occasions have they been successful in forcing the government to adopt a policy they have independently formulated and advocated'. Industrial militancy 'may have some limited impact on policy-making *but if and only if* the power elite decided to respond to their demands so as to maintain the stability of the existing structure of reward allocation'.[22]

The unions' exclusion has been aided by the educational background of senior civil servants and the tradition of *amakudari* ('descent from Heaven') whereby on retirement (in his 40s) a civil servant will begin a second career in business or politics. Senior civil servants are a well educated elite drawn disproportionately from graduates of Tokyo University; this and *amakudari* powerfully reinforces the interlocked political, bureaucratic and business elite. Whilst this elitist interlocked policy network provides continuity, there is an inevitable tendency for groups not drawn from this background to be excluded unless their participation is regarded as politically desirable.

The Ministry of Labour dates from the post-war reconstruction period and came to be regarded as labour's representative, sponsoring a wide range of consultative bodies on which unions are represented. It is regarded with suspicion by both business and the unions: the former regard it as sympathetic to labour, the latter as an instrument of control, not influence. Compared to Ministry of International Trade and Industry (MITI) the prestige of the Ministry of Labour is low, its concerns are regarded as 'ideological' not 'technocratic', and the confrontational nature of much labour politics contrasts starkly with the subtlety and confidence of business. [23]

Japan has been seen as a partial exception to the corporatist rule. Nevertheless, Japanese history indicates a tendency for 'corporatist' solutions to domestic crises caused by instability in the world economy, and government has a tendency to spawn large numbers of commissions investigating issues relevant to a ministry. These will have members drawn from politics, 'neutral experts', and group representatives. A decline in LDP electoral support in the 1970s coincided with an economic crisis which increased the political attractiveness of cooperating with the unions in the national interest. [24]

Company corporatism grew in importance as companies and their enterprise unions discussed industrial trends, international trade and Shunto, and lobbying by particular industries in an era of rapid change increased. A key private sector organisation was *Sangyo Rodo Konwakai* (Sanrokon, Industry and Labour Round-table Conference); established in 1970 under the auspices of the Ministry of Labour it meets monthly to discuss wages, prices, and employment. Ministers attend (the Prime Minister once a year). Though a deliberative body with no decision-making powers it has been increasingly consulted and is regarded as worthwhile. The public sector equivalent, *Korokon* (Roundtable Conference for Public Corporations and National Enterprises Labour Problems), established in 1978, has been less successful. Finally, tripartite advisory committees have always existed in the Ministry of Labour to comment on draft bills and policy proposals. These developments were described in unambiguously corporatist terms:

> Amidst the complexities of modern society, it is vitally important for the three parties (government, labor and management) to deepen mutual understanding through talks and discussion and duly play their own roles for the purpose of achieving economic and social development, *thus gaining a public consensus* on the desirable policy-making [sic]. *This will also open up a way for labor unions to participate in policy-making.* [25]

The result was a considerable structure of tripartite consultation; there is no significant change in the operation of the policy process.

The United States of America

It is a common judgement that organised labour is amongst the best organised and most influential of American interest groups. Whilst tripartite structures are absent unions have, nonetheless, enjoyed an important political role. After unification in 1955 the AFL–CIO could plausibly claim to be labour's spokesgroup, but long term socioeconomic change led to a dramatic decline in union political influence in the 1970s.[26]

A Democratic Congress does not confer automatic influence on the AFL–CIO, so political influence requires a sophisticated lobby strategy. This has always been so, but declining influence reflected a loss of interest in union questions by legislators now concerned with inflation and wider social questions. This required greater sophistication from the Department of Legislation (which manages lobbying and whose reputation for professionalism remained) in creating a pro-labour attitude on the key Congressional committees.[27] Union lobbyists never use crude pressure to influence Congressmen, and they do not bargain but aim to establish a reputation for authoritativeness based on a thorough knowledge of issues, Congressional procedures and Congressmen. The Department of Legislation and COPE are kept separate. Lobbying implies presenting a 'non-partisan' case to Congress, whereas COPE's function is electoral (influencing Congress's composition) and therefore partisan. These cannot be isolated but Congressmen accept the distinction as a convention of political life. This 'soft sell' confirms the non-viability of the Gompers Doctrine: lobbyists do not and dare not hint of reward and punishment, a partial exception being the COPE ratings.[28]

Unions have been most influential when part of a broad liberal coalition. They have consistently failed to secure major concessions on issues which affect them, such as modification of the Taft–Hartley Act because when lobbying on labour law they are perceived as a sectional, not a public, interest. In a more sophisticated and independent Congress avoiding the taint of sectionalism is vital. Growing interest in 'social' issues squeezed out 'economic' issues; labour's task was to show how they were interconnected to attract legislative support. The 1966 and 1976 Congresses were two of the most potentially pro-labour in history. Labour was less able to secure legislation in the 95th (1976) whereas it did not lose one key vote in the 89th (1966). Change in the Democratic Party, union decline, greater independence by Congressmen and the dominance of the presidency by the Republicans reduced labour influence. So, Democratic control did not guarantee influence, but the rise of 'New Liberalism' did not eradicate it: support merely became harder to win. The style of lobbying changed to match Congressional change; it was no longer sufficient to buy a Congressman lunch, a strong and persuasive case had to be made.[29]

The importance of party is reduced by the tradition of bi-partisanship which permeates the committee system. In 1985–6 there were 15 Senate and 22 House Standing Committees, excluding Select Committees and Joint Committees. The complexity and scope of public policy means Standing Committees have a galaxy of specialist sub-committees: the Senate *Labor and Human Resources Committee* has seven, the House of Representatives *Education and Labor Committee* eight. Proposed legislation is sent to committees for investigation. Committee recommendations are seldom changed on the floor of Congress, to do so would slow down an already cumbersome legislative process. Labour and the Democratic leadership have traditionally cooperated to ensure that Education and Labor and Human Resources were sympathetic to labour so the advent of a Republican Senate and President (1980) seemed to bode ill. The appointment of Orin Hatch (Republican, Utah) as chairman of the Senate committee caused the AFL–CIO to brace itself for conflict. In fact, Hatch pointedly announced his willingness to cooperate with the unions despite his personal commitment to policies detested by labour. Democratic control was re-established by the 1986 mid-term elections.

The Department of Labor and its Secretary traditionally act as labour's advocate in government even when union–administration relations are poor. Carter's Secretary of Labor, Ray Marshall (a University of Texas labour economist) interpreted his role thus. He was personally close to Carter, enjoyed excellent relations with union leaders, and was favourably regarded by both parties in Congress. Reagan's victory brought about a significant alteration. Raymond J. Donovan (a building contractor who managed Reagan's campaign in New Jersey) was an ultra-loyal supporter; both sides nonetheless made obeisance to the conventions. Relations, nevertheless, remained poor and Donovan resigned in March 1985. W. E. Brock, his succesor, was very different. Brock spent 14 years in Congress and was a successful Republican National Committee Chairman and was appointed to rebuild links with labour: 'He's the best you can hope for. There's a feeling that at least there will be more of an open door at the Labor Department'.[30]

The Labor Department is in a difficult position: unions question its impartiality, employers regard it as being in the unions' pocket. Its role as labour's lobby is limited by its lowly status as its Secretaries carry little weight; it is small and its tasks are not likely to make or break an Administration. Given the split between political appointees and career administrators (the former suspect the latter of undermining the Administration's policies, career bureaucrats fear the disruption of relationships) it is hard for a coherent departmental view to emerge. The Department has had a difficult time, 'conservative members of Congress say ... the Labor Department has been too timid in confronting organised labor ... Supporters commend the department for avoiding a bloodbath'.[31]

Union participation in the policy process is most visible in the legislatures and in the bureaucracy, with the exception of the United States where the legislature routinely enjoys real decision-making power. The legislative process in parliament is, for the most part, of symbolic importance. The bureaucracy, as the source of the most legislation, is their most important target. In all the systems considered unions enjoy considerable access to decision-makers and are represented on large numbers of governmental bodies. Much of this participation is, however, essentially symbolic and is confined to the details of policy. Despite visibility and access unions are subordinate political actors and their influence, as we shall see in the final section, is easily countered.

Corporatism and the Politicisation of Industrial Relations

Though the configuration, timing and extent of union–government involvement varied, it was inspired by a common motivation: to improve governability. The greater the areas of consensus, the more issues were depoliticised, the easier and more effective government would be. Though logical, this formulation soon revealed a paradox. Governments found that the more they extended their reach, intervention meant the politicisation of industrial relations, especially when governments concluded that wage bargaining was the prime cause of domestic inflation. All the states considered (at different times, using different methods) sought to integrate the unions in the policy process and persuade them to behave 'in the national interest'.

From government's perspective the problem was how to persuade unions to behave in the national interest by, for example, not exploiting their potential market power, contributing to inflation and, thereby, threatening profitability and jobs. Surely, government argued, it was rational for unions to forgo immediate returns in return for long-term gains? This is based on two assumptions. First, that there is a generally accepted definition of rationality. A union exists to secure the best rewards for its members, but from a different perspective a union not maximising its market power might be accused of irrationality, risking repudiation by its members. The second assumption is that union leaders can impose a policy on their members, or at least secure their acquiescence by offering compensatory gains such as low inflation and full employment. Furthermore, conventional political wisdom in many industrial political systems held that any attack on the unions' interests would produce a conflict which was not certain to be resolved in government's favour. Hence the popularity of exchange politics.[32]

This section considers the changing union–government relationship in the inflationary decade of the 1970s, which saw a marked decline in union influence. We shall begin with the least integrated (the United States) and conclude with the most (Sweden). In four political systems the political elite's response was to roll back union influence and challenge the position they had built up since 1945. In Japan, the response was different. As the Japanese economic miracle came under threat government *broadened* the range of influences on policy-making and one of these influences was *some* unions.

The United States

With the exception of wartime and the Nixon experiment of 1971–4, the United States had little experience of wages–prices policy as a mechanism for managing the unions. Such a policy challenged many of the assumptions common to employers and unions, and the political–industrial system which emerged out of the New Deal. By the late 1970s the Administration of President Carter was seeking a new strategy to control inflation (for which unions were partly blamed); the means available were limited as Carter ruled out deflation and compulsion; this left exhortation. Carter sought to maximise political acceptability to boost technical effectiveness by encouraging bargainers to act 'rationally' – accepting lower wages for lower prices.[33]

At a time of inflation the AFL–CIO opposed wage controls and the President's relationship with the unions was poor. Furthermore the mineworkers' strike of 1978 was a severe blow to the Administration's hopes, coming as it did at a time of escalating energy prices. If the miners' settlement breached Carter's policy other unions would do the same but a long battle would damage the economy and cost Carter political support in the run-up to the 1980 election. The White House's main interest was to settle at whatever the cost. The coal strike broke the anti-inflation policy, no other union accepted the mineworkers were a special case and business opposed government intervention.[34]

Though the 1978 guidelines were frustrated, the AFL–CIO was constrained in its response because it feared the consequences of a Republican victory in the Presidential election. Carter thus tried to rebuild his links with labour; in 1977, Carter had been 'too busy' to address the AFL–CIO convention but at the August 1979 building unions convention he offered more jobs and support for union goals in Congress. As one union official commented, 'He was well received – he promised us the moon'. In January 1979 meetings began which resulted in the tripartite Pay Advisory Committee and Price Advisory Committee and the 'national accord' (October 1979) whereby the Administration agreed to consult the unions on economic policies and the AFL–CIO agreed to cooperate with the anti-inflation programme.[35] Neither the Administration nor the AFL–CIO had any means of securing compliance, Congress was sceptical and drawn to monetarism, and a politically resurgent business community dismissed the deal as unwarranted interference giving too much power to the unions. The difficulty facing the Administration was clear:

People correctly believe that their individual behavior has no national impact and blame any collective problems ... on the obvious agency of collective action, government. But government is not omnipotent. It can succeed ... only by collective individual actions ... The guidelines attempt to do this ... they won't work unless backed by a threat – recession.[36]

In the USA there was no basis, technical, political or institutional, for a collective solution.

Carter's defeat and the onset of the 'Reagan Revolution' was accompanied by an assault on the unions' established position in the political economy. Deregulation, technical change and deskilling, greater industrial mobility, foreign competition and a slowing of economic growth altered the unions' environment:

> In industries where unions are established, employers have raised serious challenges, capitalizing on the unions' eroding bargaining strength to create more favourable bargaining terrain and even attacking, through decertification, the unions themselves. Where unions do not exist, employers have redoubled their efforts to keep them out ... employers have sought to alter the administration of labour law so as to curtail union rights and stymie union efforts.[37]

Inflation transformed the unions into a scapegoat of Democratic and Republican administrations. Hitherto, government sought to capitalise on the unions' 'insider' status. Reagan's election led to a reaction against this status in a way that would have been unthinkable for previous Republican administrations and was reflected in the appointment of a Secretary of Labor and agency heads who were unsympathetic to labour. Labour's political response was muted by the decline of their influence in Congress.[38]

Individual unions and the AFL–CIO were acutely aware of the importance of Reagan's election in 1980. The result was an upsurge in union political support for the Democrats and organising activity in industry to block or at least slow down the Reagan Revolution. The AFL–CIO interpreted the Reagan's victory as marking the end of bi-partisan acceptance of the position accorded labour under the New Deal and that the unions now had to mobilise to create a new settlement.[39]

The United Kingdom

Few other political systems have as much experience of incomes policies as the British. All have failed. The 1944 White Paper *Employment Policy* pledged the continuation of full employment but the 1945–51 Labour government became increasingly concerned at its inflationary consequences, a concern shared by its Conservative successors. Nevertheless all governments strove to adhere to the 1944 commitment.[40]

By the early 1960s both parties believed incomes policy to be essential as a contribution to solving the 'trade union problem'. It was a short step to concluding that if the unions would not reform themselves, the state would oblige. This began with Labour's *In Place of Strife* (1969), continued with the Conservative's 1971 Industrial Relations Act (both negated by union action), culminating with the 1980, 1982 and 1984 Acts. After 1964 only the Heath government (1972–4) and the post-1979 Conservative government eschewed *formal* incomes policy. Three Prime Ministers (Wilson in 1970, Heath in 1974 and Callaghan in 1979) could blame the unions, in part, for electoral defeat.

The politicisation of collective bargaining was, then, a notable feature of the destabilisation of British politics in the 1970s. Decentralised wage bargaining and the transfer of power to local leaders ensured that though the TUC sought a cooperative relationship with government, this could not be institutionalised. Corporatist politics requires the subordination of the 'sectional' to the 'general', and British unions, though willing to cooperate insisted this should not lead to the regulation of union activities. The conundrum: to what extent was it justifiable, or even possible, to limit autonomy, and what response was available if the unions and their members rejected the corporate agreement? was not successfully addressed by any government until 1979.[41] Even if exchange politics had not degenerated into wage restraint and if the unions and their members had accepted the restraint of money wages 'in the national interest', the exchange would have remained unstable because not all participants could derive equal benefit. Some would inevitably declare themselves 'special cases' and defect, others would follow. The political and economic dangers of a breakdown of exchange politics were appreciated, but when power had been transferred down the union structure, when prices were rising rapidly and in the absence of a powerful ideology to overcome sectionalism, collapse was inevitable.[42]

There were two unsuccessful attempts in the 1970s to establish stronger corporatist arrangements. The Heath government was elected in 1970 to 'roll back' union power; though he was never a committed free marketeer, Heath was impressed by West Germany's Concerted Action (see p.124) believing it could be transplanted to Britain. Faced by growing industrial unrest and rising inflation Heath offered the TUC and Confederation of British Industry (CBI) a partnership to achieve full employment, low inflation and high profits. The TUC was interested but would not agree to wage restraint unless this was part of a wider interventionist strategy and the Industrial Relations Act was withdrawn. Though Heath wanted a deal some policies, notably the Industrial Relations Act, were not negotiable. Talks broke down in November 1972 and a pay and price freeze was imposed and any hope of tripartite bargains foundered.

The second attempt, the Social Contract, was (given the unions' links with Labour) a far more rigorous affair. It emerged out of the conflict surrounding the Labour government's union reform proposals and the need to rebuild the party–union relationship after defeat in 1970; in addition, there was a desire to combine full employment and low inflation. Negotiated between 1970 and 1974 the Social Contract's purpose was that in return for granting legal concessions and greater participation in economic decision-making to the TUC, the TUC would strive to control the inflationary impact of collective bargaining. Despite efforts on both sides to make it work the Social Contract failed between 1974 and 1976 because the Labour government could not and would not cede decision-making power to the unions and the unions simply could not deliver the support of their members for pay restraint. The problems facing the government were not solvable solely by domestic political action. At a time when change in the global economy necessitated greater mobility for capital the TUC was advocating greater control over capital flows. The Labour government had neither the desire nor the capacity to engage in conflict with domestic and international capital and when the crisis came in 1976 it was not resolved through the Social Contract or tripartism but by calling in the IMF. In so doing the Social Contract, and ultimately the government, were destroyed in the 1978–9 'Winter of Discontent'.

Union–government relations followed a common pattern of courtship and fragmentation. Both unions and government sought and advocated a mutually productive relationship which could not be institutionalised. Tripartism was politically attractive, emphasising the national interest and offering non-coercive curbs on group autonomy. Intervention generated strains which could be contained neither by parliamentarianism nor by weak tripartism, whose failure stimulated the search for a new configuration of political authority to protect the state from the turbulence, *not stability*, generated by tripartism.

Initially the unions and the TUC believed that the Thatcher government would, like Heath, return to the established quasi-constitutional norms of consultation. This did not happen. Government policy since 1979 reflects both tripartism's failure and a reassertion of parliamentarianism in reaction to union power. What is so fascinating about the 1970s, however, is the *weakness* of union power in key decision areas. Union leaders failed to affect government policy significantly, the TUC played little role in ministerial deliberations, and the decision to call in the IMF was taken by the Prime Minister and Chancellor of the Exchequer. We must be careful, therefore, not to draw too sharp a distinction between pre- and post-1979 union–government relations. The history of this relationship is one of illusion: physical presence inside Whitehall, and access to Ministers and Prime Ministers never conferred significant influence, so the post-1979 situation more accurately reflects the real relationship than the froth of tripartism.

The Federal Republic

The DGB was heir to a long corporatist tradition and after the victory of the social market economy in the 1950s it sought an accommodation with capital. From 1956, the Economics Ministry published annual economic forecasts to encourage 'responsible' bargaining and the Bundesbank warned frequently of the inflationary threat, believing that problems stemmed from a lack of understanding between the *Tarifpartners* (bargaining partners) which could be remedied by education.[43] The entry of the SPD into government in 1966 encouraged a government–union commitment to inflation free growth and full employment. This found expression in the explicitly corporatist *The Law for Economic Stability and Development* (1967) which the SPD portrayed as the socio-economic equivalent of the Basic Law and from which grew *Concerted Action*.

Quarterly meetings were held at the Economics Ministry involving about 50 representatives drawn from the major political and economic groups to prepare *Orientierungsdaten* (guidelines) on the wage and salary increases that the economy could sustain. A smaller inner group emerged to agree on basic perspectives and specialised working parties were established to consider specific or intractable problems. Concerted Action was not a talking shop but was designed to promote consensus amongst the social partners; it did not strive to eradicate conflict but to limit the issues which caused conflict and, when there was conflict, to prevent it generating turbulence. The social partners recognised that neither the guidelines nor Concerted Action could be imposed, but both enjoyed considerable authority amongst bargainers.

From 1969, however, political acceptability of Concerted Action declined as bargainers sought to evade its restraints. The holding down of wages by the DGB in the interests of the SPD in government provoked a furious response. The September 1969 strikes came as a surprise and were led by shop stewards against their own union leaders. During an unofficial miners' strike in the Saar union leaders were charged with 'sleeping on the job' and officials who tried to persuade them to end their strike were shouted down. Union leaders were attacked as *Arbeiterverater* (traitor to the workers), unions advocating continued cooperation were dubbed *Kanzlergewerkschaften* (Chancellor's unions) and their SPD supporters as *Kanalarbeiter* (sewer workers), terms indicative of strain in both the party–union and union–government relationship. A DGB survey conducted after the 1969–70 outburst found a high degree of hostility to union leaders who, to re-establish their support and authority, responded with high wage demands so defeating one of the main reasons for involvement with government. Formal Concerted Action ended when the DGB walked out of the 40th meeting in July 1977; this was not especially significant for the political system as the participants had by 1977 recognised Concerted Action to be a failure. 'Informal concerted action' continued under Chancellor Schmidt, and even under the conservative Kohl government the DGB sought to maintain the ethos of social partnership.[44]

Chancellor Schmidt enjoyed good personal and political relations with the DGB leadership which he exploited, using *Koali-
tionswang* (the pressure of coalition) and the prospect of a CDU
government to win acquiescence in unpopular economic policies.
By 1972 the Council of Economic Advisors were hinting that the
wage bargaining guidelines should be binding, the Economics
Ministry's advisors believed unemployment could be used to
chasten the unions, and the 1974 oil crisis and subsequent recession made employers more cost conscious. Faced by politically
resurgent employers' organisations and an ideological offensive
against the 'union state', the unions had little choice other than to
stick to the SPD. There were, however, limits to this support. One
limit, as we have seen, was internal instability but also important
was the DGB's commitment to independence in the interests of
pluralism. Likewise from the government's point of view too close
a relationship with interest groups might infringe Article 20(2) of
the Basic Law ('All state authority emanates from the people by
means of elections and voting'). Integration, therefore, was opposed
not only by the employers and their party allies, but ran counter to
the spirit of the Basic Law and the social market philosophy, the
DGB's own programme and the wishes of many union members.
Integration would have required a state, capital and union coalition far in advance of anything sustainable in a liberal
democracy.[45]

The Federal Republic rode the crisis of 1973–4 and 1978–9
better than most industrialised countries partly because of continued tripartite cooperation in the national interest. In the 1976
elections the SPD proposed a version of the Social Contract –
Modell Deutschland – a nationalistic modernisation policy based
on close tripartite cooperation and closely identified with Schmidt.
By 1980, however, inflation and unemployment had undermined
the SPD's electoral appeal. This led to the defection of the Free
Liberals (FDP) from the SPD coalition to the CDU in 1982 and
the entry into government of the CDU–FDP coalition under
Chancellor Kohl.

Integration would require state and capital to cede to the unions
a far greater degree of influence over 'private' economic decisions
than had been conceded under the codetermination system. The
West German dual representation system is asymmetrical and the
DGB has not and will not receive the degree or type of concessions

it believes its status as a social partner merits in either the industrial or political systems. After 1982 the DGB was forced further onto the defensive, striving to combat the 'social dismantling' of the Kohl government whilst its 'stabilising' role in the polity forced the DGB to take a defensive and accommodationist stance.[46] The DGB's 'state fixation' has three flaws: bargaining is neither compulsory nor between equals, the desire to cooperate in 'the national interest' denies it a potent weapon (non-cooperation), and the state fixation closes off certain strategies such as mass mobilisation.

Sweden

The LO believes that corporatism means interference in matters best left to bargainers and ultimately a degree of state intervention incompatible with pluralism; nevertheless they rejected 'free collective bargaining' as injurious to both social justice and to the economy. Despite a willingness to cooperate the LO could not resist pressure for higher wages from their members when inflation and/or profits were high and demand for labour was buoyant. Unions could not behave with 'restraint' in such circumstances, because if they did the result was wage drift, the damming of expectations and wage explosions. The alternative was the active labour market policy and wage solidarity, and central negotiations between the LO and SAF would impose order and predictability. From 1952, LO–SAF negotiations were annual, between 1956–66 negotiations were biannual, and triennially thereafter. At its height the LO and SAF agreed basic percentage wage increases which were then applied to the conditions prevailing in each sector. This system worked well until the late 1960s and early 1970s when it came under strain from wage drift and inflation.[47]

Attempts to stabilise the system using the Wage Formation and the Economy Report drawn up by LO, SAF and TCO economists (the EFO Report, 1970) were unsuccessful because of worsening international conditions and domestic decisions which accelerated inflation. From 1973 the Swedish political economy destabilised: the SAP bloc narrowly held on to office between 1973–6, between 1976–9 a three-party bourgeois coalition formed the government, followed by a minority Liberal government. A three-party coalition reformed, only to collapse in the spring of 1981 and be replaced by a Liberal–Centre Party coalition. The SAP returned to government in 1982. In this period profits fell, exports declined, wage costs increased, inflation accelerated, unemployment grew and the economy stagnated. By 1980 the Swedish Model was on the verge of collapse.[48]

The destabilisation of the Swedish Model was the consequence of fundamental change producing greater labour market complexity. Under the LO–SAF centralised bargaining system settlements in the manufacturing export sector set the standard for the remainder of the economy; domestic costs had to be kept in line with international costs. However, the growth of the public and private service sector (which are not involved in international trade), and the decline of blue-collar employment and the consequent rise in the importance of the white-collar federations (TCO and SACO–SR) made coordination far more difficult. Furthermore, there was in the late 1960s a reaction against centralisation reflected in events such as the LKAB strike and wage drift (a tendency in the public and private sectors to negotiate increases in addition to those negotiated centrally). As the 1970s progressed important bargainers, such as those in the engineering industry, expressed doubts about the LO–SAF system, many private sector workers expressed resentment at the high taxes required to pay for the public sector, whilst public sector workers resisted any attempt to hold down their wages. Attempts to bolster a national consensus on pay and prices (by, for example, the Haga Palace discussions of 1974–5) involving government, groups and the opposition parties were a failure.[49]

Three foundations of the system were eroding. First, moderation and wage solidarity were feasible only when wage earners felt able to forgo short-term gains because of guaranteed long-term gains from economic growth. Second, private sector workers were coming to believe that public sector growth was destroying their competitiveness, and finally, LO–SAF centralisation was breaking down. The task facing the SAP when it returned to office in 1982 was to restabilise corporate politics. Traditionally, crises in the political economy have been resolved by group cooperation not electoral competition or state intervention. A new compromise of the old type was not possible because of both divergence amongst the parties over labour market policy and the growing complexity of the labour market. The Haga Palace talks were a hint of the likelihood of greater state intervention; this became more likely with the re-election of the SAP in 1982 which was committed to a 'Third Way' in economic policy. This involved a massive 16 per cent devaluation of the Krona and a price freeze, and the unions were warned not to seek compensatory pay increases. This contributed to 'The War of the Roses', a public row between the LO chairman and the SAP Finance Minister over economic policy.

By the mid-1980s the Swedish Model as traditionally understood had collapsed. Though the Third Way policy was to prove a relative success, this did not alter the fact that Sweden's dependence on the international economy and its high domestic costs made it essential that a new arrangement be speedily found.

Japan

Earlier it was suggested that Japan was anomalous as unions were excluded from political participation. In the 1950s industrial relations were bitter and fragmented unions were picked off by the resurgent employers. Unions responded with *Shunto* (the Spring Labor Offensive) – enterprise bargaining could not be eradicated but could, Sohyo believed, be coordinated. In 1955 Sohyo recommended the submission of a unified minimum wage demand to the employers supported by coordinated joint action. In that same year Shunto was launched.[50]

Whilst not enthusiastically welcomed, employers appreciated that Shunto offered the stable domestic environment and a flexible workforce required by the large corporations as the economic miracle accelerated. To supplement this they promoted enterprise unionism, lifetime employment, wages based on length of service and company welfare schemes. The unrest of the 1950s convinced employers and many employees that trials of strength were in no-one's interest. Shunto promised to institutionalise and regularise conflict: it was, in effect, a 'social contract'. Four points should be borne in mind: joint struggle does not mean the imposition of a nationally negotiated settlement. Second, bargaining determines only broad outlines; negotiations take place at enterprise level within the parameters established by Shunto, so ensuring that settlements meet the needs of each enterprise. Third, industrial action is synchronised carefully and is usually symbolic. Fourth, despite the breadth of the demands made at the beginning of

Shunto, the political demands are ignored. Though essentially a wage bargaining process, its scope has broadened in recent years.

Japan's exposure to the international economy on which its economic success depended would seem to make it a prime candidate for a corporatist incomes policy. 'In Japan', however, 'the specific characteristics of the labour market and of the process of wage determination ... have *produced some of the results that certain types of "incomes policy" seek to obtain in other countries.*'[51] Elsewhere incomes and corporatist politics were a response to a failure of collective bargaining, but in Japan enterprise unions in the very large export oriented corporations voluntarily limited themselves obviating the need for a state led incomes policy. The identity of interest between these corporation and their enterprise unions generated a *privatised incomes policy* which, because of the dominance of these corporations, was imposed in the domestic economy via cost pressures on medium- and small-scale suppliers whose workforces were largely unorganised. Nevertheless, in the 1974 Shunto the unions won increases of 32.9 per cent; business and government warned of the consequences and that government intervention might be necessary if the 1975 Shunto followed the same path. In the mid-1970s the Japanese political economy seemed to be at a crossroads: Shunto and wage costs appeared to be running out of control but a compulsory incomes policy risked an upsurge of industrial unrest with obvious adverse political and economic consequences. A response had to be found which would contain incipient political instability and maintain economic growth.

An event of epochal significance was the establishment of *Zenmin Rokyo* (the Japan Private Sector Trade Union Council) on 14 December 1982 with a membership of 3.8m from 39 unions; by January 1986 it embraced 5.4m members and 62 unions. Zenmin Rokyo originated from Shunto, private sector union disquiet at the militancy of the public sector, and the state's desire for a consensus on economic development at a difficult time.[52] Soon after its inauguration Zenmin Rokyo was embraced by the Ministry of Labour, was invited to talks at MITI on future industrial policy, and to the Ministry of Health and Welfare to discuss social policy. Such contacts gave Zenmin Rokyo a status and prestige greater than that of any other labour organisation. Zenmin Rokyo also evoked a favourable response from the LDP. On 20 November

1987 *Rengo* (Confederation of Private Sector Trade Unions) was formed to supersede Zenmin Rokyo (see Chapter 2). Rengo is, potentially, a major step towards increased political influence, though the public–private sector cleavage remains an obstacle. The projected inclusion of Sohyo's public sector unions reduces its attractiveness to the political and economic elite, a factor recognised by other elements in Rengo. At Rengo's founding conference Domei's chairman, for example, declared that further unification could come only on the basis of accepting Rengo's ethos of non-partisan and democratic trade unionism concentrating on bargaining, not political, issues. This was interpreted as a rejection of the political and industrial militancy associated with Sohyo's public sector affiliates whereas Rengo represents a type of trade unionism more congenial to the Japanese political and business elite. The projected integration of Sohyo's public sector unions into Rengo in 1990 therefore make it unlikely that Rengo will wield significant influence. Japanese unions remain fragmented, density is declining, free market policies and attacks on the public sector limits the political space available for corporatism and sustains labour's suspicion of the LDP and the Japanese state.

By the mid- to late 1970s the established mechanisms for managing the politics of industrial relations throughout the industrial world were collapsing under the impact of economic crisis. At the time it was common to speculate on a 'crisis of governability' but no liberal-democratic industrial state collapsed, and the period marked the beginning of a transition to a new governing style in which unions were to play a very different role.

Conclusions

Union–Government Relations: Purpose and Limits

Government–union relations developed as a response to the industrial and political presence of organised labour, and were designed to integrate (and control) unions. They failed because union political interests could not be confined within a single structure. Labour ministries, originally established as the unions' channel of political access, declined in importance and were replaced by wide ranging consultative institutions and processes covering virtually every aspect of policy. Despite the multiplicity of government–union relationships they are all variations on the theme of subordination. Unions have access to decision-makers, some are integrated into the policy process, but all find their interests subordinate to those of capital.

The influence of unions is limited by, first, the fact they are a minority which encourages defensiveness and are vulnerable to charges of unrepresentativeness. Second, unions are divided ideologically and occupationally and, of course, not all workers join unions. Third, in liberal democracies political legitimacy springs from the electoral process, not from group interaction; governments can challenge union participation by citing a higher political authority. Finally, the degree of integration is limited by the ability of union leaders to persuade their members to accept bargains which the latter may not perceive to be in their immediate interests. Sooner or later, no matter how corporatist the political system, union leaders must respond to their members' wishes, or risk schism. This inevitably destabilises the union–government relationship.

From government's perspective the problem was to persuade unions to behave in the general interest by, for example, not exploiting their market power. Surely it was rational for unions to forgo immediate returns for long-term gains? This makes two assumptions: that there is a commonly accepted definition of 'rationality', and that union leaders can impose a policy on their members. In many industrial polities it was axiomatic that any attack on the unions would result in major political conflict and economic disruption, producing serious political and electoral consequences; in the long run, the governing process was made more difficult. Four political systems attempted a political exchange. In the United States and Britain this proved impossible because of decentralised bargaining and poorly integrated unions unable to adhere to any agreement within political systems unable to reconcile exchange politics with liberal democracy. In West Germany and Sweden exchange was preserved, but with difficulty. The collapse of Concerted Action, the departure of the SDP from government and rise of conservatism did not produce an assault on the DGB. The DGB was weakened but it made significant gains (on working hours, for example) and the social partners agreed on the need to maintain economic growth achieved not by tripartism but through a common perception of the economy's needs. This attitude was bitterly resented by many DGB members. Sweden's problems were similar but because of SAP dominance and the long history of cooperation the destabilisation of this long established system was more threatening for the polity. However this, and Sweden's dependence on the international economy, encouraged speedy adaptation.

The anomaly is Japan. Whilst Japan did not have a state led corporatist system it had a corporatistic network based on the LDP–bureaucracy–business elite to which a *section* of the unions gained access. As in West Germany and Sweden the need to maintain competitiveness was recognised, but was pushed further in Japan by the community of interest between the manufacturing export corporations and their enterprise unions who via Shunto dominate the rest of the economy.

Those political systems which have successfully managed the politics of industrial relations have not been the most corporatist in structure or institutions but those with a common perception of the economy's international vulnerability. This does not mean there exists in Sweden, Japan, or West Germany management–union–government unanimity: bitter conflict remains, but is counter-balanced by a recognition of economic vulnerability. Unions have retained, and in Japan may be on the point of increasing, their influence.

The Relevance of the Post-war Boom, and its End

The dramatic expansion of world trade after 1945 ('the Great Boom') and its attendant domestic consequences (full employment and inflation) were crucial in the development of union–government relations. In Britain, West Germany, the United States and Sweden post-war economic policy was directed at avoiding 1930s-style mass unemployment; any recurrence was expected to produce massive unrest. However inflation, not unemployment, became the dominant economic problem and governments sought to engage unions in a cooperative relationship to control inflation as savage deflation (and therefore high unemployment) was not believed to be a viable option. The Great Boom also eased resource constraints on government by permitting improvements in pay, increased profits and more public services.

It was assumed by many at the end of the 1950s that many of the problems of industrial society were solved and that politics in a post-industrial society would be about the problems of managing prosperity.

From the mid-1960s, however, the Great Boom was running out of steam. The instability of the international economy increased as the ability of the US economy to sustain it declined, and both domestic inflation and unemployment increased. As the boom slowed, greater stress was placed on the union–government relationship as governments sought to stem rising inflation and unemployment, but the oil shocks and 'stagflation' broke these arrangements. As growth slowed the surplus available for wages, profits and public spending shrank and governments were forced to take hard decisions and priority was given to the maintenance of profitability. Tripartite politics had, to a greater or lesser degree, mitigated the effects of market inequalities to the advantage of the unions. The end of the Great Boom initially saw greater emphasis placed on these arrangements, but ultimately their collapse produced an increased commitment to a lower level of government activity and a greater role for the market. In these circumstances, union political influence suffered.

Variations in the Corporatist Experience

Though all the systems analysed were subjected to the same general experience, their responses varied considerably. Four systems (West Germany, Sweden, the United States, and Britain) responded with state led tripartite systems of varying rigour, whilst Japan (until the 1970s) opted for a 'private' version.

The degree of institutionalisation varied considerably. In all the systems there developed a large network of consultative bodies, many of which had tripartite representation. Some, such as the Swedish AMS had decision-making power, though most were similar to the British MSC lacking such power. The intrusion of such institutions into collective bargaining was rare – it should be remembered that Swedish government was not a participant in the highly centralised LO–SAF system and West German Concerted Action (like the NEDC in Britain and COWPS in the United States) could only make recommendations. The physical absence of government did not mean that the views of government were not integral to their deliberations. In Japan, of course, such a system was not needed given the symbiotic relationship between big business (including enterprise unions) and government, and the dominance they exercised through Shunto over wage levels.

The corporatist experience was essentially an extension of interest group politics. It is logical to assume there can be no corporatist political system without corporatist political institutions involving government, employers and unions jointly exercising executive power. These are very rare. The political systems we have considered are parliamentary-liberal democracies in which governments, ultimately responsible to electorates, were reluctant to surrender their sovereignty (and possibly their political survival) to non-elected organisations representing sections (albeit important sections) of society.

The Corporatist Experience in Historical Perspective

Corporatism emerged as a response to the legacy of the 1930s, evolving after 1945 as a response to the inability of the institutions of traditional parliamentary democracy to solve these problems. Securing agreements (formal or informal), institutionalised or not, was attractive to politicians as they promised to ease the problems of governing a complex polity. Is corporatism of some type therefore inevitable, or does its collapse show it to be a temporary phenomena?

Liberal-democratic political systems are characterised by a formal separation of the polity and economy in which the state can project itself as a neutral force. Capitalism's development creates tensions which cannot be easily contained by the institutions of parliamentary democracy – the state (concerned to maintain the conditions for continued accumulation) embraces the unions making concessions in an attempt to secure their quiescence. On this basis, unions have secured significant gains, albeit at the cost of surrendering a degree (sometimes considerable) of autonomy. In the final analysis these arrangements were intended to control the unions in the interest of the status quo by giving unions an illusory sense of influence. All prudent governments wish to know the views of major interests, but consulting or involving unions in tripartite politics is not corporatism. Unions are kept far from the centres of power and once tripartism served its purpose, failed or collapsed, it was abandoned.

6

The Politics of the New Working Class

Chapter 6 examines, first, the replacement throughout the industrial world of the 'old' working class based on traditional manufacturing by a 'new' non-manual working class. To what extent is this new working class different in its political aspirations, ideology and behaviour? Second, the chapter considers the political consequences of the public sector's growth. Public sector unions were central in the politicisation of industrial relations and the reaction against union 'power'. Finally, change in the political economy in the 1970s gave an impetus to exclude, marginalise or neutralise union political influence. Since then unions have been seeking a *modus vivendi* in an unsympathetic environment as a base for resurgence of influence. What form has this taken? Will it be successful? How will the unions be managed in the 1990s?

The White-collar Phenomenon

Why in all the systems considered (except Sweden) is union membership and density declining even though the labour force is growing? Highly unionised manual industries (mining, steel, heavy engineering) are declining, whilst expanding industries (services, electronics, information industries) either have no tradition of unionisation or are difficult to organise, problems compounded by employer resistance (Table 6.1). Over the last quarter century in all the states (except Japan) the percentage employed in manufacturing and industry has declined; the corollary is an increase in non-manual employment in the public and private sectors (Table 6.2).

135

Table 6.1   *Economically active population, % employment by industry, 1986*

Industrial sector	United States	Japan	West Germany	Sweden	United Kingdom
Agriculture	3.1	8.5	5.1	4.7	2.1
Mining, Forestry	0.9	0.2	1.2	0.3	3.6
Manufacturing	19.2	24.4	30.6	21.9	20.6
Electricity, Gas, Water	1.3	0.5	0.9	0.9	2.8
Construction	6.7	8.9	6.8	5.9	6.3
Wholesale, Food, Hotels	20.5	22.1	15.0	13.4	17.2
Transport, Communications	5.5	5.8	5.6	6.7	5.9
Financial Services	9.9	6.5	6.2	7.3	7.0
Community, Social Services	30.5	20.1	26.3	36.0	24.5

Note:
This table excludes those in the armed forces, groups not adequately defined and the unemployed.

Source: ILO, *Year Book of Labour Statistics 1986*, 46th edn (Geneva: ILO, 1986) Tables 1A and 2B.

Are White-collar workers 'Different'?

The 'new working class' has the same problems as the old. When organised they are charged with lacking 'class consciousness', concerned to preserve differentials from encroachment by manual workers; white-collar unionisation is portrayed as the consequence of proletarianised working conditions and blue-collar affluence, a product of 'status panic' coupled with a reluctance to engage in industrial or political action. However, 'just as the blue-collar workers do not always see themselves as a proletariat, the white collar workers are not all conservative and anxious not to lose status'.[1] The evidence indicates a growing *congruence* between blue- and white-collar attitudes; the latter are less likely to be partisan, and less likely to take industrial action, but blue-collar workers and unions have moved towards these 'white-collar' attitudes. *All* unions exist to defend and better the pay and conditions of their members and 'the adoption of collectivist methods for achieving material gains is compatible with a wide range of political and social attitudes which may be strongly antipathetic to collectivism as a general political philosophy'.[2]

Politics have been critical for white-collar growth; low concen-

Table 6.2 *Sectoral employment, % of civilian employment, 1960–84*

	1960–7	1968–73	1974–9	1980–4	1960–84	Change
(a) Industry						
United States	35.2	34.0	31.0	29.1	32.7	− 6.1
Japan	31.5	35.8	35.7	35.0	34.2	+ 3.2
West Germany	47.7	47.9	45.1	42.6	46.1	− 5.1
United Kingdom	46.7	44.0	40.0	35.0	42.1	−11.7
Sweden	41.3	38.5	34.8	30.7	37.0	−10.6
OECD average	*36.3*	*36.6*	*34.7*	*32.3*	*35.2*	*− 1.1*
(b) Manufacturing						
United States	26.8	25.8	23.0	20.8	24.4	− 6.0
Japan	23.7	26.9	25.4	24.7	25.1	+ 1.0
West Germany	35.3	36.6	35.1	33.0	35.1	− 2.3
United Kingdom	37.4	36.1	32.7	27.7	34.0	− 9.7
Sweden	31.4	28.3	26.4	22.9	27.8	− 3.6
OECD average	*26.9*	*27.2*	*25.3*	*23.2*	*25.8*	*− 3.7*
(c) Services						
United States	57.9	61.5	64.9	67.4	62.3	+ 9.5
Japan	42.9	47.5	52.3	55.3	48.7	+12.4
West Germany	40.4	43.6	48.4	51.8	45.4	+11.4
United Kingdom	49.1	52.8	57.3	62.4	54.6	+13.3
Sweden	46.1	53.4	59.0	63.8	54.5	+17.7
OECD average	*45.1*	*49.8*	*54.3*	*58.1*	*51.0*	*+13.0*

Source: OECD Historical Statistics, 1960–84 (Paris: OECD, 1986) Tables 2.10 and 2.11.

tration of numbers, status and employer resistence made 'spontaneous' growth difficult; the Wagner Act in the United States was, for example, vital.[3] Similar measures were taken after Japan's defeat, but enterprise unionism and the lifetime employment system created an occupational category (*the permanent worker*) transcending the occupational divide. Enterprise unionism reduced status and reward differences, making unionisation acceptable and familiar to Japanese white-collar workers.[4] In 1931 Swedish engineering industry foremen and bank employees formed a central organisation, and a public sector centre emerged in 1937. The LO regarded these as a major breach of the industrial union principle, arguing that all workers should join the appropriate industrial union. The *Right of Association and Collective Bargaining Law* (1936) encouraged white-collar unionisation and in 1944 TCO was formed.[5] White-collar unions grew rapidly in

Britain until the early 1960s, stagnating until the 1970s. Economic factors, especially inflation, promoted renewed growth which was sustained by a sympathetic Labour government which passed several Acts making recognition easier. So substantial was the upsurge that it altered the character of the TUC and its politics and, to a lesser degree, the party–union relationship.[6] West Germany is slightly different. Qualms about the DGB's social democratic heritage underpinned the formation of the *Deutsche Angestelltengewerkschaft* (DAG, German Salaried Employees' Federation) in 1949, which believed that industrial unionism could not express adequately the complex interests of industrial society and that non-manual interests would suffer; it is nevertheless organised on industrial lines.[7]

The political impetus behind white-collar unionisation was crucial, both in terms of government action and the growth of the public sector. Even though many of these unions sought to generate an ethos different from blue-collar unions they have gradually become more involved in many of the activities traditionally associated with blue-collar unions.

Is There a 'White-collar' Ideology?

There are, broadly speaking, two schools of thought, each based on the assumption that white-collar workers constitute a new working class. One sees them as a revolutionary force supplanting the industrial proletariat, the second as hostile to 'traditional' working class politics. White-collar workers are sometimes portrayed as victims of false consciousness, doomed to merge with the working class but refusing to recognise their true interests. A later interpretation saw the shift to knowledge based industries creating a new revoluntionary force better able to exploit the contradictions of capitalism. There is, however, scant evidence to show that white-collar workers are revolutionary.[8] Their emergence has undoubtedly modified union politics, encouraging a more individualistic view of society; white-collar workers tend to insist on non-partisanship from their unions, and they have a more cooperative view of their industrial role.

In Britain the overlap between TUC and Labour Party affiliated unions and the dominance of blue-collar giants created a common ideological base. Shifts in the occupational structure were reflected in changes in selecting the General Council which boosted the influence of the white-collar unions. Many white collar unions are not party affiliated and were unhappy with both the party–union–TUC relationship and the corporatist drift of TUC politics in the 1970s, *but so were many manual unions*. The 1987 TUC Agenda did not reveal a distinctive white-collar ideology. Resolutions were proposed, seconded and amended by a bewildering combination of manual and non-manual unions drawn from the public and private sector, conveying the impression of concerns spanning occupational, industrial and sectoral boundaries. Poll evidence indicates little difference in the attitudes of trade unionists. All workers, irrespective of occupational category, approve of unions as a defender of their interests and do not regard unions as too powerful, though the attitudes of clerical workers diverge sharply. Blue-collar workers have the most positive view of the unions' contribution to industrial efficiency, white-collar workers the least. There was a clear occupational divide over party politics: non-blue-collar workers were most likely to reject the party–union link. White-collar workers were evenly divided on whether or not unions were dominated by extremists: both blue-collar and clerical workers were equally convinced that unions were dominated by militants. The findings on the party-political connection are interesting as every white-collar union with a political fund and which was affiliated to the Labour Party voted to maintain their funds in the ballots held under the 1984 Act.[9]

A survey of the US labour force found that a majority regarded unions as powerful social and political institutions. White-collar workers were *more* likely to believe this. A substantial majority agreed that unions were necessary for protection (80 per cent), but white-collar workers were *less* likely to agree. Some 28 per cent of white-collar workers (39 per cent of blue-collar) would vote for union representation. White-collar union members were more concerned with pay inequities and fringe benefits than the absolute level of wages, more interested in participation in decision-making, more likely to support unionisation if dissatisfied with job content, and tended to hold a negative view of the labour movement. There was little variation in union satisfaction ratings accorded by blue- and white-collar. This 'reinforc[ed] the view that American workers approach the decision to unionize in very pragmatic terms. They are apparently less influenced by their general image of labor in society or by their general views of the labor movement than they are by their judgements about what unions actually do for their members.' The 1984 elections revealed a plurality of union voters in all occupational categories for Mondale, except the upper white-collar (56 per cent Reagan, 44 per cent Mondale) and white-collar union voters were less concerned about social security, unemployment and the political influence of working people, and more concerned about the budget deficit, taxes, and the Soviet Union than union voters as a whole. They tended to be closer to the Republicans on social issues. [10]

In Japan the 'company member' concept and the organisation of blue- and white-collar in enterprise unions makes it difficult to distinguish separate interests. Further, the marxist legacy leads Sohyo especially to regard workers as in a common relationship to the means of production, not members of occupational categories. Electoral evidence shows the unionised–non-unionised cleavage to be more important than an occupational cleavage. The Japanese Election Survey found that 50 per cent of its sample described themselves as working class, but when asked to locate themselves in one of five strata 27.0 per cent described themselves as upper middle, 46.2 per cent lower middle, and 15.3 per cent upper low. Only 25.8 per cent of the sample were union members, 70.8 per cent had no union members in their immediate family, most (35.1 per cent) were affiliated with Sohyo and 48.3 per cent supported the JSP; however, 50 per cent did not know to which national federation their union affiliated. There was, therefore, a reluctance to be identified as working class and join unions, and a lack of interest in unionism above the enterprise level. Substantial numbers nevertheless support *policies* identified with unions: 55.7 per cent were concerned about government policies on unemployment and inflation, 44.5 per cent wanted more schools and hospitals, and 45.2 per cent more social welfare; the July 1983 survey found that 33.2 per cent believed government should do more to represent the interests of wage earners. Survey evidence suggests that Japanese workers (blue- or white-collar) have broadly similar concerns, but support for union-type policies does not translate into union membership because of the low esteem unions enjoy. [11]

The DAG and TCO do have distinct programmes, but to what extent do these differ substantially from the DGB and LO? The DAG's *Social Policy Programme* dating from 1971 lays great stress on the extension of worker participation, stressing that left to itself the market cannot satisfy worker needs; but, like the DGB, it accepts the market's primacy. DAG and DGB programmes are, therefore, variations on a theme. The DAG emphasises the extension of share ownership, the DGB codetermination, and like the DGB it calls for a greater state role in promoting prosperity and full employment. This programmatic similarity is a product of the post-war environment established in reaction to Nazism and the acceptance by labour market organisations of the social market economy. The DAG is disadvantaged competing for members, as it operates a closed recruitment strategy even though the distinction between manual and non-manual is fading and the sheer size of the DGB reduces the DAG's attraction.[12]

TCO projects itself as the natural home of non-manual workers, its 'task is to promote the common interests of salaried workers as employees'. TCO recognises that these have changed over the years from (for example) pensions, to pay and conditions and, latterly, to politics. Despite its claim to occupational exclusivity TCO willingly cooperates with LO, though the latter has been scathing about TCO 'free-loading'. Merger remains impossible whilst TCO insists on the existence of separate white-collar issues which LO regards as a significant weakening of *the wage earners' front*. Both the TCO and LO support high growth, the active labour market policy and full employment, though TCO has criticised eroding pay differentials. The reports discussed at TCO's 1985 Congress give some idea of its concerns. *Codetermination* discussed the extension of the legislation passed in the early 1970s, the *Welfare Report* advocated a new welfare consensus recognising growing cost and the danger of resentment from taxpayers, the *Personnel Education Report* advocated greater retraining and workplace education, the *Pay Report* examined the development of collective bargaining and government policy, the impact of taxation, and the extension of profit related pay, and finally the *Service Society Report* considered the impact of structural change and called for the production and delivery of public services to be as efficient as possible.[13]

There is little evidence to suggest that white-collar unions generate either a distinctive ideology or are 'revolutionary'. Originally more concerned with status issues, the concerns of blue- and white-collar have converged as structural change exposed both groups to similar problems; both are *instrumental* in their behaviour.

Public Sector Trade Unionism

State employment is one of the most politically contentious aspects of the labour market, its cost being identified as a major burden on the 'productive' (private) economy, and as government is the employer public sector industrial relations are inevitably politicised. Public employment in our five systems has been about 3 per cent higher than for the *Organisation for Economic Cooperation and Development* (OECD) states as a whole. Between 1960 and 1973 public employment (Table 6.3a/6.3b) in the USA grew by an average of 2.4 per cent, in West Germany 3.7 per cent, in the UK 2.5 per cent, and Sweden 5.8 per cent, but between 1974 and 1984

Table 6.3a   *Employment in government, % of civilian employment, 1960–84*

	1960–7	*1968–73*	*1974–9*	*1980–4*	*1960–84*	*Change*
United States	16.7	17.8	17.2	–	17.0	[0.5]
Japan	–	–	6.5	–	–	–
West Germany	9.4	11.6	14.2	15.5	12.3	6.1
United Kingdom	15.5	18.5	20.8	21.8	18.8	6.3
Sweden	14.6	21.2	27.3	31.9	22.7	8.1
OECD average	*12.1*	*13.7*	*14.8*	*15.3*	*13.8*	*1.7*

Source: *OECD Historical Statistics 1960–84* (Paris: OECD, 1986) Table 2.13.

Table 6.3b   *Employment in government, average year to year, % change, 1960–84*

	1960–7	*1968–73*	*1974–9*	*1980–4*	*1960–84*
United States	4.0	0.7	1.4	–	1.9
Japan	–	–	1.9	0.7	–
West Germany	3.7	3.7	2.2	1.0	2.8
United Kingdom	2.4	2.5	1.6	−0.5	1.6
Sweden	5.2	6.3	4.9	2.2	4.7
OECD average	*3.2*	*2.3*	*2.1*	*0.8*	*2.2*

Source: OECD, *Historical Statistics, 1960–84* (Paris: OECD, 1986) Table 2.13 and Table 1.13.

the figures were 1.4 per cent, 1.6 per cent, 1.1 per cent, 3.6 per cent and 1.3 per cent for Japan. The economic crisis of 1973–4 marks a watershed in the politics of the public sector. Cost makes public employment sensitive; public sector workers judge their pay and conditions with reference to the private sector and govern-ments have often conceded these claims feeling constrained by the need to be seen as a good employer and because these workers deliver services paid for and consumed by electors. As costs mounted at a time of economic crisis it is hardly surprising some of the bitterest disputes were in the public sector.[14] Public sector workers join unions for the same reason as any other group, but all governments are suspicious of public sector unions. The disruption of government and public services reflects badly on government and is less tolerable politically than the interruption of market traded goods. Any threat (real or imagined) to the state from its own 'servants' is bitterly resented.

The Public Sector in Sweden

Up to 1950 the state sector was small, growing between 1950 and 1960 but exploding between 1960 and 1980 from 31.6 per cent to 61.6 per cent of employment, something closely related to Social Democracy's political dominance.[15] The public sector is heavily unionised by the LO, TCO and SACO–SR but its composition has changed dramatically: in 1950 the bulk were blue-collar and members of LO, whereas half are now members of the white-collar TCO and SACO–SR.

   Growth and economic crisis made the public sector politically contentious, provoking major assaults from the SAF. Its first national congress (September 1977) committed SAF to resisting state intervention and public sector growth, claiming that the public sector was stifling initiative and political liberty. The Swedish Centre for Working Life warned of an impending fiscal crisis provoked by the burden of a bloated state sector 'crowding out' productive investment and stifling entrepreneurialism through high taxation. As the public was financed by the private that latter, it argued, must take priority. The third SAF congress (November 1984) advocated greater commercial input, increased use of private services and more competitive tendering in the public sector. One remedy the SAF advocated was greater participation by businessmen in politics. In the 1982 Riksdag elections, for example, 31 per cent of MPs originated from the public sector compared to 19 per cent from the private sector.[16]

The labour movement has always laid great stress on the public sector contributing to full employment and the growing interest of LO, TCO and SACO–SR on 'quality of life' issues in the 1970s prompted them to advocate greater public provision. The Social Democratic government, though ideologically committed to the public sector, was concerned by SAF militancy, and the economic consequences of a public sector which by 1982 absorbed 66.6 per cent of Sweden's Gross Domestic Product (GDP). Hereafter, public sector *growth* was to be restrained in favour of household consumption and private manufacturing investment. The government had, in effect, accepted the core of the SAF's case: 'it is important that public service is provided as effectively as possible ... Bureaucracy and controls will have to be reduced while promoting efficiency and a service spirit'.[17] Government intervention was resented by public sector workers. After the granting of full union rights to the civil service in 1966 the politicisation of the public sector increased. A teachers' strike (1966) was followed by a strike of senior civil servants (1971) which was declared illegal by a special law, and in 1980 and 1985 there were major and widespread disputes. Public sector workers are in a difficult position, trying to avoid alienating public sympathy whilst disrupting government, and government is under pressure to preserve the welfare state and ensure that it does not inhibit the private sector.

The Public Sector in the United States

The public sector has grown dramatically, but growth in the total labour force means it has remained stable in overall terms. Growth has also been restrained by traditional hostility to 'big government', the dominance of a free enterprise culture, and federalism. The bulk of public sector employees are employed by state and local government. Education, for example, employs 6.75m (36.4 per cent of public employment) but only 23 000 are federal employees; 3.4m teachers are employed by state and municipal governments, a 64 per cent increase since 1952. The bulk of public employees (92.3 per cent) are employed by organisations headed by elected officials: federal government 4.0m (23.7 per cent), state government 3.7m (21.7 per cent), and local government 9.3m (54.4 per cent).[18]

Union density has risen from 10.3 per cent (1952) to 22.1 per cent (1978). The main unions are the *American Federation of State, County and Municipal Employees* (AFSCME, 1.1m members), the *American Federation of Teachers* (AFT, 100 000 members), and the *National Education Association* (NEA, 1.7m members), these embrace 13 per cent of public sector membership. Federal government has 78 separate organisation, the largest is the *American Federation of Government Employees* (AFGE, 679 000 members), the postal service has two unions, the *American Postal Workers' Union* (APWU, 232 000 members) and the *National Association of Letter Carriers* (NALC, 186 000 members). All, except NEA and AFSCME (between 1976 and 1985) are AFL–CIO affiliates.

Up to 1962 the collective bargaining rights of federal workers were limited. President Kennedy's Executive Order 10988 (January 1962), though not a law, extended to federal employees most of the rights in the Wagner Act (except for the right to strike) and their pay and conditions are ultimately determined by Congress.[19] Congress is unlikely to respond, as public employees lack public sympathy and their fragmentation makes it impossible to present a united front. The major federal unions are often rivals despite their common interests. The *National Treasury Employees' Union* (NTEU), 90 000 members), the *National Federation of Federal Employees* (NFFE, 130 000 members), and the *National Association of Government Employees* (NAGE 80 000) are not affiliated to the AFL–CIO, unlike the AFGE. Affiliation, they contend, is inappropriate as the AFL–CIO is dominated by private sector, blue-collar unions. Merger seems logical but AFGE overtures have been rebuffed. There are structural problems; the AFGE (for example) is 45 per cent blue-collar and its membership is spread through 70 departments and agencies, while the NTEU is based on highly skilled professional workers at the heart of federal government.

Public sector unions spend a large proportion of their time and resources on politics. The AFSCME and the NEA, for example, have substantial numbers of members in many states whose livelihoods depend on government; they are more likely to be registered to vote and vote Democrat. In the 1984 elections AFSCME targeted 15 states whilst the NEA sent 3 letters and made 3 phone calls to every member to encourage them to vote. In the 1983–4 election cycle the NEA PAC raised $2.4m, the AFSCME $1.4m, and the AFT spent $771 000. Federal unions raised and spent less. NALC raised $1.3m, APWU $769 000, the AFGE $704 593 and the NTEU PAC $313 057.[20]

In the 1950s there were few public sector strikes but after the late 1960s they increased and by the 1970s had become common. In 1965 there were 432 strikes involving 23 000 employees, in 1980 there were 538 involving 247 000. As recently as 1962 no state had collective bargaining legislation for its employees; by 1980 13 had extended full collective bargaining rights and 23 had made some concessions. Strikers face severe retribution. In 1981 the *Professional Air Traffic Controllers' Association* (PATCO) struck in pursuit of a pay increase even though this was illegal and they had been warned of the consequences. President Reagan dismissed 11 000 controllers, massive fines were imposed and several union leaders were imprisoned. Ironically PATCO was the only AFL–CIO union to endorse Reagan for President in 1980. The crushing of PATCO demonstrated government willingness to resist public sector unions, and it had echoes at state and municipal level. In 1986 however the *National Air Traffic Controllers' Association* (NATCA) was established as a replacement for PATCO. NATCA is forbidden to strike but its founding was seen as a major victory for the AFL–CIO and for federal government unionism.[21]

The assault on the public sector begain under Carter but the Reagan Administration was regarded as particularly hostile, and there was an upsurge of protest against proposals to limit the pay of existing workers and the entitlements of the retired. To resist this and attract increased numbers of public sector workers into union membership the AFL–CIO's *Public Employees' Division* (PED) was restructured into the *Federal/Postal Division* (FPD) and the *State/Local Division* (SLD). A PED report found that of 6.5m eligible state and local government employees in the 27 states and District of Columbia with collective bargaining laws, 71 per cent voted for union representation. In the 23 states lacking such legislation only 14 per cent of the 4m eligible workers were unionised. In the bargaining states union representation grew from 60.1 per cent (1976) to 71.2 per cent (1982) but membership density ranges from 18.2 per cent (North Dakota) to 98.6 per cent (New York) and 23 unionised states have densities of 40 per cent

+ and 7 of 80 per cent +. Density in the non-bargaining states fell from 16.1 per cent to 14 per cent (1976–82), and densities range from zero (North Carolina) to 54.2 per cent (Nevada); 9 have densities below 10 per cent. There were significant gains in Ohio from 41.6 per cent (1982) to 51.6 per cent (1986), and Illinois (45 per cent to 80 per cent) after the passage of collective bargaining laws in 1982.[22] This suggests that the politicisation of the public sector will continue as unions strive to secure the passage of collective bargaining laws at state level and constant pressure to check federal spending will have the same effect at national level.

The Public Sector in West Germany

The fastest growing sectors have been education (1950 288 000, 1980 913 000), health care (1950 350 000, 1980 1 139 000), and social welfare (1950 251 000, 1980 453 000). Employment in public trading bodies (for example, posts, telecommuncations, transport, manufacturing, energy and public utilities) has increased from 1.4m (1950) to 2.3m (1980).[23] At the summit of state employment are *Beamte*, permanent state officials appointed in law and traditionally regarded as a *Stand* (Estate) whose training, functions and ethos confers the status of public *servant* not public *employee*. Their salaries and conditions are determined by the state and they are forbidden to strike. *Beamte* are a minority (about one-third of civil service employment), the remainder are *Angestellte* (Employees) and *Arbeiter* (Workers) who lack the status and tenure of *Beamte* and whose wages and conditions are regulated by contract agreed through collective bargaining.

Seven DGB unions have civil service members: Mining and Energy 229 (0.06 per cent of total union membership), Education and Science 138 741 (74.7 per cent), Railway Workers 182 110 (47.9 per cent), Public Service and Transport 87 389 (74 per cent), the Police Union 141 614 (84.5 per cent), Agriculture 2694 (6.3 per cent), and the Postal Workers 270 069 (58.9 per cent). In total civil servants comprise 10.6 per cent of DGB membership, white-collar workers 21.7 per cent and blue-collar 57.8 per cent. The *Deutscher Beamtenbund* (DBB, German Civil Service Officials' Federation) organises 820 000 civil servants but in the public sector as a whole the DGB affiliated *Public Service and Transport Union* (OTV) with 1 173 525 members (15 per cent of total DGB membership) dominates. The DGB and DBB are based on competing organisational principles (industry versus occupation) whilst the latter stresses its social exclusivity and its activities are directed at preserving *Beamte* status.

The legal position of public workers and civil servants is complicated. Article 9(3) of the Basic Law concedes a general right to organise unions and strike, but says nothing specifically about unions. However, Article 7(3) gives the Federal authorities exclusive rights over 'the status of persons employed by the Federation and by Federal corporate bodies under public law'. Civil service unions may not regulate working conditions by collective agreement so 'it is doubtful whether [the DBB] should be termed a union federation at all. It does not negotiate with the government since its members are all tenured civil servants for whom collective bargaining is prohibited. *It is thus mainly a lobbying organisation*'.[24]

The DGB regards the public services as essential for a civilised society and full employment but recognises that this sector is directly dependent on government decisions. Whilst supporting the public sector the DGB is acutely aware of its, and West Germany's, dependence on a prosperous manufacturing sector to provide the surplus for public spending. So whilst rejecting 'cuts' it approves of the 'efficient delivery' of public services.[25]

Concern over the public sector stemmed from both a primordial fear of cost and the belief that the public sector was a bastion of left-wing sentiment. The conservative Kohl government regarded the public sector as a political and economic problem but was caught in an ideological dilemma. The social welfare state was financed by rapid economic growth as envisaged by social market theorists; to challenge this would be to challenge the ideological hegemony of the social market economy. The Kohl government proclaims its loyalty to this heritage whilst doubting the future ability of the tax base to finance public provision of services at their present level. The government has increasingly stressed the market aspect of the social market and the need to use the public sector to provide an environment conducive to private industry. This required the 'exercise [of] strict discipline in public-sector spending . . . we have to restrict the growth of public expenditure. At all levels of government therefore economic budgeting is the catchword'. A commission was appointed in 1985 to explore the opening up of posts, telecommunications and railways to market forces and a privatisation programme is underway. The social security and health care systems were to be restructured to reduce costs and place greater emphasis on civic and personal responsibility.[26] These policies imply a break with the past, and it seems unlikely that government can achieve its goals without conflict with the public sector unions.

The Public Sector in Japan

Before the war public sector unions were, with the exception of the teachers, predominantly right-wing, but the upsurge in militancy in the wake of defeat led directly to restrictions on the rights of public sector workers who were in the vanguard of the unions' revival. Article 28 of the Constitution, the Trade Union Law, and the Labour Relations Adjustment Law do not apply to the public sector; the *Public Corporation and National Enterprise Labour Relations Law* (PCNELR) guarantees the right to organise and bargain collectively but not to strike, whilst the *National Public Service Law* (NPSL) and the *Local Public Service Law* (LPSL) bars national and prefectural civil servants from concluding collective agreements or engaging in political or industrial action. Public sector union politics is based on competing legal principles enshrined in the Constitution. Article 15 states that *'all public officials are servants of the whole community and not any group thereof'*, whereas under Article 28 *'The right of workers to organize and to bargain and act collectively is guaranteed'*.[27]

Pay and conditions are negotiated by the *National Personnel Authority* (NPA) but these are *recommendations*. Public sector wages and conditions are effectively determined by the government which has regularly restrained public sector pay. Government–union relations were worsened by ideological differences, governments having been conservative, the public sector unions having close connections with the left. Article 102 of the NPSL bans civil servants from all political activity except voting, and this has been strictly defined by the Supreme Court and vigorously enforced. The Teachers' Union has been in frequent conflict with government in resisting attempts to rewrite history textbooks and promote a conservative-nationalist ethos at odds, the Teachers claim, with the Constitution. To avoid conflict and compensate for these legal disabilities government created the *Public Corporation and National Enterprises Labour Relations Commission* (PCNELRC), the NPA and the *Personnel Commission* (PC). These have been a failure, as has the *Roundtable Conference for Labour Problems in Public Corporations and National Enterprise* (Korokon) established in 1978 to build up confidence between management and employees in the public sector.[28]

The Japanese public sector is therefore highly politicised because of the government's attitude in collective bargaining and because of the legal restrictions. It is hardly surprising that union densities are highest in the public sector. Strikers are (potentially) subject to criminal and civil liability as well as internal disciplinary action, and although reform has been under discussion since 1965 nothing of substance has changed. The *Council of Public Corporations and National Enterprise Workers' Unions* (Korokyo), a Sohyo affiliate, frequently holds 48 or 96 hour strikes during Shunto and others (such as the rail unions) pursue 'legal action' (go slows, strict observance of safety laws and so on). Though ritualistic they are often illegal and can, as happened with the 1975 strikes, cause considerable disruption especially in public transport. However, the restrictive attitude of the courts is supported by public opinion. The Japanese Election Survey asked respondents whether or not they agreed that the right to strike ought to be extended to the public sector: 20.2 per cent agreed or agreed somewhat, 22.7 per cent were neutral, and 44.7 per cent disagreed or disagreed somewhat. When asked about the importance of this issue 26.1 per cent thought it very important/important, 48.6 per cent saw it as not important/not at all important.[29] Public sector workers have been criticised for what many Japanese see as favourable treatment in terms of old age pensions and retirement benefits when compared to the private sector and many (given the degree of commuting in Japan) are hit badly by public sector disputes. The preparation of privatisation proposals for some public sector activities indicates that government patience is exhausted. At a time of economic restructuring the 'featherbedded' public sector is, of course, an easy political target and convenient scapegoat.

The Public Sector in the United Kingdom

The typical UK public sector employee is white-collar, providing a service in health, education or welfare in central or local government or via the public corporations. Up to the 1940s the public sector was small (10 per cent of total employment) but it tripled between 1938–1951 as a consequence of war, nationalisation, and the growth of the welfare state. In the 1950s it shrank by 341 000 but in the 1960s and 1970s growth began, accelerating between 1966 and 1976 and subsiding thereafter. The main growth areas between 1951 and 1981 were education (162 per cent), health care (167 per cent), and social services (219 per cent); employment in state industries has declined dramatically despite recurrent bouts of nationalisation because of the rundown of labour intensive industries such as coal mining and the railways. The public sector's share of total employment has remained broadly unchanged at about 20 per cent.[30]

Except for 1927–47 when civil servants were denied the right to strike and their unions were forbidden to affiliate to the TUC (prohibitions which apply to the police) and events such as the withdrawal of union rights at the Government Communications Headquarters (GCHQ) and the suspension of teachers' collective bargaining rights in 1986, public sector workers are not subject to legal discrimination. The public sector is traditionally heavily unionised, density rose by only 4 per cent between 1951 and 1974 (from 71 per cent to 75 per cent), and they constitute 40 per cent of total union membership. Its composition has changed dramatically; it is now primarily non-manual and white-collar with a growing tendency to engage in industrial and political action.[31]

These unions have become increasingly influential in the TUC in the last decade. In 1986–7, for example, 20 out of 48 General Council members came from unions with a significant membership in the public sector. Three of the TUC's Industry Committees (Health Services, Local Government, and Energy) and the Public Services Joint Committee are concerned with the affairs of the public sector and its workers. Public spending restraint after 1976 and, after 1979, ideological hostility produced a high level of politicisation. This had two distinct but related phases. First, resistance to government efforts to restrain public spending led to the phase of *economic conflict*; the second phase was that of *ideological conflict* generated by the questioning of the public sector's legitimacy initiated by the Conservative government. Between 1979 and 1987 12 major state owned enterprises were privatised and the numbers employed in the civil service were cut.

This was portrayed as an essential element in reversing the pattern of post-war political development. The result was conflict.

Education, local government and the civil service illustrate developments. There is a dissonance between the teachers' 'professional' ethos and hostility to government policies. Teachers have become increasingly militant as the consensus on education collapsed. The National Union of Teachers (NUT), for example, published General Election manifestoes. *Our Children, Our Future* (1983) stressed the threat to public education; *For All Our Children, Vote For Education* (1987) stressed the damage done to education by the Conservative government. Neither implied or made a voting recommendation because the broad political loyalties of the NUT's membership meant that an overt party endorsement might lose membership (industrial militancy did cost the NUT members) and second, the NUT did not have a political fund under the terms of the 1984 Act. In the 1970s, and especially after 1979 the National Association of Local Government Officers (NALGO), adopted a higher political profile. A policy document *NALGO In The 80s* declared that NALGO needed both a political fund and Labour Party affiliation but both were rejected by the membership in 1981. Before the 1983 and 1987 election NALGO mounted expensive political campaigns, *Put People First* and *Make People Matter*, to challenge the ideological assault on public provision. As in the case of the NUT no partisan voting recommendation was made. The main civil service unions (the Civil and Public Servants Association (CPSA), the Society of Civil and Public Servants (SCPS) and the Civil Service Union (CSU)) were in a similar position. Since 1979 employment has declined by 108 000 (14.8 per cent) to its lowest level since 1945 and government intends to make further reductions. Civil service unions moved from being concerned primarily with wages to challenging the fundamentals of government policies. A by-product of this was the merger of the CSU and the CPSA in October 1987.

The Royal College of Nursing (RCN) is the tenth largest union (251 157 members) but is not affiliated to the TUC; it is the only union to have the Queen as its patron and its members enjoy total public sympathy. It is both non-partisan and rejects industrial action. The RCN was politicised by spending cuts, low wages and poor working conditions. Since 1982 (after flirting with TUC affiliation) the RCN has become openly critical of government policy after it became clear that its traditional virtues gave it little influence in the National Health Service (NHS) policy process; as industrial action was rejected, their only remaining option was a higher political profile. In 1985 the RCN appointed a parliamentary liaison officer, in early 1986 it mounted a £250000 press campaign opposing government policy, and a *Manifesto for Nursing Health* (1986) and *Nurses: Power and Politics* (1987, written by the RCN's General Secretary) were published.[32] The experience of the RCN shows both the climate of public sector politics in Britain and the rapid politicisation of its unions.

Industrial militancy did not deflect government policy and cost public support, hence the adoption by public sector unions of political strategies designed to influence public opinion. This new political style was jeopardised by the 1984 Trade Union Act, which broadened the definition of 'political' to include pressure group as well as electoral activity by a union. Such activity required a political fund approved by a ballot of the membership. The politicisation of white-collar workers and the diversity of their political activities were threatened by the 1984 Act as most of the unions involved did not have political funds. In the spring of 1987 the courts ruled that NALGO could not finance its *Make People Matter* campaign out of general funds as its intention was to influence voting behaviour. The inevitable consequence was that public sector unions decided in increasing numbers to create political funds, despite government claims they were not needed. This will most likely result in a high and increasing level of conflict with the public sector unions in the 1990s as government policy strives to reduce both the cost and size of the public sector.

Managing the Unions in the 1990s

The recession of 1973–82 marks the end of one era in government–union relations and the transition to another. The decade saw a re-ordering of the international economy which necessitated domestic industry becoming capable of operating in highly competitive global markets which required the removal of obstacles to the flexible use of capital and labour. Throughout the industrial states unions were perceived to be an obstacle to be overcome; how this was to be achieved varied from state to state. Since 1979 (or thereabouts) governments have been searching for new means of managing the unions; these have varied from coercion (Britain) to semi-incorporation (Japan). Unions have not, however, been totally quiescent but have sought to adapt to their new environment.

Thatcherite Conservatism and the Unions

The British experience demonstrates both the attraction of tripartism and that the strains it generated could be neither contained nor resolved by weak tripartite structures; failure meant discredit and the search for a new configuration of political authority.

The Conservative government's strategy had three elements. First, there would be no intervention to prevent unemployment rising, which would both help restructure industry and chasten the unions. Second, a programme of incremental legal reform would cumulatively impose moderation on the unions by making effective industrial action difficult and union leaders accountable to the members who were presumed to oppose militancy. Finally, a new climate would be encouraged by an ideological offensive stressing individualism and not collectivism and the identity of interest between employers and employees, and by highly visible demonstrations of the government's determination to defeat strikes. By the 1987 General Election the Conservatives could claim to have transformed British politics:

> Is it really only such a short time ago that inflation rose to an annual rate of 27 per cent? That the leader of the Transport and General Workers' Union was widely seen as the most powerful man in the land? . . . And that Labour's much-vaunted pay pact with the unions collapsed in the industrial anarchy of the 'winter of discontent', in which the dead went unburied, rubbish piled up in the street and the country was gripped by a creeping paralysis which Labour was powerless to cure?[33]

The TUC believed the Thatcher government would return to consulting the unions when the political and electoral consequences of recession and unemployment struck. When neither materialised the TUC began to grope towards a response. This came at the 1983 TUC Congress, the 'New Realism' Congress.

The TUC found itself asking questions about its and the unions role in society and politics, and refighting battles it believed had been won years before. 'New Realism' involved accepting the electorate's decision, responding to the wishes of the membership and adapting to the new environment. Though New Realism received a setback with the banning of unions at GCHQ and the coal dispute, for example, it could not be stopped. Individual unions, led by the Electricians and the Engineers began to modify both their political and industrial strategies and to negotiate new forms of collective agreements which fitted the requirements of the 'Thatcher Revolution'.[34]

The policies of the government were distasteful to the unions, but not to their members. Traditionally, the remedy for the TUC was to help secure the electoral defeat of the Conservatives, but the Labour Party and its policies aroused little enthusiasm. So, the TUC is in the unenviable position of seeking political change to ease its environment but the party most likely to do this appears to be incapable of denting Conservative dominance. Of course, a change of government would not and will not transform the unions' position – for example, the change in the labour market (both demographically and structurally) is beyond government control so the unions must respond. The TUC recognised painfully slowly that a new epoch was dawning in which a change of government would not solve the unions' problems and that salvation lay in their own hands: 'If the Movement, in the longer term, is to establish firmly its right to consultation and involvement in decisions about national economic and social issues, then it must shoulder the responsibility for collectively framing its own priorities'.[35]

This implies a reduction in the prominence given to partisan politics in the 1970s and a greater directing role for the TUC, which would require unions to surrender some of their jealously guarded sovereignty. This, given the TUC's inability to forge a consensus over the types of agreements negotiated by some unions, seems unlikely, and bodes ill for the revival of union political influence. Of more long-term significance are the efforts of the TUC and individual unions to attract workers into membership: from greater numbers greater political influence may ultimately spring. Unions have, as a result of the political fund ballots, seen the need to improve their communications and have become more concerned to explain themselves and their actions to their members and potential members rather than take consent for granted. Legislation on strike ballots and union elections has gone some way to improving communication between leaders and their members and will serve to strengthen trade unionism. These moves towards a flexible, members oriented strategy are at an early stage, but offer the best prospect for a resurgence of union political influence in the 1990s though it will never return to the scale or visibility of the Social Contract era, something which many unions welcome.

Reaganism and Rebuilding the Unions

Accelerating relative economic decline in the 1970s accompanied an upsurge of business political activism and a decline of union influence in the United States. Deregulation (begun under Carter) was seen as essential if business was to compete effectively and the bargaining system was blamed for both labour market rigidity and inflation; both had at their core hostility to the unions. Such sentiments underpinned change in what had hitherto been regarded as a satisfactory employer-union relationship based on the New Deal and the compromises thrashed out between 1936 and 1947, guaranteed and policed by government. Mass production – symbolised by the automobile industry – required a stable, organised and controlled workforce; this was provided by the labour laws of 1936–47 and the contract based collective bargaining system which evolved in tandem. The decline of mass production and increased foreign competition led to a change in the political–economic framework, as stability was no longer an asset.[36]

The change can be seen in the new role of the NLRB. Established by the Wagner Act and modified by the Taft–Hartley Act to police and mediate industrial politics, in the last decade its role became more partial as employers became more aggressive and the climate of opinion shifted. In the 1960s they were winning about 59 per cent NLRB of organising elections, by the 1970s they were winning about 45 per cent and the absolute number of elections fell dramatically. This took place under both Democrat and Republican Administrations but under Reagan's NLRB chairman, Donald Dotson, the NLRB ruled against management in only 55 per cent of unfair practice cases, and in representation cases NLRB supported management in 75 per cent of its decisions. More generally, its interpretation of labour law became more restrictive, it ceased to be a help to the unions and became a powerful and effective mechanism for their subordination. Although the crushing of PATCO was an unambiguous signal to the private sector, the Administration did not use labour law against the unions, but sought to reduce its effectiveness by emphasising the avoidance of intervention. At the Department of Labor, for example, Donovan promoted an 'arm's length' regulatory style (or 'hands off', depending on one's viewpoint); he began a 'long difficult and sometimes painful process of reevaluation and restructuring ... [the Department] is leaner, more efficient and more purposeful'.[37] Critics claimed it and its agencies (especially in health and safety) were also less effective and pro-business.

This process was aided by the shift of the political agenda in the 1970s away from labour because of the sympathy of many Democrats in the Congress and electorate for aspects of the Reagan agenda. By 1980 labour's agenda and its political support coalition was in retreat with many union leaders and members feeling profoundly pessimistic about the future. Industrial, technical and political change conspired to produce speculation that so fundamental a transformation was underway in the political economy that the unions were locked into a spiral of decline which would culminate in their extinction. In the past 25 years the death-knell of American unions has been rung prematurely many times and this speculation ignored the possibility of any effective political response to the environment facing the American unions.[38]

After 1980 the AFL–CIO responded by, first, modifying its role in the Democratic Party's presidential candidate selection procedures and second, its Congressional lobbying activity. The former was not a conspicuous success (for reasons beyond the AFL–CIO's control) and it made no similar intervention in 1987–8 largely because of the plethora of Democratic candidates in the early stages. Once Michael Dukakis received the nomination, however, the AFL–CIO swung behind the party ticket. In Congress, however, labour was more successful especially when Democratic control was restored, and it won some important victories (for example, on plant closure notification) in the teeth of Presidential opposition. Aware of its weaknesses at the grassroots the AFL–CIO and its affiliates have also opted for a long-term membership oriented strategy to reverse the decline in membership and thereby boost labour's political influence.

The Changing Situation of Workers and Their Unions stressed that the decline in membership was not the result of a wholesale and principled rejection of union membership by workers, or ineffectiveness (on average union workers were paid one-third more than non-union workers), but was due to the impact of recession on heavily unionised industries. To win these sympathetic millions (27m potential new members were identified) unions were urged to improve their services and benefits and in February 1986 the AFL–CIO launched the *Union Privilege Benefit Programs* (UPBP) and the *Associate Membership Program* (AMP): 'From these tens of thousands can gain come and greater strength in the legislative halls and political arena'.[39]

These developments, though at an early stage, indicate an effective response to decline. Many of the ideas in the UPBP and AMP have been taken up by the TUC but American unions have a far easier task in reasserting their political influence. To some extent the political pressure has been reduced by the mid-term elections and the lame-duck nature of the Reagan presidency. After 1986 the Administration became less hostile and Congress more sympathetic; the separation of powers means that more effective union political organisation can have a significant effect in Washington (particularly in Congress), whereas party government in Britain means that no matter how effective union political organisation, the interconnection of legislature and executive blocks union influence. Union membership, however, continues to decline and technical change and corporate diversification continues to break up the traditional bases of American unions. The AFL–CIO's strategy offers the best and only hope of expanding the political influence of the unions, but if it is the economic climate which is so hostile, can union political influence significantly effect it? In the 1990s American unions will for the most part retain the position they have.

The Federal Republic: Reaction Postponed?

In the 1970s doubts about continued growth limited the willingness of the state and employers to make concessions to the unions. The aim of economic–industrial policy was to restructure industry to maintain competitiveness and profitability, even if the cost was an increase in unemployment. An increasingly conservative political climate put the unions on the defensive, a situation made worse by the electoral problems of the SPD and a crisis of confidence in the movement over the nature of the representation provided by the DGB. This has considerable implications for the polity.

Union strategy had been to defend their members within a consensus embracing the government (irrespective of party), the Bundesbank, the BDA/BDI (Federation of German Employers Associations and Federation of German Industry) and the DGB based on a sensitivity to West Germany's dependence on the world economy.[40] The departure of the SPD from government in 1982 confirmed the already established drift away from Keynesianism (the DGB's preferred policy) and the CDU–FDP coalition produced an alliance of traditional conservatives unhappy with union involvement in decision-making with free market liberals who saw unions as obstacles to the market's operation. The Kohl government continued to talk to the unions knowing full well the strength of the DGB's anxiety about competitiveness: 'the government does not run much risk because the trade unions are very much interested in [the economy's] success and, for lack of alternatives, are forced to cooperate when they are no longer a courted participant in the modernization cartel'.[41] Observers noted in these attempts to maintain the economic miracle a potential for destabilisation:

> In addition to splitting West German industry, the union movement, and the working class into export-dependent 'winners' and increasingly domestic market oriented 'losers', this economic strategy [export led growth] became ever more risky in a world of sluggish demand replete with uncertainties. A serious setback for West Germany's exports would mean a severe curtailment of the surplus necessary to maintain the high quantity and quality of 'carrots' presently comprising the all-important welfare ingredients of the model.[42]

To economic instability was added political instability.

The DGB's 1981 Basic Programme reiterated the positive role unions played in the Federal Republic's political development, rejected accusations of economic irresponsibility, and advocated progress towards the 'social state'. Though essentially defensive the unions won significant victories; for example, IG Metall engaged in a nine week strike in 1984 to win reduced working hours. This was interpreted as the limit to which it was wise to push the DGB and there were no further significant attacks on the unions. The bankruptcy of *Neue Heimat* (New Home, a DGB housing cooperative) due to a combination of greed and mismanagement by union officials cost the unions DM5bn. Though rescued by the banks the collapse raised questions about the type of trade unionism hitherto dominant in the Federal Republic. The *Neue Heimat* scandal undermined the authority of senior figures who were not involved and caused some union members to demand that the unions get out of peripheral activities and concentrate on the more aggressive pursuit of better wages and conditions. Employers, politicians, and some union leaders fear *Neue Heimat* will act as a focal point for demands for radicalisation, and will reduce the room for manoeuvre hitherto open to union leaders in their economic and political activity. Both IG Metall and OTV have hinted at the need for the DGB to move towards a 'British' model of adversarial trade unionism coupled with a withdrawal from social partnership. In late 1985 and early 1986 there were widespread, if brief, 'political' strikes when DGB workers stopped work to 'discuss' proposed changes in the labour laws which the DGB claimed would limit the right to strike. These changes were widely interpreted as a riposte to the 1984 engineering dispute and again IG Metall and OTV were prominent. In December 1986 the Ruhr was brought to a standstill in protest by the DGB at the projected loss of 30 000 jobs in the steel industry; a similar number were also to go in the coal industry. Protesters occupied bridges and the SPD government in North Rhine–Westphalia ordered the police not to intervene. In April 1987 the employers and IG Metall came very close to a massive dispute on hours; the unions wanted a reduction from 38.5 to 35 but compromised on 37 in return for greater flexibility. Industrial politics in Federal Republic are thus in something of a ferment.

Politically there is also flux. As a result of long-term electoral change and a series of poor performances in Bundestag and Landtag elections, the SPD is distancing itself from the DGB. In the run-up to the January 1987 Bundestag elections the fallout from the *Neue Heimat* scandal contributed to an increase in anti-union sentiment which reflected badly on the SPD and helped the CDU. The 1987 elections saw the Greens gain ground (increasing their share of the vote from 5.3 per cent in 1983 to 8.3 per cent and their Bundestag representation from 27 to 42 seats) and subsequently move leftwards, whilst the SPD sustained losses (its vote fell from 38.2 per cent to 37.0 per cent and its seats from 193 to 186). As a result, the SPD began a rethink of both image and policy which involved a distancing from the unions. This was led by Oskar Lafontaine (SPD Prime Minister in the Saarland) who urged unions not to push for higher wages and so encourage job creation and who expressed scepticism about the traditional SPD–DGB policy accord. Lafontaine's ideas were denounced by many DGB unions, but many in the SPD welcomed this challenge to political orthodoxy as offering the SPD a chance to win over new groups of electors unresponsive to traditional cues and convince them that the SPD could run the economy efficiently.

Conservative politicians, meanwhile, contend that the surge in the mark's value and the onset of the European market in 1992 demands a fundamental re-examination of the level of wages, fringe benefits, working hours, and welfare provision. Conservatives have claimed that the veto exercised by the DGB has produced an immobilism in the West Germany political economy which has serious implications for the 1990s. There remains considerable readiness within the DGB to compromise but if the economy stagnates, pressure for change will grow and confrontation will become more likely.[43]

Sweden: Consensus Maintained?

After 1973 the Swedish political economy destabilised. Electoral politics became more unstable, profits fell, wage costs rose, economic growth slowed dramatically, and the collective bargaining system was breaking down. In 1983 the Engineering Employers' Association and Metalworkers' Union rejected the SAF–LO role, negotiating a separate agreement. In 1984, for the first time since 1956, there were no central LO–SAF talks. This fragmentation was too serious for government to ignore. It must be remembered that non-intervention by the state was always more apparent than real:

> It would ... be wrong to accept too readily the conventional Swedish view of the relatively minor part played by governmental authority... The power of the state is considerable. This is no corporatist system in which interest groups are endowed with legal privileges and act as independent semi-sovereign entities ... *they are the instruments of public policy used by the state, wherever this is feasible, in the place of its own paid servants.*[44]

The Finance Minister, Karl Olof-Feldt, referred to bargainers as 'lunatics', threatened retaliation, and 'invited' bargainers to talks.

The classic Swedish Model depended on the centralisation provided by LO–SAF and dominance of industrial workers and manufacturing companies. The growth of services, the public sector and, therefore, the growing prominence of TCO, SACO–SR, and non-manufacturing unions in the LO made the bargaining system infinitely more complex. This was compounded by the economic problems of the 1970s which raised doubts about the cost of the public sector and the burden of the tax system which led the Engineering Employers to demand more decentralised bargaining. In turn, this increased the level of inter-union (public–private) and inter-sectoral conflict, further reducing the ability of the LO and SAF to police the system.[45]

The future configuration of collective bargaining is not yet clear, but the old system cannot be recreated:

> organizations originally built from the bottom up had to adapt themselves to a centralized umbrella organization run very much from the top. This 'superstructure' has become progressively more complicated. It consists not only of the executive boards [of] LO, TCO, and SACO/SR but also of a range of special negotiating cartels ... when the Government makes demands of the labour market organizations it addresses itself to their leaderships, just as it did in the 1930s. *It is they who can be assembled round a conference table.*[46]

The bargaining system that developed after 1945, despite periodic amendments, became incapable in the 1980s of handling an increasingly complex economy and labour market and itself became more unwieldy, producing crude decisions which were evaded (wage drift) by wide sections of the labour market.

Changes in the international economy will shift the balance of power against the unions in the 1990s unless the unions can recreate their former solidarity. Bargaining in the 1980s was characterised by growing pressure, especially in engineering and other export sectors, for industry level settlements. The LO was forced to concede a looser form of 'wage solidarity' which recognised that changes in the labour market, union fragmentation, and decentralised bargaining in the private sector made it impossible to control wage negotiations as in the past. These developments excited considerable alarm in government, an alarm compounded by a growing sense of impending industrial conflict – for example, there was a three week lockout of white-collar workers in the engineering industry in January 1988. On the other hand, there was also an awareness of the implications of these difficulties as both the LO and SAF struggled to reassert some control by producing a new model of labour market behaviour (the FOS model, the revised labour market model of 1987) and the SAF imposed a massive Kr1m fine on the bakery employers for conceding an excessive wage increase.

Three possible developments have been identified. First, a *state imposed incomes policy*. Though there are precedents, this option is unlikely except as a short-term crisis expedient: it runs counter to the ethos of Swedish political life and would undoubtedly create more problems than it solved. Second, the SAF now supports *federation/industry level negotiations*, and these correspond with the economy's evolution. If it was the only way, the LO would reluctantly accept it even though bargaining would be further fragmented and would be resisted by the public sector and the low paid. Third, *full decentralisation* would be supported only by the SAF. This would widen differentials both within the private sector and between the public and private sector, the active labour market policy would collapse, inter-union competition would increase and the politics of collective bargaining would be dominated by the Engineering Employers and the Metalworkers. Government would, as a result, be forced to take a far more interventionist stance, which would provoke a political crisis. The first and third options are impossible as long as SAP political hegemony remains intact; the most likely development is the extension of industry bargaining, with government trying to boost the regulatory authority of the LO and SAF.

The solution sought by the unions, employers and government would appear to be 'coordinated decentralisation', but in the 1990s the level of overt government participation will be higher. In the 1980s government became steadily more prominent in negotiations; the tripartite Rosenbad Meetings of 1984–5 (Rosenbad is the location of the Prime Minister's residence) secured agreement on wage increases of 5 per cent, and the process was repeated in 1986, though the public sector proved difficult. Subsequently bargainers expressed concern at government's role and government declared its non-intervention whilst warning it would intervene if bargainers did not act responsibly. There were, therefore, no central negotiations in 1987–8. The emerging model is one of binding tripartite agreements to achieve full employment and low inflation. Neither the union nor the employers are particularly enthusiastic but they are mindful of the alternative. Government has resurrected the pre-Saltsjobaden threat: if bargainers cannot cooperate in the national interest at national level, then government will act to secure that interest. The piecemeal interventions of the 1980s are giving way to a 'negotiated incomes policy' for the 1990s involving the traditional bargainers but with a much higher profile for government than in the past. There are powerful forces ranged against this (for example, inter-federation rivalry, sectoral rivalries, wage drift, demands for greater labour flexibility, internal competitive pressure) and politically it will depend on the continuation in government of the Social Democrats, the party most trusted by the unions.

Japan: Divide and Rule

After 1975 Shunto underwent a significant change. Accelerating international inflation was a major threat to the Japanese system, given its dependence on imported oil and exporting manufactures. Shunto, covering 70 per cent of unionised workers, was clearly crucial especially as a formal state led incomes policy had been rejected. In the 1974 Shunto, however, the unions won increases of 32.9 per cent and both government and employers warned of the adverse consequences if this was repeated. Great hope was invested in the moderation of the enterprise unions in the export sector, and government did all it could to sensitise them and the public to Japan's international economic vulnerability, but did nothing which might threaten the moderation of these key unions. These unions' leaders, enjoying intimate relationship with corporate leaders, accepted the impossibility of money wages keeping pace with inflation without seriously damaging the economy. They were worried about lay-offs and threats to the lifetime employment system and were, therefore, willing to barter pay for jobs.[47]

In the 1975 Shunto wage increases fell from 32.9 per cent (1974) to 13.1 per cent (1975); two interpretations were advanced to explain this. First, the traditional flexibility of management–union relations and a concern for the national interest which embraced their members enabled the collective bargaining system quickly to adjust. Alternatively, it was argued this adjustment was imposed on tame enterprise unions worried at the loss of their privileges and, through Shunto, on the rest of the labour force who were unorganised and outside the charmed circle. There are elements of truth in both interpretations but the enterprise unions were acutely aware of the new economic situation and were anxious to avoid government intervention which, in the past, had been coercive and repressive. Political fallout was largely avoided by a successful propaganda campaign which portrayed stabilisation as being in the national interest.[48]

In a longer perspective, however, the outcome of the 1975 Shunto seems to have been less of a watershed. Ministry of Labour statistics show that after 1970 Shunto outcomes corresponded to what industry claimed it could afford to pay in increased wages; in 1975 industry calculated that the economy's performance warranted an increase of 15 per cent; 14.9 per cent was awarded. So, in terms of the preceding fifteen years *what should have happened did happen*. Second, the system of labour–management consultation produced a significant political result. Though Japanese unions enjoyed little autonomous political access or influence the generation of 'corporate consciousness' through the enterprise union system in the large export oriented corporations enabled their views to be integrated with those of management who then transmitted this consensus to government through the LDP–business–bureaucracy network. As in other examples of corporatism, in Japanese 'company corporatism' union interests remained subordinate. Corporate consciousness, company corporatism and the distinction between core and periphery workers onto whom the burden of restructuring could be placed allowed the maintenance of job opportunities for permanent employees. Consequently, 'Unemployment remained low despite the severe external shocks of the 1970s, and the flexibility of institutions and practices has allowed macro-economic policies directed towards curbing inflation to be particularly effective'.[49] By the mid-1980s, however, problems were appearing.

Wage moderation continued through the 1980s, the 1983 Shunto increase (4.4 per cent) being the lowest since 1955 but the pace setting industry (steel) was depressed and could not therefore establish the sort of increases which might be justified according to the profitability of other sectors – for example, electronics. Union demands for a new pace setter received a very cool reception from employers and government, but the decline of basic industries such as steel (general throughout the industrial world) will mean that demands will be renewed for a new pace setter and this represents a significant threat to the consensus on wages built up since 1975. Similarly, the formation of Rengo represented a formidable threat to this consensus because of the projected integration of Sohyo's public sector unions in the 1990s. Furthermore, it must be remembered that this consensus has been built by transferring the costs of restructuring to the weakest groups in the labour market. One of Rengo's key policies is the extension of union membership; if these hitherto marginal groups were drawn into membership then they might not be so acquiescent as in the past. The OECD has identified a potential for instability in the labour market: 'there has been a marked deterioration in the quality, if not the quantity of jobs offered. The conditions of women; the precarious job tenure and insufficient hours of work of part-time and other employees; the situation of men over 55 years old and the conditions of "dispatched workers" have led to increased pressure for protective legislation.'[50] Such legislation is, of course, costly.

Shunto and company corporatism successfully reconciled enterprise interests and those of the macro-economy, obviating the need for overt and massive government intervention. Japan's privatised corporate state has provided political and economic stability for the very large export oriented corporations whose interests were encapsulated by the policy network. Problems might arise if the interests of these corporations and the government diverged, for example, over government urging workers to work less, spend more on imports and take more holidays, or when companies run down their domestic operations and relocate overseas to circumvent the high value of the yen, or if the potential for domestic unrest caused by restructuring prompts the state to promote costly welfare measures to avoid instability. This might result in the politicisation of Japanese industrial relations to a degree not seen since the late 1940s and early 1950s; however, the current situation suggests that the management of the unions in the 1990s will follow the pattern of the 1970s and 1980s, with the emphasis being placed on the enterprise unions in the large export corporations.

Conclusions

The Politics of White-collar Trade Unionism

Much of the literature on white-collar trade unionism hints at a degree of wonderment at the upsurge of union membership amongst this group, implying that white-collar workers are 'different'. This is because of the supposed divergence of temperament between the two groups: the former are more collectivist, industrially militant, and politically motivated, whereas the latter are individualistic, moderate and non-political. The blue-collar workers' direct relationship to production, a relationship not softened by better working conditions, fringe benefits and higher status of the white-collar employee, made blue-collar workers more inclined to join unions for self-defence. Whatever the past validity of this, the evidence shows that the organisational and ideological gap between blue- and white-collar workers has been narrowing; both readily accept the need for trade union organisation.

The reasons for this are quite straightforward. First, the number of blue-collar workers has declined (in some cases dramatically) whilst the number of white-collar jobs has increased, so that the number of white-collar union members could be expected to rise. Second, white-collar workers have become more willing to join unions. As the nature of work has changed many white-collar jobs (most of which are of low status) have become similar to routine blue-collar work: boring, repetitive and demanding little skill. White-collar work has thus become 'proletarianised', similar to that of blue-collar workers, and consequently white-collar workers have become more favourably disposed to joining unions. Third, many skilled, higher status white-collar workers perceived themselves threatened by blue-collar union membership and resorted to union membership to defend their existing differentials. As the threats multiplied unionisation and aggressiveness in defence of white-collar interests increased. So explaining white-collar unionisation is not especially difficult: it is a rational response by an increasingly significant number of workers to their changing work environment. More problematic is the belief that white-collar workers have a different ideology to blue-collar workers.

The Politics of Public Sector Trade Unionism

Traditionally white-collar workers, because of a low density of membership and their service ethos, were reluctant to participate in politics, especially partisan politics, although the public sector was an exception. The evidence shows, however, that whereas white-collar workers are less committed to party-political action they are politically active. Indeed, the point is not that white-collar workers are becoming more like blue-collar workers but that the two groups have converged to an instrumental model of unionism. The spread of collective bargaining amongst white-collar groups and collective bargaining's inability to meet all membership demands inevitably draws white-collar unions as interest groups into political activity lobbying the executive and legislature. Political activity does not require partisanship.

Though there are differences it is difficult to argue that white-collar trade unionism generates an ideology radically different from blue-collar unions (or vice-versa). White-collar workers cannot be regarded as a 'new working class', either radical or conservative, and the upsurge in white-collar union membership is for basically the same reasons as blue-collar unionism: self-defence. Much of this applies to the public sector: the typical public sector worker is a white-collar employee providing a service. Many public sector workers, not necessarily those in the highest grades, were imbued with a service ethos which militated against union membership; there were often prohibitions on organisations and on their political activity.

The politicisation of the public sector stems from these workers' direct relationship with the state. The state is the employer; it is also the source of public policy and the target for group activity, therefore union–government relations are unlike those in the private sector. Relationships are worsened by the state's reluctance to lose control over those responsible for implementing government decisions, and by poor comparability of wages and conditions with the private sector. A further twist was provided by economic crisis and an ideological assault on the public sector prompted by the cost of public provision which was portrayed as a drain on the 'productive' economy struggling to overcome recession; recovery would be aided by restraining the cost of the public sector. Fiscal conservatism was part of a wider critique of 'big government', blamed for sapping initiative and enterprise, and ultimately threatening liberty.

Politically there was a swing to the right, even in systems supportive of public sector provision. Public sector workers found their wages and conditions restrained, and in some systems efforts were made to break public sector unionism; government transferred public functions to the private sector and commercialised the residuum. Public sector workers resisted, not only by joining unions (public sector union growth was well established) but by engaging in industrial and political action. The politicisation of the public sector is one of the most noteable developments in the politics of the advanced industrial states and some of the bitterest and protracted industrial disputes in the late twentieth century will be in the public sector.

Managing the Trade Unions in the 1990s

The management of the unions in the 1990s stems from the perception of actual, or potential, economic decline as a result of changes in the international economy. Governments responded by seeking to remove the maximum number of obtstacles to the restructuring of economic activity, but – whether politicians like it or not – unions are not going to disappear. But how influential will they be?

American and British unions have converged on a similar

response to decline. This involves a membership oriented strategy designed to make unions attractive to the unorganised. From increased membership stems political influence, though crude numbers are not, of course, a guarantee of influence. British unions have been pushed out of the political process to a greater degree than in the USA because of Britain's unitary–party government; the separation of powers and the permeability of Congress gives American unions greater opportunities for influence. Nevertheless, unless British and American unions can halt their decline they will remain marginal to the political process.

In Sweden and West Germany the problem is slightly different. In Sweden, the continued dominance of Social Democracy will help maintain union influence, whereas the West German unions suffered a loss of influence when the SDP left office. In both systems, however, we must not over-estimate the prior extent of union influence when considering the situation in the 1990s. There was a significant political mobilisation of business influence in the 1970s and growing concern was expressed by government and employers at the vulnerability of economic success to international economic turbulence. Concerned to protect profitability, business and government were able to persuade unions accustomed to consensus politics to accept their remedy for the ills of the economy; this put the unions on the defensive and cost them influence. Swedish and West German unions are powerful enough to prevent an assault, but in the 1990s they will be under constant pressure to adapt to capital's needs.

Japanese unions were not essential to the political process, but again the perception of economic vulnerability brought change. The integration of the enterprise unions in the export oriented sector and the modification of Shunto were the most notable changes, and these will most likely be maintained in the 1990s as corporations relocate manufacturing abroad. This will be coupled with the privatisation of public sector industries and constant pressure on the remainder. Rengo is a development of potentially great significance representing either a powerful single centre or, alternatively, a further opportunity for divide and rule. In the 1990s the traditional hostility to the public sector will be maintained coupled with greater openness to the enterprise unions in the large corporate sector. This is likely to change only if, first, there is a savage deterioration in Japan's economic performance and, second, if the sectoral cleavage between public and private is resolved, or if union membership penetrates those groups in the labour market who have so far borne the burden of economic change. None of these seems likely on the basis of past evidence.

7

Unions, Power and Politics

The purpose of Chapter 7 is twofold: to provide the book's conclusions and to present theoretical observations on the political role of trade unions and locate them in the power structure of industrial capitalism. The first section sets out briefly the various analytical perspectives (pluralism, elitism, marxism, corporatism and collective action theory) used in this book to analyse the unions' political role. The second and third sections build on this using a model of unions' political action derived from the Webbs. The next two sections explore the unions' reactive political role using perhaps the most powerful tool for the analysis of unions (marxism), and their powerlessness, using the work of Lukes. The chapter concludes by considering four questions: are unions too powerful, are they irredeemably defensive, have they found a new political style, and, finally, has the need for union political activity increased?

Analytical Perspectives

The book adopts no single model or theory to analyse union political activity and rejects the idea of comparative politics as a 'science', since it is incapable of generating 'law-like generalisations'. Nevertheless, political analysis is essentially comparative and comparative analysis can elicit general trends and repeated patterns of political behaviour.[1] In analysing the role of unions in the politics of the advanced industrial states this book draws on a number of analytical traditions which need to be briefly described.

Pluralism

This is the dominant analytical perspective in comparative politics and in the analysis of trade unions.[2] Unions are regarded as a major socioeconomic interest and, therefore, one of the major political actors in liberal-democratic capitalist society. In these societies power is dispersed and politics is generated by the inter-action of multiple interest groups and between interest groups and the state. Conflict is real, and at times bitter, but is generally re-solved peacefully through a process of adjustment and comprom-ise between groups and government. Political actors adjust de-mands to achieve broadly acceptable compromises according to the commonly understood 'rules of the game'. Of course, plural-ism does not assume all groups to be equal in their resources and influence, but no one group is sufficiently powerful so as to be able consistently to impose its desires on society or ensure the primacy of its interests in a majority of cases. The state has two roles: as an umpire supervising the process of group interaction and imple-menting authoritative decisions which are accepted by the major-ity of actors as legitimate even if they disagree, and second as an arbiter deciding between the claims of competing groups. In both instances the state can be seen as an interest group in its own right; the state is neither passive nor neutral.

Elitism

Elite theory conceives of society or an organisation divided into two segments: the rulers (the minority) and the ruled (the majority).[3] Unions can be seen as an organisation of the 'mass' hitherto excluded from political participation by the elites. As the masses organised and achieved political consciousness they threatened the elite dominated status quo. Eventually, their interests had to be incorporated into the elite consensus. However, it was union leaders who gained access to elite status and from this it is a short step to postulating their 'seduction' by the elites from their primary loyalty. Instead of threatening change in the power structure, union leaders become one of its guarantors by mod-ifying and accommodating mass demands in return for elite recognition and minor concessions. Trade unions, dominated by the professional bureaucratic leadership stratum, become agents and instruments of social control not political change, thereby helping preserve a status quo inimical to their real interests. Union leaders do not become full members of the elite: they remain, literally, outsiders and therefore vulnerable to exclusion when the elites feel they can dispense with their services, though this will happen only if there are other mechanisms to act as guarantors of the elite's dominance.

Marxism

Unions constitute both a threat and a support for the status quo.[4] Irreconcilable conflict between labour and capital generates trade unionism for worker self-protection in the market order. Organisation amplifies the power of the individual worker to the point where the status quo is threatened and capital makes concessions. Though union led industrial conflict is a serious problem it cannot, of itself, change significantly (let alone overthrow) capitalism. This is because unions are, by definition, sectional and as such they offer the ruling class an opportunity to divide and rule by not only making economic concessions to powerful groups of workers but by conceding equal political rights to the working class, even to the extent of permitting a working class party to form a government, splitting the working class into reformist and revolutionary wings. Trade unions play a major role, as they develop conflict conscious-ness amongst the working class, but they are sectional and are invariably tied to reformist-parliamentary politics so blunting the working class's revolutionary ardour. Once again, union leaders are incorporated into a political process whose operation is fundamentally hostile to the real interests of the working class.

Corporatism

Corporatism, essentially a variant of pluralism, applies specifically to unions (and employers) as it envisages the integration of capital and labour into the policy process to create a political exchange between groups and government to preserve economic and politi-cal stability.[5] Participating groups secure a role in the formulation and implementation of policy and recognition as the legitimate and authoritative representative of their members' interests. The state gains both group expertise and their cooperation in the implemen-tation of policy; the purpose of such arrangements is to promote the governability of the industrial polity by depoliticising sensitive issues. There are, broadly speaking, two views of corporatism: the first holds it to be a natural response to the political and economic complexity of the modern polity all liberal-democratic political systems are, therefore, to some degree 'corporatist'. Alternatively, it is regarded as a temporary response to crisis in the political and economic systems and is used by ruling groups to limit the impact of trade unionism. Once the crisis is resolved unions are, once more, excluded from the political process.

Collective Action

Instead of examining the relationship of unions as organisations to politics, collective action theory seeks to understand union political behaviour by analysing the motivations of union members.[6] Why workers join obviously influences union political behaviour: do they join to promote collective (group or class) interests, or for personal reasons? Collective action theory argues for the latter. If the benefits of union action are available to all workers in a group there is no incentive to join as these benefits can be denied only by compulsory membership (the closed or union shop). The implications of this for union political activity are that whilst political action is portrayed by union leaders as an essential supplement to collective bargaining it is often not seen to be directly relevent to the individual member's personal interests and is therefore controversial. A union's political preferences may not be those of the member, so too great a stress on political action, especially partisan politics, to achieve collective gains can produce membership disquiet and unrest. This means there is an inherent limitation on union political involvement (what the membership will accept), and unions are always on the defensive because they can never mobilise their full potential strength or embrace the whole working population. Legislation won by unions, for example, benefits working people as a whole, be they members of the union or not, and even if the legislation is restricted to small groups of workers the same point applies.

   One of the frustrations of comparative political analysis is the plethora of competing analytical approaches. This book uses elements from all of the above perspectives: pluralism offers insights into the unions' role in the policy process, elitism points to their essentially subordinate role in the political system, marxism enables us to penetrate the contradictory position of unions in capitalist society, corporatism is useful for analysing the evolution of union–government relations, and collective action offers valuable insights into the motivation and behaviour of union members. None, however, tells us why, or how, unions became involved in politics, and that is the purpose of the next section.

Definitions and Strategies

A trade union is a *'continuous association of wage earners for the purpose of improving the conditions of their working lives'*.[7] Let us break this down into its component parts for analysis.

1.   Continuous association
Unless an organisation can stabilise itself it cannot generate the resources of numbers, solidarity, ethos and policy which underpin the winning and use of political influence. Unions emerged and evolved in a hostile environment and are, in part, motivated by powerful historical memories of that struggle. After all, 'Unity is Strength' is the universal trade union ethos.

2.   Wage earners
Unions are formed from the propertyless masses – Marx's proletariat – called into being by industrialisation. Technological change transforms the organisation of work and the structure of the labour market but the vast bulk of the population remain wage earners with no resource other than their labour power, which they sell. No matter how affluent workers become, no matter what civil and political rights are won, the unequal power relationship between the buyer and seller of labour power remains intact.

3.   Improving conditions
This is the purpose of trade unionism. The broad sweep of union development indicates an ability periodically to take the offensive and promote change when the balance of economic and political forces is favourable. This, however, never affects the basic power structure of society; the political economy in which they operate raises too many obstacles to unions seeking to change the distribution of power or rewards.

4. Working lives

Unions focus their activities on the problems which emanate from the immediate situation of their members. This implies concentration upon workplace issues and problems. The nature of work and its consequences, however, means that unions cannot remain confined within the workplace as the range of influences affecting the workplace is infinite. Nevertheless, this orientation towards one aspect – albeit a very important one – of their members' lives often limits their activities.

There is nothing in the Webbs' definition which refers specifically to 'politics' but, after reflection, it is clear that politics is central to their analysis of trade unions. The birth of trade unions was a political struggle, the winning of recognition was a political struggle, and the lives of millions are profoundly influenced by political decision-making at the local, national and international level. If unions are doing their job of 'maintaining or improving' their member's interests they cannot avoid politics and they must seek a relationship with government, the body charged with the political ordering of society. The organisation of large numbers of individuals and the pursuit of *representative* rights and status symbolises this. Unions are political, and they define politics as 'who gets what, when and how'.

If all unions are political what motivates their political action? This brings us to the choice of strategy. Again, following the Webbs, three main union strategies suggest themselves:

1. Unilateral regulation

This is where unions formulate and impose their own policies on the supply of labour, largely without reference to employers. This is the 'purest' form of trade unionism, but in reality it can apply only to small numbers of very highly skilled craftsmen in a proto-industrial economy.

2. Collective bargaining

This entails joint regulation of working conditions with employers, though joint regulation does not require equal power. This covers a wide range of issues but some matters – for example, private investment decisions – are seldom covered. Collective bargaining requires continuous association and mutual organisation by both employers and employees.

3. Statutory regulation
This was regarded by the Webbs as 'second best' to collective bargaining. It is, however, vital as it explicitly introduces politics. Where unions are not powerful enough to bargain collectively they engage in pressure group and electoral politics using their numbers and organisation to secure legislative concessions from the state to circumvent employer economic power and achieve those things not achievable by collective bargaining. Here is the origin of both corporatist and social democratic–labourist party politics. Unions seek joint regulation through collective bargaining. Confronted by employer resistance they naturally seek for a countervailing force to neutralise that power; they find it in politics, and then deploy their numerical superiority and their organisation. They can follow such a strategy because of the *formal political equality* (one man, one vote) and civil liberties (freedom of association, for example) of liberal-democratic capitalism.

Collective bargaining, its strengths and weaknesses, is the motor for union political activity. Though concerned primarily with employment issues it has progressively widened to include social policy and macro-economic policy and it brings together capital and labour as organised forces in a relationship which could devastate society should it run out of control.

Collective bargaining is, therefore, highly political and is one of the mechanisms whereby liberal-democratic societies regulate conflict. It is an activity too important to be left to unions and employers, hence the interest of the state in the course and consequences of collective bargaining; but the state's interest is not that of a neutral umpire.

The politics of collective bargaining is present in all capitalist industrial states but how this politics is organised and conducted depends on the history, culture, legal framework and so on of each national union movement. The Webbs regarded collective bargaining as superior to legal enactment, hinting that the two were competing strategies. In fact, they conceded that legal enactment was crucial for a stable system of collective bargaining. Union pressure for statute law could guarantee the legal existence of the unions and regularise collective bargaining, help secure basic rights for poorly organised workers and provide minimum working standards. Law could provide collective bargaining with a degree of stability not achievable in face-to-face negotiation; the bonus for the employer and the state was a mechanism for controlling social conflict.

Union–government relations are of central importance in the politics of the advanced industrial states. Whilst making due allowance for differing national experiences the role of the state has, generally, shifted from repression to accommodation and thereafter to regulation. In some states the role of the law has been very much more influential (for example, in the USA and West Germany) in determining industrial relations than in other states (for example, Britain where the law was relatively unimportant as a regulator until the 1970s). In Japan, trade union law moved from being favourable to the unions to being restrictive as a response to industrial militancy, whilst in Sweden law has been used to support the private relationship between unions and employers. Once unions achieved legal existence and political legitimacy the state's main interest became securing an equilibrium between capital and labour, but equilibrium was not necessarily an equal balance. After 1945 the economic role of the state became pre-eminent in the union–government relationship. The growth of the welfare state made governments considerable employers in their own right as well as responsible for maintaining economic prosperity. By the 1970s the union–government relationship was dominated by the supposed inflationary consequences of trade union power. The result was the politicisation of industrial relations.

Methods of Trade Union Political Action

Union political activity stems for their primary purpose: the defence and enchancement of their members' individual and collective interests. Though workers join unions for essentially 'economistic' reasons (better wages and working conditions) the pursuit of these inevitably draws unions into politics. Union political activity has two broad manifestations:

Party-political Involvement

Unions enjoy a close relationship with a political party because they have long recognised that collective bargaining cannot achieve all their desires whereas legislation is generally applicable and less easy for employers to avoid. The specific party-political relationship, however, varies enormously.

In Britain, the Labour Party originated within the unions, something reflected in the party's dependence on union money, their votes at the party Conference and the presence of union leaders on the National Executive Committee. Organisationally, the party–union link is the strongest considered in this book. In the United States the AFL–CIO and its constituent unions reject formal affiliation with the Democratic Party and deny the need for (and viability of) a labour party. The absence of close organisational links does not, however, alter the fact that the AFL–CIO and the Democratic Party are politically interconnected. Sweden and West Germany come somewhere between the UK and the USA. Like the AFL–CIO both the LO and the DGB do not affiliate nationally to their respective Social Democratic Party. In Sweden, affiliation occurs at the grassroots and in West Germany there is a similar tradition, but neither have the formal links characteristic of the British model. Yet, as in the case of the United States, the existence of a close party-political link cannot be denied. On the face of it the party–union relationship in Japan is closer to that of the United States, Sweden and West Germany. In fact, in some respects the Sohyo–JSP and Domei–DSP connection is closer than in Britain. Both the JSP and DSP suffer electorally from being identified as extensions of their respective union sponsors.

Are these 'trade union parties'? The party–union relationship is complex but the general answer is 'no'. In Britain, for example, the unions do not behave as a monolithic bloc inside the Labour Party and historically they have been very reluctant to assert themselves, whilst in Japan Sohyo has been striving to distance itself from the JSP and encourage it to take a more independent stance to boost its electoral prospects. In the United States the unions are only one element (albeit an important one) in the Democratic Party coalition, and have recognised that they cannot dominate the party and must work with the newer social groups. The LO and DGB have relied on personnel and ideological overlap to ensure that their interests are embraced by their respective parties.

Strong organisational connections do not necessarily produce political harmony, as the British experience shows. In fact, the strongest and most harmonious party–union relationships

(Sweden and West Germany) depend on the existence of a powerful ideological and programmatic consensus buttressed by self-interest and a collectivist ethos. In this way party and union recognise their interdependence and strive to ensure that neither damages the other's vital interests. Unions accept that the party should have primacy in electoral matters. They have deferred to the party's conception of its electoral interests, accepting that too visible a role by the unions costs votes on the grounds that there is little point in supporting a party which is electorally unattractive. They support a party because they expect sympathetic legislation when it achieves power. In Japan the unions have failed to achieve a 'catch-all party' and, as such, have been excluded from electoral success. The party–union connection has not prevented the progressive dealignment of working class and trade union members from voting for the unions' preferred party. In the British, Japanese and West German general elections and the American Presidential election of the 1970s and 1980s large sections of their members rejected the unions' partisanship.

Interest Group Activity

Unions are major interest groups and the target of their activity is the state. The reasons for this are simple: the state is the source of legislation and is regarded as responsible for economic prosperity. Furthermore, the state is a significant employer and its employees have, in recent years, joined unions in large numbers. Collective bargaining's content and effects inevitably places the unions in a direct relationship with the state.

What factors make unions influential? Though they are industrial organisations unions are reluctant to use industrial action for political purposes. The history of trade union politics in many systems shows that any union movement doing so risks massive state retaliation. However, industrial action does have political consequences – for example, disputes in major industries can compel government intervention or change government policy, and strikes in the public sector challenge government policy directly. Nevertheless, government perceptions of the disruptive power of trade unions has profoundly influenced the government–union relationship, a relationship which originally emerged to avoid such disruption. The characteristic feature of this relationship is a greater or lesser degree of corporatism. In making this assertion I do not intend to imply that corporatism is either the natural or normal form of the government–union relationship, or that all liberal-democratic industrial political systems are corporatist. Pluralism, marxism, elitism and, to some degree, collective action theory agree that, for varying reasons, unions have become participants in the policy process. The scale of this integration not only varies from system to system, but varies over time within these political systems.

Two contradictory attitudes influence the government–union relationship. Unions cooperate, and seek cooperation, with government as a response to their *weakness* in collective bargaining, whilst the government has promoted cooperation out of a belief in the disruptive *power* of the unions. Participation in the policy process is part of a wider process of minimising the possibilities of serious conflict; integration (as in Sweden) is an exception but in all the political systems analysed in this book (including Japan) there exist extensive tripartite and/or consultative institutions. The relative absence of tripartism in the United States is compensated for by the separation of powers which enables AFL–CIO lobbyists to use Congressional committees as conduits for their influence. This is especially important at a time when executive bodies such as the Department of Labor are unsympathetic to the unions.

Union–government relations are vulnerable to political change. This is most obviously so in the United Kingdom where union influence over government peaked in the mid-1970s, declining rapidly after the accession of the Conservatives to government in 1979. This government pursued a conscious strategy of removing and marginalising the unions' influence in the policy process. Hitherto, this was the policy of Japanese governments but when confronted by economic difficulties the government's reaction was to integrate the private sector manufacturing unions into the policy process to supplement the existing system of company corporatism. In Sweden and West Germany the unions have largely retained their position in the policy process. In the former, this was helped by the presence of a Social Democratic government, though significant political concessions were secured from the LO; in the latter DGB influence was limited by a conservative government after 1982 which forced the DGB onto the defensive.

Trade unions have in the post-war period secured access to the policy-making process. They are consulted on a wide variety of issues through a myriad of structures. This consultation and cooperation is not, however, between equals as government remains the dominant partner within the relationship and retains sufficient power and resources to negate union influence, whilst the dominant interests in the political process remain those of business. This brings us to the position of trade unions in the politics of capitalist industrial society.

Unions, Politics and Capitalism

A question often asked about unions is: are they grave-diggers or angels in marble? Are they a threat to capitalism or do they signify working class acceptance of and integration into capitalism?[8] Marx and Engels doubted the ability of the unions significantly to affect the workers' economic position. As power relations between capital and labour are inevitably unequal the worker would always lose, so collective bargaining could only constrain capitalism. Politically, however, the role of the unions was far more significant: 'They are the military school of the working-men in which they prepare themselves for the great struggle . . . they are the pronunciamentos of single branches of industry . . . as schools of War, the Unions are unexcelled'.[9] Here, Engels is referring to the politics of *industrial* action; the unions' wider political involvement elicited a more ambivalent response.

Politically they were a check on the unfettered power of capital, but their sectionalism obscured an appreciation of wider class issues. The material attractions of bourgeoise society and their leaders' search for respectability and acceptance encouraged a false distinction between 'trade union' and 'political' activity. So, even when unions were united in pursuit of some common 'political' goal they were, in reality, engaged in limited action which posed no major threat to the status quo. 'As to the limitation of the working day', for example:

it has never been settled except by legislative interference. Without the working men's continuous pressure . . . That interference would never have taken place . . . the result was not to be attained by private settlement between the working man and capitalists. This very necessity of general political action affords proof that in its merely economic action capital is the stronger side.[10]

Nonetheless, Marx and Engels remained confident that the political maturity of the working class would be advanced by the struggle for legislation and political concessions. So, 'out of the separate economic movements of the workers there grows up everywhere a political movement ... a movement of the class, with the object of enforcing its interests in a general form'.[11] Trade union politics, of themselves, could not change anything of substance. Marx and Engels recognised in the day-to-day struggle the danger that this would come to predominate and that unions would attack not the cause of their problems (capitalism) but its effects (wages and conditions).

This is, of course, more or less what happened. These developments were accelerated by the separation of economic and political conflict and the consequent institutionalisation of class conflict. The initial stages of industrialisation can be seen as marked by a unity of economic and political unrest. The impact of class struggle is, however, limited by the political and organisational immaturity of the nascent industrial working class, as well as by the repressive reaction of the state. As the working class matures and gains in numbers, organisation and confidence the state reduces the level of repression and makes concessions. These include legal recognition of the unions, their gradual involvement in a web of rules and procedures with both employers and the state, and the progressive extension of the vote to the (majority) working class culminating in the formation of working class political parties. Cumulatively, these developments 'separate' the economic and political aspects of class struggle into collective bargaining and electoral politics. Each sphere has *separate* rules and procedures, so institutionalising and blunting the impact of class conflict. So powerful is institutionalisation, and so strong are the barriers between the two spheres, that liberal capitalist society can even be governed by a working class party with a socialist ideology with no major consequences for the fundamentals of that society.[12] The consequence is the integration and political neutering of trade unions.

The institutionalisation of class conflict and the weakness of trade unions in capitalist society was analysed by Lenin in *What Is To Be Done?* Unions, he argued, could pose no major threat to the stability of capitalism; unions were sectional not class organisations and their behaviour was, therefore, essentially conservative. The workers' economic struggle is based on their place of work and conditions of employment and was concerned with 'the common demands for the removal of the most glaring evils'. For Lenin, industrial strife (as for Marx and Engels) serves as a starting point for the awakening of class consciousness but strikes are *directly* relevant only to the group of workers involved, except as an example. The unions' objective is a better price for labour power, a better deal from the existing system, not its abolition. As a marxist Lenin could not regard trade union struggle as 'political', only class struggle was truly political; unions organised groups of workers not a class, and industrial conflict was therefore containable within capitalism.[13]

The concession of the vote to the working class was initially seen by Marx as a potentially revolutionary step; as there were more workers than capitalists, the workers could capture the state.[14] However, as the workers continued to disgrace themselves by voting for their employers' parties or collaborationist parliamentary socialist parties (described by Lenin as 'parliamentary fakers and traitors to the working class') the formal political equality of capitalism came to be regarded as one further survival mechanism at the disposal of the ruling classes.[15]

The separation of economic and political questions and the institutionalisation of class conflict creates two categories of issues: control issues and economic issues. *Issues of control* are intractable: it is impossible for control over fundamental decisions (for example, investment decisions or the distribution of power) to be shared. Inequality can be camouflaged and fudged, but control is essentially indivisible: one either takes decisions, or one is subject to them. On *economic issues*, however, conflict is more easily resolved. Some groups of workers can be bought off, whilst others can be resisted and defeated. General concessions – for example, a welfare state – can be made which do not jeopardise the status quo and, in fact, strengthen it.

For a marxist trade union struggle could never reveal, let alone challenge, the power structure of capitalism and the concession of formal political liberty and equality obscures an appreciation of their 'real' social and economic interests. Political consciousness could not be generated by economic struggle as even the most 'reactionary' trade union leader could pursue an aggressive and militant industrial strategy. So the structure of trade union politics in the advanced capitalist industrial states is a product of the separation of economic and political struggle, each having their separate organisations: parliamentary parties and trade unions. They are inter-linked but their relationship and structures vary according to history, law and culture; but in all capitalist industrial states working class politics would be fragmented. This fragmentation makes it impossible for unions to behave other than conservatively. Concessions are illusory and temporary: in boom conditions unions cannot (because of their sectionalism) assert themselves collectively; at times of recession they cannot resist the inevitable reaction as they lose members and confidence. In both instances, unions aspire to accommodate themselves to the status quo and defend their position within it.

Marxism, therefore, holds there *should* be a relationship between working class status, union membership and class consciousness, but that class consciousness is very rare. *Conflict consciousness* is not class consciousness, and is the natural form of trade union consciousness and not a debased mutation of 'true' class consciousness, a variety of false consciousness. This book accepts the thesis that class conflict is bifurcated and institutionalised but it is not the case that economic and political conflict are aspects of the same phenomenon in the early stages of industrialisation after which, as capitalism matured, they separated and were blunted. In fact:

> the institutional separation of (the *manifestations* of) class conflict in the industrial and political spheres, far from making the transcendance of capitalism, is *the normal mode of the structuration of class conflict in capitalist society.*[16]

Capitalism's strength and resilience relies, to a large degree, on the separation of the polity and the economy. Formal political equality and gross economic inequalities inevitably clash and generate conflict, but this conflict is directed at securing *integration* into, and *amelioration* of, the status quo, not its transcendence.

Even if one were to reject the view that unions are irredeemably conservative, there would remain enormous obstacles to a working class revolutionary consciousness. It has been argued a working class must pass through four developmental stages: *class identity* (defining oneself as working class playing a distinct role with others in production), *class opposition* (recognising the capitalist as an irreconcilable enemy), *class totality* (recognising the workers' individual and collective subordination in society), and finally, an *alternative socioeconomic model* embraced not as a utopian ideal but as a realistic, attainable political goal.[17]

Such a developed consciousness is extremely rare. Whilst elements are characteristic of the labour movements of advanced capitalism, nowhere have the four elements coexisted. No advanced capitalist industrial state has undergone a marxist revolution. Perhaps the nearest is the *explosion of consciousness* seen in some major political–industrial disputes.[18] The problem is that such explosions are short-lived and are essentially concerned with economic demands. They are unstable because whilst the majority of workers involved might have common economic demands they are unlikely to have the same degree of political unity. Union consciousness is complex: on the one hand unions seek integration into the status quo but at the same time they have a conflictual view of society. The tension between these contradictory impulses does not necessarilly lead to the left, and whilst strikes might radicalise they seldom revolutionise.

A crucial element in the integration of the unions into capitalism is their acceptance of *parliamentarianism* as the sole legitimate political strategy. This has blunted the political impact of the unions in two ways. First, unions were historically strongly committed to the ideals of pluralism in capitalist liberal democracy, as these were seen as essential for union legitimation. Loyalty to these norms has led unions to stress working within the parliamentary system; this represents a 'self-denying ordinance' whereby the unions *themselves* limit their political options in a political process which operates according to the opponent's rules. Second, the conflict between the 'political' and 'industrial' wings of the labour movement also limits the unions' impact. When a society industrialises unions emerge, and subsequently, a political party to represent union interests. Eventually this produces a conflict of primacy. Whose interests should predominate? This is usually resolved by an agreement which entails the unions deferring to the party's conception of its electoral interests and what is electorally acceptable. This not only bifurcates the movement's impact but, once again, means *conforming* to rules made by the economically and politically powerful.

This interpretation suggests that the essential characteristics of trade union politics are *subordination and powerlessness*. The next section considers why this is so, and applies the concept of power to trade unions.

Unions and the Problem of Power

This book contends that unions are defensive and reactive in their behaviour and are, as organisations, often conservative. In reality they have very little power – defined as the ability to bring about intended effects in the face of opposition. In the literature on trade unions three groups of explanations for this can be identified. The first might be termed *the betrayal thesis*. The membership's radicalism is betrayed by the defection of leaders motivated by a desire to protect their status and the material rewards of union office. Union leaders are seduced into cooperation with the state and employers under the illusion that their *personal* interests are coterminous with the *collective* interests of the working class. The state goes so far as to buttress the official, 'responsible' leaders against the rank-and-file. Their dominance is reinforced by the apathy and passivity of the bulk of the members, who are reluctant to challenge the experience of the leaders or to offend against the union ethic of unity and solidarity.

The second theme stresses the *sectionalism* of unions and union memberships. Initially composed of smug, self-satisfied skilled artisans, it was expected that the organisation of the unskilled would remedy this. It did not. Today unions are often portrayed as the bastions of middle-aged, male industrial workers: a social group now in terminal decline because of technological change. Unions tend to ignore the interests of women, part-time workers and ethnic minorities; their ingrained biases makes union membership unattractive to the new working class of the sunrise and service industries.

A third explanation highlights *affluence*. Assessment of the impact of union behaviour ranges from the crude idea that the working class has literally been bought off by higher wages paid for by the exploitation of the unorganised and the Third World, to the more sophisticated versions of the 'affluent worker thesis' which portrays workers as increasingly instrumental in their behaviour. These themes overlap, but have at their core the belief that the maintenance of living standards and consumption is the workers' prime motivation in joining a trade union, a motivation which is profoundly conservative but which does not exclude the possibility of militant industrial action. The political implication is that affluence blunts working class radicalism and deflects the unions away from promoting social and economic change into consumerism, securing 'more' from the status quo. The result is a privatised, passive labour force unresponsive to collective goals or mobilisational politics.

Betrayal, sectionalism and affluence cast light on the motivation of trade union politics, but even when taken together they give little appreciation of the *location* of trade unions in the power relations of industrial capitalism. Pluralism 'involves a focus on *behaviour* in the making of *decisions* on *issues* over which there is an observable *conflict* of (subjective) *interests* seen as express policy preferences revealed by political participation'. Non-decision-making, as a qualified critique of pluralism, 'allows for consideration of the ways in which *decisions* are prevented from being taken on *potential issues* over which there is an observable *conflict* of (subjective) *interests*, seen as embodied in express policy preferences and sub-political grievances'. A final aspect of power is 'the operation of social forces and institutional practices or through individual decisions [which] can occur in the absence of actual, observable conflict [which] may never in fact be actualised. What one may have ... is a *latent conflict* between the interests of those exercising power and the real interests of those they exclude'.[19]

Trade Unions and the First Dimension of Power

There is a vast body of literature analysing unions from the pluralist perspective. Unions are, after all, a collectivity which has a legitimate right to participate in political life. The rationale for national trade union centres is as labour's authoritative representative in the policy process. In the post-war period unions became highly visible actors in the politics of the industrial democracies, though their role varied from system to system. What conclusions about influence can be drawn from the fact of participation in the policy process?

There is a grave danger of misinterpreting *visibility* and *access to decision-makers* as manifestations of influence and power. Whilst unions have the resources (organisation, wealth and numbers) to act as interests in a pluralistic policy process, they are by no means the most powerful group; furthermore the incrementalism of the policy process provides a means whereby the state can reconcile antagonistic group preferences in 'the general interest'. As participants, unions are subject to the 'rules of the game' which encourage the acceptance of sub-optimal outcomes in return for continued participation. Access to the policy process often comes at the end of a long period of bitter struggle and there is a tendency for a group to misinterpret securing access as elite acceptance of the integration of their interests as fully equal to those of hitherto dominant groups. The state is not, however, neutral. The social attitudes of the governing elite (embracing those elements drawn originally from the working class) are seldom those of organised labour; furthermore, even in those political systems where there is a cooperative relationship between the state and the unions, the need to maintain the confidence of capital (both domestic and international) and the support of the electorate are far more important to the state than the relationship with the unions.

Trade Unions and the Second Dimension of Power

On a closer analysis, then, the influence of trade unions in industrial liberal democracies is circumscribed by the *mobilisation of bias* inherent in both political institutions and the attitudes of those who staff them. Unions are usually at a disadvantage as their interests do not coincide easily with the system's bias. This bias will organise some issues into politics, whereas some will not enter the political agenda. This can be achieved by symbolic action such as token appointments to committees, minor concessions, appeals to the 'national interest', loyalty, and so on. The cultural similarities between the governing and other elites generates a degree of mutual understanding which does not necessarily or inevitably exclude the unions, but it does make it difficult for them to gain entry to the policy process, and access becomes an end in itself. From the point of view of trade union politics this mobilisation of bias serves to confirm their conservative and reactive role. Unions find it very difficult in this context to *initiate* policy; their influence is traditionally confined to *blocking* policies. As this usually involves the use or threat of industrial action, unions are vulnerable to the charge of behaving in an anti-democratic manner, seeking to thwart the will of an elected government. The role of bias can be seen from the fact that industrial unrest is commonly conceived to be a major problem, but in terms of days lost, human suffering, and economic losses industrial injuries are far more significant, yet the latter have never achieved the salience of the former as a political issue. Similarly, whilst union wage claims have been blamed as a major cause of inflation, little attention has been devoted to the question of low pay. There is in this a strong element of *non-decision-making*: union behaviour is modified by the process whereby they 'learn' which issues are likely to elicit a favourable response from government. Unions are unlikely constantly to raise an issue and devote scarce resources to a demand when there is no response from decision-makers. Unions will tend, therefore, progressively to downgrade demands and replace them with more 'realistic' goals.

Trade Unions and the Third Dimension of Power

The third dimension deals with the cultural mechanisms whereby a system perpetuates and defends itself from hostile ideas and perceptions which might come to influence political behaviour in a significant way. This involves the internalisation of belief patterns and cultural traits which makes any alternative to the status quo (literally) unthinkable, or so inconceivable as to be in the realm of a utopia. In liberal-democratic societies this is achieved via the mass media, the education system and the wider socialisation process which inculcates an acceptance of the status quo as legitimate and normal. Perhaps the clearest illustration of this can be seen in the media's treatment of trade unions and their activities. They are seldom portrayed positively: unions are (explicitly and implicitly) presented as militant, unreasonable, irrational and dictatorial sectional interests, wielding massive power to the detriment of the community as a whole. Social and economic relations are, on the other hand, portrayed as consensual and cooperative until disrupted by alien doctrines supported by a militant minority who manipulate and dupe the moderate majority in pursuit of their political interests. Once again the structure of power acts so as to limit the options *unions believe are open to them*, again confirming their role as objects of the political process in capitalist states. Countries with a vibrant social democratic and trade union press have been better placed to stem, to some degree, the hostility of the media. The best example of this is, of course, Sweden.

From this it is clear that trade unions as political actors can achieve certain goals, but that there are limits to what can be achieved. The major obstacle to union political influence is not necessarily a society's political institutions, for under liberal capitalism formal political equality and democratic ideology can be exploited by the unions. The critical limitation on trade unions in capitalist society, and the one most difficult to identify and challenge is its *ideological hegemony* which determines what is, and what is not, politically feasible and permissible. The following argument is based on the work of Gramsci, though the use of these ideas is not intended to imply that any of the union movements considered here are engaged on a revolutionary enterprise.

Hegemony can be achieved only by winning the support of other groups and social forces, so transcending sectional interests: achieving hegemony or challenging an existing hegemony comes through various stages. The first stage is *simple solidarity* between workers, which underpins the emergence of trade unions for mutual insurance and protection. The organisation of workers by trade or occupation does not imply any collective consciousness. The second stage is *economic solidarity*, and corresponds to the struggle for economic and political rights described by Marx and Lenin, 'winning politico-juridical equality with the ruling groups ... to participate in legislation and administration, even to reform these – *but within the existing fundamental structures*'. The final stage is *political struggle* between two competing ideologies, only one of which can be victorious. Here, unions recognise that they cannot themselves challenge the status quo and require the support of other groups, so creating a broad ideological consensus. Within this process the state plays a very important role resolving the conflicts between capital and labour:

the State is seen as the organ of one particular group ... the dominant group is coordinated concretely with the general interests of the subordinate groups, and *the life of the State is conceived of as a continuous process of formation and superseding of unstable equilibria* ... between the interests of the fundamental group and those of the subordinate groups – equilibria in which the interests of the dominant group prevail, but only up to a certain point.[20]

From this perspective, the state's relationship with the unions can vary dramatically over time. Equilibrium ('the balance of class forces') can be created in many different ways – by, for example, a corporatist relationship seeking to integrate the unions with the state; or, alternatively, the unions can be marginalised.

This pattern can be seen, to a greater or lesser degree, in all the political systems examined in this book. In both the United States and the United Kingdom unions were able to achieve a recognised position in the political process; in the UK this took the form of tripartism whilst in the United States the fragmentation of political institutions allowed the AFL–CIO to win a reputation as the most effective Congressional lobby. However, in both the United States and United Kingdom the unions were speedily and easily marginalised by the Reagan and Thatcher Administrations. In Japan, of course, marginalisation was the normal characteristic of union–government relations but as the Japanese political economy came under increasing stress the LDP sought a new equilibria by integrating unions in the very large, export oriented corporate economy. In Sweden no attempt was made, or could be made, to marginalise the unions without shattering the political system. Neither the bourgeoise coalition (1976–82) nor the Social Democrats could do anything other than to maintain the traditional government–union relationship. The commitment to full employment, continued economic growth and corporatism could not alter the fact that the Swedish unions were forced on to the defensive. The West German unions were powerful enough to resist the conservative political attack after 1982 because of their intrinsic strength and position in the political economy. West Germany's dependence on the international economy and the unions' desire to safeguard economic growth and employment placed them on the defensive, though they were able to secure several significant concessions.

The political analysis of trade unions has suffered from an undue concentration on surface attributes and behaviour. Their visibility in, and access to, the political process has been misinterpreted by both analysts and union leaders as representing real power. Institutional penetration and political activism disguises their *structural weakness and vulnerability*; trade unions do play an important role in the politics of capitalist liberal democracy, but what they can achieve is limited by their concentration on the first dimension of power. So, 'If the powerless are to redress their situation, they need to surmount the obstacles intrinsic to the third and second dimensions of power – to change perceptions of a situation and of the feasibility of alternatives, *and then to conquer institutional barriers.*[21]

It is therefore very misleading to talk of the 'power' of trade unions as if power was a commodity possessed rather than a relationship generated by shifting economic and political forces. At times the balance of these forces favours the unions, at others it does not. Thus, in the national strike of 1974 the British National Union of Mineworkers was 'powerful', in the strike of 1984–5 it was 'powerless'. Despite their reputation for power unions have failed, for example, significantly to alter the distribution of rewards in society; they have not prevented the growth of unemployment; they have been unable to prevent the state from regulating their internal activities; and they have been unable to alter the ingrained suspicion of trade unionism. At best we can regard the unions as influentials.

Unions, Politics and the Future

In the late 1970s it was widely believed in the industrial democracies that power had shifted too far to the unions, and that a corrective was required:

> The public ... considers only the people who write advertisements, sell insurance and peddle cars – hardly pillars of public trust – as less ethical than union leaders. In the popular mind, union leaders are dinosaurs waiting for the comet to hit and put them out of their misery.[22]

In all the systems considered recession provided that corrective, though in some (notably the United Kingdom) the legal balance was altered against the unions; the unions are undoubtedly on the political defensive.

Unions are under attack from two directions. Not only are they facing a hostile political environment, but the labour market is changing in ways hostile to trade unionism. The dominant image of trade unionism is of a male, manual worker employed in manufacturing; the expanding groups in the workforce are traditionally difficult to recruit, difficulties compounded by hostility amongst these (and more traditionally organised workers) to many aspects of trade unionism. Evidence from our five states shows considerable animus against the defects of the unions' democratic processes and their political pretensions, but there remains general support for the protective role of unions. So unemployment, industrial and occupational restructuring, and a hostile political climate pose severe difficulties for unions in the politics of the advanced industrial states.

Not all is doom and gloom, however. In the industrial states trade unions retain considerable numerical and organisational strength, and there is potential for growth as the workforce is expanding and there remains pools of unorganised workers in traditional industries. As union densities have, with the exception of Sweden, been falling an effective response from the unions, radically different from their previous strategies, is necessary.

This problem is clearest in the Anglo–American unions. Structural change and a hostile political environment forced the AFL–CIO to rethink strategy, as we have seen, to promote a more positive image amongst existing and potential members as well as the general public. Addressing the 1987 TUC Lane Kirkland proclaimed the vitality of trade unionism but that they must adapt to a changing environment. This call was taken up by the TUC General Secretary and Congress which approved a resolution calling for a full review of TUC and union services as a means of attracting new members. In Japan, Sohyo has similarly recognised that unless it divests itself of its poor image unions will remain marginalised. The chosen method of regeneration is the unification of labour movement organisations, though the public–private sectoral cleavage remains the major obstacle. Swedish union leaders, on the other hand, have not been fooled by comprehensive membership. They have long recognised that whilst Swedes join unions in vast numbers, their participation rate is low and great efforts have been made to boost industrial commitment though the results have been disappointing. A similar situation applies in the Federal Republic.

The point is, of course, that an essential element in solving a problem is to recognise that a problem exists. Up to the mid-1970s trade unions throughout the industrial world appeared insufferably complacent. The AFL–CIO basked in its reputation as the best organised Washington lobby, the TUC had a comforting self-image as a quasi-governing institution, the DGB's role as a social partner appeared secure, the LO's interests were an integral element in Swedish polity, whilst Sohyo defended tenaciously its ideological ghetto. This complacency was shattered by the economic crises of the 1970s and 1980s.

Crisis compelled these union movements to face the reality and adapt to survive as the environment which hitherto had sustained them changed. During these years it became fashionable for right-wing commentators to urge that the unions remove themselves, or be removed, from 'politics', a sentiment which evoked a positive response from many union members. This is, of course, impossible. Though they denied it, unions regarded themselves as the infallible and authentic voice of their members' economic and political interests, and expected the membership to follow their recommendations and preferences. It took the sharp smack of partisan dealignment to persuade the unions that there was no necessary connection between joining a trade union and following its prescriptions. The 'decline of working class politics' compelled unions everywhere to reorient their political and electoral activity in three ways. First, to make these activities more effective and professional in organisational terms; second to establish mechanisms and processes to establish what the members' political desires actually are; and finally, to communicate their political vision to their members and hopefully win them to that vision. This reorientation is everywhere still underway, so assessment is difficult, but there has been enough change for it to be described as significant.

The unions' response to partisan dealignment and the changing electoral environment is clear because the response is one for the unions to make. This is not the case with the relationship with government. The crisis of the 1970s led governments to question their perceptions about the role of the unions in the political system as, quite simply, governments progressively recognised the emperor had no (or, at least, very few) clothes. This awareness provided the signal for the exclusion of the unions from the policy process, an act which a few years previously would have been unthinkable and which left the unions dithering about their response. For a time unions strove to revive their traditional role, but with no success: in the United States, the United Kingdom and West Germany the AFL–CIO, the TUC and the DGB accepted that this option was no longer available and slowly, painfully began to reorient themselves away from 'high' politics towards re-establishing their position at the grassroots. By so doing, they reasoned, they might once again compel their respective governments to concede a place at 'the top table'. In Sweden the LO's institutional position has not been challenged but the political mobilisation of business created a powerful countervailing force which balanced its influence with government. The LO is still working on a response. Japanese unions faced the most complex situation. Traditionally excluded from the policy process certain sectors of the union movement found themselves being courted by the good and the great of Japanese politics. The potential for the seduction of major unions was high and the prospect not unalluring, but seduction of the few meant rejection for the majority. Sohyo strove quite successfully to block this whilst at the same time taking advantage as far as it could of a more open climate. Once again, these are straws in the wind, no more than indications of a higher level of strategic political thinking within the union movements of the advanced industrial states. The contrast, however, with the sterility of much of the pre-crises period is noteworthy. Obviously, the configuration of the government–union relationship of the 1990s is not clear. What is certain is that it will be a more distant relationship than in the past. Not only will governments seek to maintain an arm's length relationship, but the unions themselves will be reluctant to be drawn into their embrace.

Flux in the labour market and economic structure means that unions will, for the foreseeable future, remain in the role of supplicants. In terms of their regeneration this is no bad thing, for the weakening of the state fixation will force them to direct their attention to their only source of power: their members and the even greater numbers of potential members. Economic crisis, mass unemployment, and ideological challenge compel the unions on pain of continued decline to begin to forge a new contract with their members by going back from whence they came – to the factories, the mills, the mines, the offices, the warehouses and so on, to plant and nurture the seeds of their own revival.

Recommended Reading

The place of publication is London, unless stated otherwise.

1 Historical Background and Political Development

The two volumes authored by H.A. Clegg *et al.*, *A History of British Trade Unions Since 1889, Volume 1, 1889–1910* and *Volume 2, 1911–1933* (Oxford: Clarendon Press, 1964 and 1985) are magisterial. H. Pelling, *A History of British Trade Unionism*, 4th edn (Harmondsworth: Penguin, 1987) and C.Cook and B. Pimlott (eds), *Trade Unions in British Politics* (Longmans, 1982) provide shorter introductions. For America P. Taft, *Organised Labor in American History* (New York: Harper & Row, 1964) provides an overview and C.L. Tomlins, *The State and the Unions. Labor Relations, Law and the Organized Labor Movement in America, 1880–1960* (Cambridge: Cambridge University Press, 1985) brilliantly analyses the interplay of law, ideology and politics. There is no comprehensive survey of Swedish labour history and politics. D. Blake, 'Swedish Trade Unions and the Social Democratic Party: The Formative Years', *Scandinavian Economic History Review*, 8 (1960) pp. 19–44 is indispensable and S. Kololik (ed), *Sweden's Development from Poverty to Affluence, 1750–1970* (Minneapolis: University of Minnesota Press, 1975) contains a number of useful essays; S. Hadenius, *Swedish Politics in the Twentieth Century* (Stockholm: The Swedish Institute, 1985) is a clear description of recent Swedish history. A good introduction to the complex history of the pre-Hitler German labour movement are the two volumes by J.A. Moses, *Trade Unionism in Germany from Bismark to Hitler, Volume 1, 1869–1918* and *Volume 2, 1919–1933* (New York: Barnes & Noble 1982); for the remaking of the unions see E.C.B. Cullingford, *Trade Unions in West Germany*, (Wilton, 1975) and the indispensable A.S. Markovits, *The Politics of West German Trade Unions. Strategies of Class and Interest Representation in Growth and Crisis* (Cambridge: Cambridge University Press, 1986). S.L. Large, *The Yuaikai, 1912–1919. The Rise of Labour in*

Japan (Tokyo: Sophia University Press, 1972) examines the antecedents of Japanese unions and J. Moore, *Japanese Workers and the Struggle for Power, 1945–1947* (Madison: University of Wisconsin Press, 1983) examines the early post-war period. K. Okochi *et al.* (eds), *Workers and Employment in Japan* (Princeton, N.J.: Princeton University Press, 1974) and K. Taira, *Economic Development and the Labor Market in Japan* (New York: Columbia University Press, 1970) provide much information not only on Japanese unions but also on the development of the employment and industrial relations systems.

There are a number of edited collections dealing with the general political role of trade unions which have been used in writing this book. C. Crouch and A. Pizzorno (eds), *The Resurgence of Class Conflict in Western Europe Since 1968, Volume 1, National Studies* and *Volume 2, Comparative Analyses* (Macmillan, 1978) is a good starting point. O. Jacobi *et al.* (eds), *Economic Crisis, Trade Unions and the State* (Croom Helm, 1986). P. Gourevitch *et al.* (eds), *Unions and Economic Crisis: Britain, West Germany and Sweden* (Allen & Unwin, 1984); R. Edwards *et al.* (eds), *Unions in Crisis and Beyond: The Experience of Six Countries* (Dover, Mass.: Auburn House Publishing, 1986); and H. Juris *et al.* (eds), *Industrial Relations in a Decade of Economic Change* (Industrial Relations Research Association Series, Madison: University of Wisconsin Press, 1985). Also useful, though it deals with wider issues, is J. Goldthorpe (ed.), *Order and Conflict in Contemporary Capitalism. Studies in the Political Economy of Western European Nations* (Oxford: Clarendon Press, 1984), and an excellent one-volume study is K. von Beyme, *Challenge to Power. Trade Unions and Industrial Relations in Capitalist Countries* (Sage, 1981).

2   Structure, Politics and Ideology

M. Poole, *Industrial Relations. Origins and Patterns of National Diversity* (Routledge & Kegan Paul, 1986) provides a comparative-analytical starting point and an appreciation of R. Michels, *Political Parties*, orig pub. 1915 (New York: Collier-Macmillan, 1962) is indispensable for an understanding of power in organisations. J. Hemingway, *Conflict and Democracy* (Oxford: Clarendon Press, 1978), though based on British examples, is of wider relevance and considers a broad range of material. On union government in each system see, R.J. Willey, *Democracy in West German Trade Unions* (Sage, 1971) on West Germany; W. Korpi, *The Working Class in Welfare Capitalism* (Routledge & Kegan Paul, 1978) and L. Lewin, *Governing Swedish Trade Unions* (Cambridge, Mass.: Harvard University Press, 1980) on Sweden; M. Warner and D.J. Edelstein, *Comparative Union Democracy* (New York: Transaction Books, 1979 is a study of Britain and America; and E.F. Vogel (ed.), *Modern Japanese Organisations and Decision Making* (Berkeley: University of California Press, 1975) contains a perceptive essay on Japanese unions.

3 Trade Unions and Political Parties

The party–union relationship in Sweden, Britain and West Germany is covered in the two collections, W. Paterson and A.H. Thomas (eds), *Social Democratic Parties in Western Europe* (Croom Helm, 1978) and *The Future of Social Democracy* (Oxford: Clarendon Press, 1986). J.A. Stockwin, *Japan. Divided Politics in a Growth Economy*, 2nd edn (Weidenfeld & Nicolson, 1982) and A.H. Cook, *An Introduction to Japanese Trade Unionism* (New York, Ithaca: Cornell University Press, 1966) for Japan, and G. Wilson, *Unions in American National Politics* (Macmillan, 1979) for the USA are solid introductions.

4 The Decline of Working Class Politics?

The books cited for Chapter 3 contain much on voting behaviour but, in addition, E. Kolinsky, *Parties, Opposition and Society in West Germany* (Croom Helm, 1984), and G. Braunthal, *The West German Social Democrats, 1969–1982. Profile of a Party in Power* (Boulder, Colorado: Westview Press, 1983) are essential for West Germany as are W. Korpi, *The Democratic Class Struggle* (Routledge & Kegan Paul, 1983) and F.G. Castles *The Social Democratic Image of Society* (Routledge & Kegan Paul, 1979) for Sweden. There is a vast literature on British voting behaviour, but D. Butler and D. Stokes, *Political Change in Britain* (Harmondsworth: Penguin, 1971) contains a discussion on the relationship between voting and union membership not present in the 1975 edition, and B. Hindess, *The Decline of Working Class Politics* (Paladin, 1971) though weak on research has an important thesis. B. Sarlvik and I. Crewe, *Decade of Dealignment. The Conservative Victory of 1979 and Electoral Trends in the 1970s* (Cambridge: Cambridge University Press, 1983) covers long-term change. E. Carll-Ladd, *Where Have All the Voters Gone?* 2nd edn (New York: Norton Press, 1982) and D. McKay, *American Politics and Society*, rev. edn (Oxford: Basil Blackwell, 1985) explain US voting behaviour. For Japanese voting behaviour and the role of the unions see J. Watanuki, *Social Structure and Voting Behaviour in Japan* (Tokyo: Sophia University, Institute of International Relations Research Paper A–41, 1980) with his (plus co-authors), *Electoral Behaviour in the 1983 Japanese Elections* (Tokyo: Sophia University, Institute of International Relations, 1983), and K. Steiner *et al.* (eds), *Political Opposition and Local Politics in Japan* (Princeton, N.J.: Princeton University Press, 1980) which contains several useful essays.

5 The Rise and Fall of Corporatism

The literature on corporatism is vast, G.H. Lehmbruch and P.C. Schmitter (eds), *Trends Towards Corporatist Intermediation* (Sage, 1977)

202   *Recommended Reading*

contains several seminal essays but A. Cawson, *Corporatism and Political Theory* (Oxford: Basil Blackwell, 1986) is the best single study. Though by far the most 'corporatist' political system, there is surprisingly little on Sweden. M. Donald-Hancock, *Sweden. The Politics of Post-Industrial Change* (New York: Praeger, 1972) remains the best description of the policy process. A.S. Markovits, *The Politics of West German Trade Unions* describes the evolution of concerted action in detail. Union–government relations in Britain can be studied through K. Middlemas, *Politics in Industrial Society* (Deutsch, 1979) and *Power, Competition and the State. Volume 1, Britain in Search of Balance 1940–1961* (Macmillan, 1986); for more recent developments see A.J. Taylor, *Trade Unions and the Labour Party* (Croom Helm, 1987). The conservative–business dominance of Japanese political process is mapped out by J.A. Stockwin, *Japan. Divided Politics in a Growth Economy* and T.J. Pempel, *Policy and Politics in Japan* (Philadelphia: Temple University Press, 1982). The essay by R.H. Salisbury in Lehmbruch and Schmitter, *Trends Towards Corporatist Intermediation* is worth reading but G. Wilson, *Unions in American National Politics* remains the best introduction to the role of unions as interest groups in the policy process.

6   The Politics of the New Working Class

K. von Beyme, *Challenge to Power* provides an excellent comparative study of white collar unionism, though it excludes Japan. G.S. Bain, D. Coates and V. Ellis, *Social Stratification and Trade Unionism* (Heinemann, 1973) and R. Hyman and R. Price (eds), *The New Working Class. White Collar Workers and Their Organisations* (Macmillan, 1983) are excellent introductions to white-collar unionism. R. Rose (ed.), *Public Employment in Western Nations* (Cambridge: Cambridge University Press, 1985) presents a comprehensive and comparative analysis of public sector growth, and M. Lawn (ed.), *The Politics of Teacher Unionism* (Croom Helm, 1985) contains several useful essays on white-collar–public sector unions. On the consequences of economic crisis for union political influence, the reader is referred to volumes edited by O. Jacobi, P. Gourevitch, R. Edwards, H. Juris, and J. Goldthorpe.

7   Unions, Politics and Power

A comprehensive introduction to theories of trade unionism is M. Poole, *Theories of Trade Unionism*, rev. edn (Routledge & Kegan Paul, 1984) and the classic essay by P. Anderson in R. Blackburn and C. Cockburn (eds), *The Incompatibles. Trade Union Militancy and the Consensus* (Harmondsworth: Penguin 1967) repays careful reading. Marxism is the most challenging analytical tool for studying unions in capitalist society; R. Hyman, *Marxism and the Sociology of Trade Unionism* (Pluto Press, 1971) remains an excellent pamphlet, whilst V.I. Lenin, *What Is To Be*

Done?, first published 1902, is an indispensable source. Apart from polemics the debate on union power is best approached through M. Mann, *Consciousness and Action Amongst the Western Working Class* (Macmillan, 1973) which, though dated, remains very useful and S. Lukes, *Power. A Radical View* (Macmillan, 1974) is indispensable. J. Gaventa, *Power and Powerlessness. Rebellion and Quiescence in an Appalachian Valley* (Oxford: Clarendon Press, 1980) is a brilliant attempt to operationalise Lukes's work, and has importance far beyond its specific concern.

Notes and References

2 Structure, Politics and Ideology

1. J. Hayward, 'Trade Union Movements and their Politico-Economic Framework', in J. Hayward (ed.), *Trade Unions and Politics in Western Europe* (London: Cass, 1980) pp. 1–9. M. Poole, *Industrial Relations. Origins and Patterns of National Diversity* (London: Routledge & Kegan Paul, 1986) provides a useful introduction.
2. R. Michels, *Political Parties*, orig. pub. 1915 (New York: Collier-Macmillan, 1962) sets out the inevitability of oligarchy. Useful studies are, J.D. Goldstein, *The Government of British Trade Unions* (London: Allen & Unwin, 1952), S.M. Lipset, M. Trow and J. Coleman, *Union Democracy* (New York: Free Press, 1956), J. Hemingway, *Conflict and Democracy* (Oxford: Clarendon Press, 1978), W. Galenson, *Trade Union Democracy in Western Europe* (Berkeley: University of California Press, 1962), and A. Carew, *Democracy and Government in European Trade Unions* (London: Allen & Unwin, 1976).
3. A. Flanders, *Management and Unions*, (London: Faber, 1970) pp. 30–1.
4. A.H. Cook, *An Introduction to Japanese Trade Unionism* (New York: Cornell University Press, 1966) p. 98.
5. D. McLaughlin and A.L. Shoomaker, *The Landrum–Griffin Act and Union Democracy* (Ann Arbor: University of Michigan Press, 1979). J. Gaventa, *Power and Powerlessness* (Oxford: Clarendon Press, 1980) examines the situation in one union (the Mineworkers).
6. DGB 1981 Programme, quoted in D. Schuster, *DGB. The German Trade Union Movement* (Bonn: Friedrich Ebert Stiftung, 1985). See also, R.J. Willey, *Democracy in the West German Trade Unions* (London: Sage, 1971).
7. S. Hadenius, *Swedish Politics in the Twentieth Century* (Stockholm: The Swedish Institute, 1981) pp. 131–2.

8. W. Korpi, *The Working Class in Welfare Capitalism* (London: Routledge & Kegan Paul, 1978) pp. 234–6, and L. Lewin, *Governing Swedish Trade Unions* (Cambridge, Mass.: Harvard University Press, 1980).
9. G.K. Wilson, *Unions in American National Politics* (London: Macmillan, 1979) pp. 118–25, and M. Warner and J.D. Edelstein, *Comparative Union Democracy* (New York: Transaction Books, 1978).
10. AFL–CIO, *The Changing Situation of Workers and Their Unions* (Washington: AFL–CIO, 1985) p. 13, and A.R. Schwartz and M.M. Hoyman, 'The Changing of the Guard: The New American Labor Leader', *Annals of the American Academy of Political and Social Science*, 473 (May 1984) pp. 64–75.
11. *Democracy in Trade Unions*, Cmnd. 8778 (February 1983) para. 2, p. 1, and A.J. Taylor, *The Trade Unions and the Labour Party* (London: Croom Helm, 1987) pp. 159–68.
12. T. Shirai, 'Decision-Making in Japanese Unions', in E.F. Vogel (ed.), *Modern Japanese Organisations and Decision Making* (Berkeley: University of California Press, 1975) p. 171, my emphasis, and J. Watanuki *et al.*, *Electorial Behaviour in the 1983 Japanese Elections* (Tokyo: University of Sophia Institute of International Relations, 1986) p. 187.
13. Shirai, 'Decision-Making', p. 184.
14. R. Martin, *The TUC. The Growth of a Pressure Group 1868–1978* (Oxford: Clarendon Press, 1980), and D. Barnes and E. Reid, *Government and Trade Unions* (London: Heinemann/Policy Studies Institute, 1980).
15. Taylor, *The Trade Unions and the Labour Party*, pp. 199–205.
16. Schuster, *DGB*, p. 158.
17. Wilson, *Unions in American National Politics*, p. 187.
18. *AFL–CIO News*, 34(44) (1 November 1986).
19. AFL–CIO, *The Changing Situation*, pp. 22–6.
20. C.M. Rehmus, 'Labor and Politics in the 1980's, *Annals of the American Academy of Political and Social Science*, 473 (May 1984) pp. 40–51, and 'Declining force – increasing power', *The Economist* (14 February 1987) pp. 35–37.
21. *The Swedish Trade Union Confederation* (Stockholm: LO, 1985) p. 15.
22. L.G. Albage, 'Recent Trends in Collective Bargaining in Sweden', *International Labour Review*, 125(1) (Jan–Feb, 1986) p. 116.
23. *TCO 1986–1989 Draft Programme* (Stockholm: TCO, 1985) para. 1.5, p. 1, and, *The Unions and the Party – A Team* (Stockholm: LO, 1984) p. 1.
24. 'Sohyo's Programme', quoted in *Sohyo News*, 360 (15 July 1980) p. 2.
25. A.B. Cole *et al. Socialist Parties in Post-War Japan* (New Haven: Yale University Press, 1966) p. 317, and J.R. Soukup, 'Labor and

Politics in Japan: A Study of Interest Group Attitudes and Activities', *Journal of Politics*, 22 (1960) p. 314.

26.   *Sohyo News*, 360 (15 July 1980) pp. 3, 9.

27.   A. Flanders, 'The Tradition of Voluntarism', *British Journal of Industrial Relations*, 12 (1974) pp. 352–70, M. Rogin, 'Voluntarism: The Political Functions of an Anti-Political Doctrine', *Industrial and Labor Relations Review*, 15(4) (1962) pp. 521–3, and, S. and B. Webb, *Industrial Democracy* (London: Longmans, 1902) Chapters 2 and 4.

28.   *Royal Commission on Trade Unions and Employers' Associations 1965–1968 Report* (Donovan Commission), Cmnd. 3623 (June 1968) para. 40, p. 10.

29.   *Trade Unionism* (London: TUC, 1966) para. 149, p. 36 and para. 174, pp. 68–9, my emphasis.

30.   *TUC Strategy* (London: TUC, 1984) para. 32, p. 11, and Taylor, *The Trade Unions and the Labour Party*, pp. 84–9.

31.   C. Patten, *The Tory Case* (London: Longmans, 1983) p. 129.

32.   *Hands Up For Democracy* (London: TUC, 1983), pp. 3, 10.

33.   AFL–CIO, *The Changing Situation*, pp. 5–6.

34.   *A Guide to Basic Law and Procedures* (Washington: National Labor Relations Board, 1979) p. 55.

35.   H. Holloway, 'Interest Groups in the Post-Partisan Era', *Political Science Quarterly*, 94 (1979) pp. 117–33.

36.   *Department of Labor. 70th Annual Report* (Washington, 1982) pp. 57, 67.

37.   R.L. Trumka (President of the Mineworkers), quoted in the *National Journal*, 16 (19) (12 May 1984) p. 927.

38.   *TCO Draft Programme 1986–89*, para. 1.4, p. 5.

39.   *Swedish Trade Union Confederation*, pp. 3, 6.

40.   *The Basic Agreement*, 'General Grounds for the Basic Agreement' (1938), my emphasis. See also, L. Forseback, *Industrial Relations and Employment in Sweden* (Stockholm: The Swedish Institute, 1981) pp. 10–12.

41.   Schuster, *DGB*, p. 106.

42.   P. Schwerdtner, 'Trade Unions in the German Economic and Social Order', *Zeitschrift für die Gesamte Staatswissenschaft*, 135 (1979) pp. 454–73, and K. Burchardt, *Employment and Social Security in the Federal Republic of Germany* (Bonn: Asgard Verlag, 1980) p. 7.

43.   *The Collective Bargaining System in the Federal Republic of Germany* (Cologne: Bundesvereinigung der Deutschen Arbeitgeberverbande, 1984) pp. 2, 5, my emphasis.

44.   Cook, *An Introduction to Japanese Trade Unionism*, p. 111, and *This Is Sohyo* (Tokyo: Sohyo, 1985) p. 33.

45.   *This Is Sohyo* (Tokyo: Sohyo, 1985) pp. 17, 18.

46.   *Sohyo News*, 360 (15 July 1980) pp. 2–3.

47.   *Sohyo News*, 367 (15 August 1981) p. 12.

48.   *This Is Sohyo* (Tokyo: Sohyo, 1985) p. 45, my emphasis.

3 Trade Unions and Political Parties

1. O Kirchheimer, 'The Transformation of the West European Party Systems', in J. La Palombara and M. Weiner (eds), *Political Parties and Political Development* (Princeton, N.J.: Princeton University Press, 1966) pp. 184–5.
2. W. Freitag (DGB Chairman 1952–5), quoted by R.J. Willey, 'Trade Unions and Political Parties in the Federal Republic of Germany', *Industrial and Labor Relations Review*, 38(8) (February 1974) p. 42, my emphasis.
3. D. Schuster, *DGB. The German Trade Union Movement* (Bonn: Friedrich Ebert Stiftung, 1985) p. 206.
4. A.S. Markovitz, *The Politics of West German Trade Unions* (Cambridge: Cambridge University Press, 1986) p. 24.
5. *The Unions and the Party* (Stockholm: LO, 1985) p. 9.
6. W. Korpi, *The Working Class in Welfare Capitalism* (London: Routledge & Kegan Paul, 1980) p. 83.
7. *The Unions and the Party*, p. 8.
8. *The Swedish Trade Union Confederation* (Stockholm: LO, 1981) p. 8, and L. Forseback, *Industrial Relations and Employment in Sweden* (Stockholm: The Swedish Institute, 1981) p. 105.
9. N. Goran-Myrdal, 'The Swedish Model – Will It Survive?', *British Journal of Industrial Relations*, 28(1) (1980) pp. 57–69, and his 'Collective Wage Earner Funds. A Road to Socialism and the end of Freedom of Association', *International Labor Review* 120(3) (May–June 1981) pp. 319–33.
10. *Welcome To The Labour Party* (London: Labour Party, n.d.) p. 1.
11. For an account of the rise and fall of the Liaison Committee, see A.J. Taylor, *The Trade Unions and the Labour Party* (London: Croom Helm, 1987).
12. Taylor, *The Trade Unions*, pp. 124–32 for TULV and pp. 220–5 for TUCC. For TUFL, see *NEC Report, 1986*, p. 3, and 'Unions Aid Target Seats', *Labour Party News*, 1 (February–March 1987) p. 11.
13. H.M. Drucker, *Doctrine and Ethos in the Labour Party* (London: Allen & Unwin, 1979), and his 'The Influence of the trade unions on the ethos of the Labour Party', in B. Pimlott and C. Cook (eds), *Trade Unions in British Politics* (London: Longmans, 1982) pp. 258–71.
14. R.F. Hoxie, *Trade Unions in the United States* (New York: Appleton Press, 1920) pp. 45–6.
15. Interview with George Meany, *U.S. News and World Report*, 21 (February 1972) p. 31.
16. B. Keller, 'Organized Labor's Vital Signs Show Waning Political Clout; But Numbers Don't Tell All', *Congressional Quarterly Weekly Report*, 40(35) (28 August 1982) p. 2112.
17. These figures are calculated from '1985 Report on Congress', *AFL–CIO News*, 31(7) (15 February 1986).

208   *Notes and References*

18. G.K. Wilson, *Unions in American National Politics* (London: Macmillan, 1979) p. 135.
19. N. Ike, *Japanese Politics. Patron–Client Democracy* 2nd ed. (New York: A. Knopf, 1972) p. 53.
20. R.A. Scalapino, 'Japanese Socialism in Crisis', *Foreign Affairs*, 38(2) (1960) pp. 318, 320, 322.
21. T. Hanami, *Labor Relations in Japan Today* (Tokyo, New York and San Francisco: Kodansha International Ltd, 1981) p. 111, and J.A. Stockwin, *Japan: Divided Politics in a Growth Economy* 2nd edn (London: Weidenfeld & Nicolson, 1982) pp. 163–95.
22. Hanami, *Labor Relations in Japan Today*, pp. 108–10.
23. A. Pelinka, *Social Democratic Parties in Europe* (New York: Praeger, 1983) p. 129.
24. H. Kastendiek, *et al.*, 'Institutional Strategies for Trade Union Participation', in O. Jacobi *et al.* (eds), *Economic Crisis, Trade Unions and The State* (London: Croom Helm, 1986) p. 279.
25. G. Braunthal, 'The Social Democratic Party', in H.G. Peter Wallach and G.K. Romoser (eds), *West German Politics in the Mid-Eighties* (New York: Praeger, 1983) pp. 87–8.
26. M. Linton, *The Swedish Road To Socialism* (London: Fabian Society, 1985) pp. 24–5.
27. *The Unions and the Party – A Team* (Stockholm: LO, 1984), p. 2.
28. 'Walfardstaten' does not have the broadly negative association it has in Anglo–American political culture. Swedish welfare statism is better expressed as 'communal prosperity'. J.D. Stephens, *The Transition from Capitalism to Socialism* (London: Macmillan, 1979) pp. 129–40.
29. Stephens, *The Transition from Capitalism to Socialism*, pp. 177–94, S. Hadenius, *Swedish Politics During the Twentieth Century* (Stockholm: The Swedish Institute, 1985) p. 165, and M. Donald-Hancock, *Sweden. The Politics of Post Industrial Change* (New York: Praeger, 1972) Chapter 8.
30. L. Minkin, *The Labour Party Conference* (Manchester: Manchester University Press, 1980).
31. Taylor, *The Trade Unions*, pp. 132–42.
32. *Industrial Relations Legislation* (London: TUC, 1986), *Britain Will Win. Labour Manifesto 1987*, pp. 13–4, and TUC–Labour Party Liaison Committee, *Work To Win* (London: TUC–Labour Party, 1987) pp. 10–13.
33. Alan Fisher (then NUPE General Secretary), *Labour Party Conference Report 1981*, p. 220.
34. L. Panitch, 'Ideology and Integration: The Case of the British Labour Party', *Political Studies*, 19 (1971).
35. R. Maidment and A. MacGrew, *The American Political Process* (London: Sage, 1987) p. 91.
36. J. Cottin and C. Culhane, 'Committee on Political Education', in J.G. Smith (ed.), *Political Brokers* (New York: Liverright National,

1972), and Wilson, *Unions in American National Politics*, Chapter 2 for COPE's development.

37. AFL–CIO's News Release, Annual Carlson Lecture delivered by Lane Kirkland at the Hubert H. Humphrey Institute of Public Affairs, *Unions and the American Future*, University of Minnesota, Minneapolis (18 November 1983) p. 4.

38. D. Bonafede, 'Labor's Clout', *National Journal*, 15(11) (12 March 1983) p. 569, R. Gurwitt, 'Unions Plan Expanded Efforts to Gain More Political Clout and Elect a President in 1984', *Congressional Quarterly Weekly Reports*, 14(38) (24 September 1983) p. 1918, and D.R. Sweitzer (Democratic National Committee, Director of Finance) to author, 27 May 1987, my emphasis.

39. *Sohyo News*, 360 (15 July 1980) pp. 7–8.

40. *Sohyo News*, 361 (15 September 1980) p. 11.

41. *Sohyo News*, 372 (15 August 1982) pp. 12–13.

42. 'Sohyo's Movement Policy' (12 July 1983), *Sohyo News*, 377 (15 September 1983) pp. 41–2, and 380 (15 July 1984) pp. 10–11.

43. *Sohyo News*, 377 (15 September 1983) p. 8.

44. *Sohyo News*, 377 (15 September 1983) p. 9.

4 The Decline of Working Class Politics

1. R.J. Willey, 'Trade Unions and the Political Parties in the Federal Republic of Germany', *Industrial and Labor Relations Review*, 38(8) (February 1974) p. 43.

2. E. Kolinsky, *Parties, Opposition and Society in West Germany* (London: Croom Helm, 1984) p. 43, my emphasis.

3. Kolinsky, *Parties, Opposition and Society in West Germany*, pp. 81–7.

4. L. Edinger, *Politics in West Germany*, 2nd edn (Boston: Little, Brown & Co, 1977) p. 141.

5. W. Korpi, *The Working Class in Welfare Capitalism* (London: Routledge & Kegan Paul, 1978) pp. 104–6.

6. M. Donald-Hancock, *Sweden. The Politics of Post-Industrial Change* (New York: Praeger, 1972) pp. 180–3, 187–9.

7. *The Unions and the Party – A Team* (Stockholm: LO, 1984), p. 4, my emphasis, and R. Scase, *Social Democracy in Capitalist Society* (London: Croom Helm, 1977) p. 166.

8. Korpi, *The Working Class in Welfare Capitalism*, p. 105.

9. M. Burch and M. Moran, 'The Changing British Political Elite, 1945–1983', *Parliamentary Affairs*, 38(2) (Spring 1985) pp. 1–15, and D. Kavanagh, 'Still the Workers' Party?: Changing Social Trends in Elite Recruitment and Electoral Support', in Kavanagh (ed.), *The Politics of the Labour Party* (London: Allen & Unwin, 1982) pp. 95–107.

10. B. Hindess, *The Decline of Working Class Politics* (London: Paladin, 1971) and his 'The Decline of Working Class Politics: A

Reappraisal', in B. Pimlott and C. Cook (eds), *Trade Unions in British Politics* (London: Longmans, 1982) pp. 237–57.

11.   J.A. Chandler, D.S. Morris, and M.J. Barker, *The Ascent of Middle Class Politics* (unpublished Political Studies Association conference paper, 1982), P. Whiteley, 'Middle Class, Militant and Male', *New Statesman* (6 January 1980) pp. 40–1, and A.J. Taylor, 'The Modern Boroughmongers? The Yorkshire Area (NUM) and Grassroots Politics', *Political Studies*, 32 (1984) pp. 385–400.

12.   K. Coates and T. Topham, *Trade Unions and Politics* (Oxford: Basil Blackwell, 1986) pp. 113–69.

13.   J.A. Center, 'The 1972 Democratic Convention Reforms and Party Democracy', *Political Science Quarterly*, 89 (1974–5) p. 326, 332, 340, 341.

14.   G. Meany, 'Interview', *US News and World Report*, (21 February 1972) p. 31, and G.K. Wilson, *The Unions in American National Politics* (London: Macmillan, 1979) p.44.

15.   J.L. Pressman, D.G. Sullivan and F.C. Arterton, 'Cleavages, Decisions and Legitimisation: The Democrat's Mid-Term Conference, 1974', *Political Science Quarterly*, 91 (1976), for detail.

16.   AFL–CIO, *16th Constitutional Convention Report of the Executive Council, 1985*, p. 89, my emphasis.

17.   *Report of the Executive Council, 1985*, p. 90, my emphasis.

18.   G. Gregg, 'Meany Retirement Pondered As AFL–CIO Chief Nears 85', *Congressional Quarterly Weekly Reports*, 37(30) (28 July 1979) pp. 1505–12, R. Gurwitt, 'Unions Plan Expanded Efforts To Gain More Political Clout and Elect a President in 1984', *Congressional Quarterly Weekly Reports*, 41(38) (24 September 1983) for detail, and Senator Tom Harkin (Democrat, Illinois) quoted in *The Machinist*, XL (November 1985) p. 3.

19.   Union Members To Rate '88 Contenders', *AFL–CIO News*, 32(8) (21 February 1987), and R. Gurwitt, 'Down But Not Out After '84, Labor Stresses Local Contests', *Congressional Quarterly Weekly Reports*, 44(18) (3 May 1986) p. 976.

20.   T. Shirai, 'Japanese Labor Unions and Politics', in Shirai (ed.), *Contemporary Industrial Relations in Japan* (Madison: University of Wisconsin Press, 1983) p. 335.

21.   'A Rude Awakening', *The Economist* (26 July 1986) p. 43.

22.   K. Koshiro, 'Political Power of Labor Unions in the Diet; An Analysis of Results of the Simultaneous Elections for both Upper and Lower Houses held in June 1980', *Japan Labor Bulletin*, 20 (January 1981) pp. 4–8.

23.   A.H. Cook, *Japanese Trade Unionism* (New York, Ithaca: Cornell University Press, 1966) p. 79.

24.   A. Markovitz, *The Politics of West German Trade Unions* (Cambridge: Cambridge University Press, 1986) pp. 82–3, 24.

25.   W.E. Paterson, 'The German Social Democratic Party', in W.E. Paterson and A.H. Thomas (eds), *The Future of Social Democracy* (Oxford: Clarendon Press, 1986) pp. 144–5.

26. G. Braunthal, 'The Social Democratic Party', in H.G. Peter Wallach and G.K. Romoser, *West German Politics in the Mid-Eighties. Crisis and Continuity* (New York: Praeger, 1985) p. 105, and Kolinsky, *Parties, Opposition and Society in West Germany*, pp. 57–9.
27. F.G. Castles, *The Social Democratic Image of Society* (London: Routledge & Kegan Paul, 1979) for a detailed examination.
28. Ole Borre, 'Electoral Instability in Four Nordic Countries', *Comparative Political Studies*, 13(2) (July 1980) pp. 141–71, and J.D. Stephens, 'The Changing Swedish Electorate. Class Voting, Contextual Effects and Voter Volatility', *Comparative Political Studies*, 14(2) (July 1981) pp. 163–204.
29. B. Sarlvik, 'Sweden: The Social Bases of the Parties in a Developmental Perspective', in R. Rose (ed.) *Electoral Behavior: A Comparative Handbook*, (New York: The Free Press, 1974) pp. 387–8, my emphasis, and A.H. Thomas, 'Social Democracy in Scandinavia', in Paterson and Thomas (eds), *The Future of Social Democracy*, pp. 186–7, 188–9.
30. R. Scase, *Social Democracy in Capitalist Society* (London: Croom Helm, 1977), p. 44, and O. Hulton, *Mass Media and State Support in Sweden* (Stockholm: The Swedish Institute, 1979) p. 11.
31. D. Butler and D. Stokes, *Political Change in Britain* (Harmondsworth: Penguin, 1971) pp. 190, 200–2, 212.
32. I. Crewe, 'The Labour Party and the Electorate', in Kavanagh (ed.), *The Politics of the Labour Party*, pp. 9–49, and B. Sarlvik and I. Crewe, *Decade of Dealignment. The Conservative Victory of 1979 and Electoral Trends in the 1970s* (Cambridge: Cambridge University Press, 1983).
33. P. Whiteley, *The Labour Party in Crisis* (London: Methuen, 1983) p. 106, and D. Butler and D. Kavanagh, *The British General Election of 1979* (London: Macmillan, 1980) pp. 339–48.
34. *The Economist* (18 June 1983) p. 27.
35. A.J. Taylor, *The Trade Unions and the Labour Party* (London: Croom Helm, 1987) pp. 252–81.
36. K. Phillips, *The Emerging Republican Majority* (New York: Arlington House, 1969), and R.M. Nixon, *Memoirs* (London: Arrow Books, 1979) pp. 658, 672–73. For the AFL–CIO's view see, *US News and World Report* (21 February 1972) pp. 31–2.
37. Quoted in *National Journal*, 12 (11 January 1980) p. 1835.
38. L.B. Weiss, 'Labor Unions, Split by Battle for Democratic Nomination, Worry About Reagan Inroads', *Congressional Quarterly Weekly Reports*, 38(25) (21 June 1980) p. 1733. See also, J.W. Singer, 'Carter in 1980 – Not Ideal, But Maybe Labor's Best Hope', *National Journal*, 11 (28 July 1979) pp. 1252–5, and, 'Courting the Labor Vote', *National Journal*, 11 (23 October 1979) p. 1815.
39. E. Carll-Ladd, *Where Have All The Voters Gone?* 2nd edn (New York: Norton Press, 1982) p. 38, and M. Glen, 'Labor Trying To

Bring Its Rebellious Members Back To The Democratic Fold',
National Journal, 14(44) (30 October 1982), pp. 1837–40.

40. AFL–CIO, *The Federationist*, 91(4) (1 December 1984) contains a
detailed analysis of AFL–CIO members' voting compared to the
wider electorate. See also, W.H. Wynn, 'The US Elections and the
Unions', *American Labor*, 8 (February 1985) p. 14.

41. J. Watanuki, *et al.*, *Electoral Behavior in the 1983 Japanese
Elections* (Tokyo: Sophia University Institute of International
Relations, 1983) p. 102, my emphasis.

42. G.D. Allinson, 'Opposition in the Suburbs', in K. Steiner *et al.*
(eds), *Political Opposition and Local Politics in Japan* (Princeton,
N.J.: Princeton University Press, 1980) pp. 116–18, and J. Halliday,
A Political History of Japanese Capitalism (New York: Monthly
Review Press, 1975) p. 235.

43. Shirai, 'Japanese Labor Unions and Politics', p. 344.

44. S.C. Flanagan, 'National and Local Voting Trends: Cross Level
Linkages and Correlates of Change', in Steiner *et al.* (eds), *Political
Opposition*, p. 138.

45. J. Watanuki, *Social Structure and Voting Behaviour in Japan*
(Tokyo: Sophia University Institute of International Relations,
Research Paper A–41, 1980) p. 33, my emphasis.

46. V.O. Key Jr, *Politics, Parties and Pressure Groups*, 5th edn (New
York: T.Y. Crowell, 1964) pp. 67–8.

5   The Rise and Fall of Corporatism

1. R. Rose, 'Ungovernability. Is There Fire Behind the Smoke?',
Political Studies, xxvii (1979) pp. 351–70 and R. Rose (ed.),
Challenge to Governance. Studies in Overloaded Politics (London:
Sage, 1980).

2. A. Cawson, *Corporatism and Political Theory* (Oxford: Basil
Blackwell, 1986) surveys the concept, whilst G.H. Lehmbruch and
P.C. Schmitter (eds), *Trends Towards Corporatist Intermediation*
(London: Sage, 1979) contains several seminal essays.

3. A. Lindbeck, *Swedish Economic Policy* (London: Macmillan,
1975) Chapters 4 and 8, and A. Martin, 'Trade Unions in Sweden:
Strategic Response to Change and Crisis', in P. Gourevitch, A.
Martin, G. Ross, S. Bornstein, A. Markovits, and C. Allen (eds),
Unions and Economic Crisis: Britain, West Germany and Sweden
(London: Allen & Unwin, 1984) pp. 193–218.

4. A.S. Markovits, *The Politics of West German Trade Unions*
(Cambridge: Cambridge University Press, 1986) pp. 61–93, and
A.S. Markovits and C.S. Allen, 'Trade Unions and Economic
Crisis: The West German Case', in Gourevitch *et al.* (eds), *Unions
and Economic Crisis*, pp. 94–102.

5. D. Schuster, *DGB. The German Trade Union Movement* (Bonn:
Friedrich Ebert Stiftung, 1984) p. 158.

6. K. Burgess, *The Challenge of Labour* (London: Croom Helm, 1980), K. Middlemas, *Politics in Industrial Society* (London: Deutsch, 1979), and D. Barnes and E. Reid, *Government and Trade Unions. The British Experience, 1964–1979* (London: Heinemann/PSI, 1980).
7. S.B. Levine, *Industrial Relations in Japan* (Urbana: University of Illinois Press, 1958), and E. Harari, *The Politics of Labor Legislation in Japan* (Berkeley: University of California Press, 1973) discuss in detail the origins and development of the post-war union–government relationship.
8. C.L. Tomlins, *The State and the Unions. Labor Relations, Law and the Organized Labor Movement in America, 1880–1960* (Cambridge: Cambridge University Press, 1985) pp. 317–28, and R. Edwards and M. Podgursky, 'The Unravelling Accord: American Unions in Crisis', in R. Edwards, P. Garonna, and F. Todtling (eds), *Unions in Crisis and Beyond: Perspectives from Six Countries* (Dover, Mass.: Auburn House Publishing, 1986) pp. 19–28.
9. C. Ham and M. Hill, *The Policy Process in the Modern Capitalist State* (Brighton: Wheatsheaf Books, 1984) provides the basis for the conception of the policy process used in this section. More specifically on the role of interest groups see, A.R. Ball and F. Millward, *Pressure Politics in Industrial Societies. A Comparative Introduction* (London: Macmillan, 1986) especially Chapters 1 and 2.
10. M. Micheletti, *The Involvement of Swedish Labor Market Organizations in the Swedish Political Process*, Occasional Paper 18 (Stockholm: Business & Social Research Institute, 1984) provides an overview of LO involvement.
11. M. Donald-Hancock, *Sweden. The Politics of Post-Industrial Change* (New York: Praeger, 1972) p. 157.
12. A. Lindstrom, *The Swedish Parliamentary System* (Stockholm: The Swedish Institute, 1982) p. 81, and Donald-Hancock, *Sweden* pp. 158–9.
13. G.K. Roberts, *West German Politics* (London: Macmillan, 1972) pp. 67–72, and L. Edinger, *Politics in West Germany* 2nd edn (Boston: Little, Brown & Co., 1978) pp. 232–3, 278–81.
14. W.E. Patersom, 'The Chancellor and his Party: Political Leadership in the Federal Republic', *West European Politics*, 4 (1981) pp. 3–17.
15. D.J. Toscano, 'Labor–Management Cooperation and the West German System of Codetermination', *Industrial Relations Journal*, 12 (1981) pp. 57–67. M. Alexis, 'Neo-Corporatism and Industrial Relations: The Case of German Trade Unions', *West European Politics* 6 (1983) pp. 75–92, and Markovits and Allen, 'Trade Unions and Economic Crisis', pp. 133–41.
16. J.J. Richardson and A.G. Jordan, *Governing Under Pressure. The Policy Process in a Post-Parliamentary Democracy* (Oxford: Martin Robertson, 1979) Section II, pp. 77–153.

17. K. Coates and T. Topham, *Trade Unions and Politics* (Oxford: Basil Blackwell, 1986) p. 34.
18. L. Panitch, *Social Democracy and Industrial Militancy* (Cambridge: Cambridge University Press, 1976), and H. Harris, *Competition and the Corporate Society* (London: Methuen, 1972).
19. C. Crouch, *The Politics of Industrial Relations* (London: Fontana, 1979) p. 169.
20. *Trade Unionism*, 2nd edn (London: TUC, 1967) para. 168, p. 66.
21. J.A. Stockwin, *Japan: Divided Politics in a Growth Economy*, 2nd edn (London: Weidenfeld & Nicolson, 1982) pp. 92–7. On the nature of the Japanese political process, see C. Yanaga, *Big Business in Japan* (New Haven: Yale University Press, 1968), H. Fukui, *Party in Power* (Berkeley: University of California Press, 1970), N.B. Thayer, *How The Conservatives Rule Japan* (Princeton, N.J.: Princeton University Press, 1960), and, E. Harari, *The Politics of Labor Legislation in Japan* (Berkeley: University of California Press, 1973).
22. T. Shirai, 'Japanese Labor Unions and Politics', in Shirai (ed.), *Contemporary Industrial Relations in Japan* (Madison: University of Wisconsin Press, 1983) p. 347, and, H. Fukui, 'Studies in Policymaking: A Review of the Literature', in T.J. Pempel (ed.), *Policymaking in Contemporary Japan* (Ithaca: Cornell University Press, 1977) p. 33, my emphasis.
23. Stockwin, *Japan: Divided Politics in a Growth Economy*, p. 158, and C. Johnson, *MITI and the Japanese Miracle. The Growth of Industrial Policy, 1925–1975* (Stanford: Stanford University Press, 1982).
24. T.J. Pempel and K. Tsunekawa, 'Corporatism Without Labor?', in Lehmbruch and Schmitter (eds), *Trends*, p. 231–70, and Japan Institute of Labor, *Labor Unions and Labor-Management Relations* (Tokyo: JIL, 1983) p. 23.
25. Japan Institute of Labor, *Labor Unions*, p. 31, my emphasis.
26. R.H. Salisbury, 'Why No Corporatism in America?', in Lehmbruch and Schmitter (eds), *Trends*, pp. 213–30.
27. A. Ehrenhalt, 'The AFL–CIO: How Much Clout in Congress?', *Congressional Quarterly Weekly Reports*, 23(29) (1979) and H. Holloway, 'Interest Groups in the Post Partisan Era: The Political Machine of the AFL–CIO', *Political Science Quarterly*, 94 (1979) p. 125.
28. G.K. Wilson, *Unions in American National Politics* (London: Macmillan, 1979) pp. 59–60, and C.H. Rehmus, 'Labor and Politics in the 1980s', *Annals of the American Academy of Political and Social Science*, 473 (May 1984) pp. 41–2.
29. M.D. Pohlmann and G.S. Crisci, 'Support for Organized Labor in the House of Representatives: The 89th and 95th Congresses', *Political Science Quarterly* 97, (1982) p. 641, J.W. Singer, 'Labor and Congress – New Isn't Necessarily Better', *National Journal*, 10(9) (4 March 1978) pp. 351–3, and J.W. Singer, 'The AFL–CIO's

Ken Young Looks For Better Times on the Hill', *National Journal*, 11(6) (10 February 1979) pp. 224–5.

30. Union official quoted in *Congressional Quarterly Weekly Reports*, 43(12) (23 March 1985) p. 549.

31. B. Keller, 'Executive Agency Lobbyists Mastering the Difficult Art of Congressional Liaison', *Congressional Quarterly Weekly Reports*, 39(49) (4 December 1981) pp. 2387–92.

32. P. Lange, 'Unions, Workers and Wage Regulation: the Rational Bases of Consent', in J.H. Goldthorpe (ed.), *Order and Conflict in Contemporary Capitalism. Studies in the Political Economy of Western Nations* (Oxford: Clarendon Press, 1984) pp. 98–123. The problem of rational behaviour is discussed extensively in C. Crouch, *Trade Unions. The Problem of Collective Action* (London: Fontana, 1982).

33. See President Carter's statement in, *Congressional Quarterly Weekly Reports*, 26(15) (15 April 1977) pp. 897–8.

34. R.J. Samuelson, 'No Hip-Hoorays for Coal', *National Journal*, 10(9) (4 March 1978) p. 355, and his, 'Maybe a Blessing in Disguise', *National Journal*, 10(12) (25 March 1978) pp. 468–70.

35. J.W. Singer, 'Courting the Labor Vote', *National Journal*, 11(43) (23 October 1979) p. 1815.

36. R.J. Samuelson, 'Guidelines in a Shambles', *National Journal*, 11(25) (23 June 1979) p. 1049.

37. Edwards and Podgursky, 'The Unravelling Accord', p. 34.

38. J. Barbash, 'Trade Unionism From Roosevelt to Reagan', *Annals of the American Academy of Political and Social Science*, 473 (May 1984) pp. 11–22.

39. *Report of the AFL–CIO Executive* (October 1985) p. 34.

40. K. Middlemas, *Power, Competition and the State, Volume 1, Britain in Search of Balance, 1940–1961* (London: Macmillan, 1986) analyses the attempts to maintain the 1944 settlement.

41. M. Moran, *The Politics of Industrial Relations* (London: Macmillan, 1977) analyses the move to legal solutions to the union problem in the 1960s.

42. G.A. Dorfman, *Government Versus Trade Unionism in British Politics Since 1968* (London: Macmillan, 1979) pp. 72–86, and A.J. Taylor, *The Trade Unions and the Labour Party* (London: Croom Helm, 1987) which deals in detail with the Social Contract.

43. J. Barbash, *Trade Unions and National Economic Policy* (Baltimore: Johns Hopkins University Press, 1972) pp. 81–110, and J. Bergmann and M. Muller-Jentsch, 'The Federal Republic of Germany: Cooperative Unionism and the Dual Bargaining System Challenged', in S. Barkin (ed.), *Worker Militancy and Its Consequences* (New York: Praeger, 1975) pp. 235–276.

44. J. Clark, 'Concerted Action in the Federal Republic of Germany', *British Journal of Industrial Relations*, 17 (1979) pp. 242–58 and M. Hudson, 'Concerted Action in the Federal Republic of Germany, 1976–1977', *Industrial Relations Journal*, 11 (1980) pp. 5–16.

45. 1981 DGB Programme in Schuster, *DGB*, pp. 151–2, and G.

Lehmbruch, 'Liberal Corporatism and Party Government', in Lehmbruch and Schmitter (eds), *Trends*, pp. 147–83.

46.   A.S. Markovits and C.S. Allen, 'Trade Unions and Economic Crisis', pp. 142–72.

47.   Lindbeck, *Swedish Economic Policy*, pp. 25–49, A Schonfield, *Modern Capitalism* (Oxford: Oxford University Press/RIIA, 1969) pp. 199–211, and L. Forseback, *Industrial Relations and Employment in Sweden* (Stockholm: The Swedish Institute, 1980) pp. 68–73.

48.   K. Lundmark, 'Welfare State and Employment Policy: Sweden', in K. Dyson and S. Wilks (eds), *Industrial Crisis* (Oxford: Basil Blackwell, 1983) pp. 220–4, L.G. Albage, 'Recent Trends in Collective Bargaining' *International Labor Review*, 125(1) (1986) pp. 119–32, and 'The Swedish Collective Bargaining System in Transition', *Current Sweden*, 337 (August 1985) pp. 2–4.

49.   This is discussed in K. Ahlen, 'Recent Trends in Swedish Collective Bargaining: The Collapse of the Swedish Model', *Current Sweden*, 358 (March 1988) pp. 1–8.

50.   K. Maekwa, 'Labour Union Movement and "Shunto" (Spring Campaign) in Japan', *Kyoto University Economic Review*, XLIX (April–October 1979) pp. 1–12.

51.   OECD, *Economic Survey of Japan* (Paris: OECD, 1973) p. 65, my emphasis.

52.   T. Inagami, 'Labor Front Unification and Zenmin Rokyo: The Emergence of Neo-Corporatism', *Japan Labor Bulletin*, 25(5) (May 1986) pp. 5–8.

6   The Politics of the New Working Class

1.   *20th World Congress of International Federation of Commercial, Clerical, Professional and Technical Employees* (FIET), Report (21–25 November 1983) p. 42 and K. von Beyme, *Challenge to Power. Trade Unions and Industrial Relations in Capitalist Countries* (London: Sage, 1980) p. 51.

2.   R. Price, 'Introduction to Part II. The Development and Character of White-Collar Unionism', in R. Hyman and R. Price (eds), *The New Working Class. White Collar Workers and Their Organizations* (London: Macmillan, 1983) p. 174. G. Bain, D. Coates and V. Ellis, *Social Stratification and Trade Unionism* (London: Heinemann, 1973) p. 67 remains an excellent introduction.

3.   E.M. Kassalow, 'White Collar Unionism in the United States', in A. Sturmthal (ed.), *White Collar Trade Unionism* (Urbana: University of Illinois, 1966) pp. 305–64, C. Wright-Mills, *White-Collar. The American Middle Classes* (New York: Oxford University Press, 1956) pp. 301–23, and J. Kocka, *White Collar Workers in America 1890–1940* (London: Sage, 1980).

4.   S.B. Levine, 'The White-Collar/Blue-Collar Alliance in Japan', *Industrial Relations* V(1) (1965) pp. 103–15, S.B. Levine, 'Union-

ization of White-Collar Employees in Japan', in, Sturmthal (ed.), *White Collar Trade Unionism*, pp. 205–60, and *This Is Sohyo* (Tokyo: Sohyo 1985) p. 58.

5. A.H. Nilstein, 'White-Collar Unionism in Sweden', in Sturmthal (ed.), *White Collar Trade Unionism*, pp. 261–304, and E.M. Kassalow, 'Professional Unionism in Sweden', *Industrial Relations*, 8(2) (1969) pp. 119–34.

6. G.S. Bain and R. Price, 'Union Growth and Employment Trends in the United Kingdom 1964–1970', *British Journal of Industrial Relations*, 10 (November 1972) pp. 366–81, R. Price and G.S. Bain, 'Union Growth Revisited, 1948–1974 in Perspective', *British Journal of Industrial Relations*, 14 (November 1976) pp. 339–355, G.S. Bain, *The Growth of White-Collar Unionism* (Oxford: Clarendon Press, 1970), and G. Routh, 'White Collar Unions in the United Kingdom', in Sturmthal (ed.), *White Collar Unionism*, pp. 165–204.

7. G. Hartfiel, 'Germany', in Sturmthal (ed.), *White Collar Trade Unionism*, pp. 127–64, and H. Bayer, Hans-Ekert Treu and I.L. Roberts, 'White Collar Unionisation in West Germany, 1960–1976', *Industrial Relations Journal*, 11 (1980) pp. 63–73.

8. A. Giddens, *The Class Structure of the Advanced Societies* (London: Hutchinson, 1973) p. 196. See also, S. Mallet, *The New Working Class* (Nottingham: Spokesman Books, 1975), A. Touraine, *The Post-Industrial Society* (London: Wildwood House, 1974), and A. Gorz, *Farewell To the Working Class* (London: Pluto Press, 1982).

9. A.J. Taylor, *The Trade Unions and the Labour Party* (London: Croom Helm, 1987) pp. 152–98. The data is from *Attitudes Amongst Trade Unionists* (London: MORI, August 1987).

10. T.A. Kochan, 'How American Workers View Labor Unions', *Monthly Labor Review*, 102 (1979) p. 27 and, *AFL–CIO Federationist*, 91(4) (1 December 1984) for electoral data.

11. J. Watanuki, *Social Structure and Voting Behaviour in Japan*, Research Paper A–41 (Tokyo: Institute of International Relations, Sophia University, 1980) pp. 27–8, and Watanuki *et al.*, *Electoral Behaviour In The 1983 Japanese Elections* (Tokyo: Institute of International Relations, Sophia University, 1986) Post-Election Survey (House of Councillors) (July 1983) questions 21, 33, 33SQ1, 33SQ3, 42–4, 42–7, 42–8, 44, 44–2, and AQ2. Pre-Election Survey (House of Representatives) (December 1983) question 23, 23SQ2 and 23SQ3. Post-Election Survey (House of Representatives) (December 1983) question 23, 30, 38, 40 and 52.

12. DAG 1971 Social Programme in *The Trade Union Movement in West Germany* (Brussels: EEC DG X/53/82EN) p. 21 and, von Beyme, *Challenge To Power*, pp. 47–9.

13. *Draft Programme 1986–1989* (Stockholm: TCO, 1985) pp. 2–5, and *Facts About Motions, Reports and Programmes. TCO Congress 1985* (Stockholm: TCO, 1984) for details.

14. S.G. Peitchinis, *Issues in Management–Labour Relations in the*

218   *Notes and References*

1990s (London: Macmillan, 1985) pp. 97–112, R. Rose and B. Guy-Peters, *Can Government Go Bankrupt?* (London: Macmillan, 1979) pp. 106–32.

15.   B. Guy-Peters, 'Sweden', in R. Rose (ed.), *Public Employment in Western Europe* (Cambridge: Cambridge University Press, 1985), pp. 203–27.

16.   *Enterprise For the 80s. Declarations and Resolutions of the 1977 Congress* (Stockholm: SAF, 1977), *A Creative Sweden or a Defensive One?* (Stockholm: SAF, 1980) p. 4, and K.O. Faxen, *The Limits to Public Sector Expenditure* (Stockholm: Arbetslivcentrum, 1981), J. Larsson, *Turning Point* (Stockholm: Timbro Publishing 1984), and *A Creative Sweden. People and Enterprises* (Stockholm: SAF, 1984) pp. 26–28.

17.   *The Swedish Budget 1985–86* (Stockholm: Ministry of Finance, 1985) p. 18.

18.   B. Guy-Peters, 'The United States: Absolute Change and Relative Decline', in, Rose (ed.), *Public Employment*, pp. 228–61.

19.   L. Troy, 'White Collar Organisation in the Federal Service', in A.A. Blum *et al.*, *White Collar Workers* (New York: Random House, 1971) for EO10988.

20.   J.W. Singer, 'The Limited Power of Federal Workers Unions', *National Journal*, 10(39) (30 September 1978) pp. 1547–51, J. Steiber, *Public Employee Unionism* (Washington: Brookings Institute, 1973) pp. 193–211, M. Glen, 'Labor looking to Local Unions to Turnout Rank and File for Mondale', *National Journal*, 16(39) (29 September 1984) pp. 1825–6, and *Final Report for '84 Elections* (Washington: Federal Electoral Commission, 1 December 1985).

21.   W.J. Lanouette, 'Sending Labor A Message', *National Journal* 13(34) (22 August 1981) p. 1515, and *AFL–CIO News*, 31(29) (27 September 1986) p. 15 and 32(24) (13 June 1987) p. 6, and S. Smith, 'Stalemate Looms on the Hill over Federal Workers Issues', *CQWR*, 14(2) (30 April 1983) p. 833.

22.   AFL–CIO, *Executive Council Report* (28 October 1985) pp. 336–40, and *One Country. . . Two Different Worlds* (AFL–CIO Public Employees Dept, February 1987) pp. 1–11.

23.   K.D. Schmidt and R. Rose, 'Germany: The Expansion of an Active State', in Rose (ed.), *Public Employment*, pp. 126–62.

24.   Von Beyme, *Challenge to Power*, p. 199, and A.S. Markovits, *The Politics of West German Unions* (Cambridge: Cambridge University Press, 1986), p. 11, my emphasis.

25.   D. Schuster, *DGB* (Bonn: Friedrich Ebert Stiftung, 1983) pp. 199–200.

26.   *Preserving Creation, Mastering the Tasks of the Future. Government Policy 1987–1990* (Bonn: Press and Information Office of the Federal Government, March 1987) pp. 19, 21 and 23–5.

27.   Y. Matsuda, 'Government Employees in Japan(I)', *Japan Labor Bulletin* 5 (1966) p. 7, and H. Ota, 'Political Teacher Unionism in Japan', in M. Lawn (ed.), *The Politics of Teacher Unionism*

(London: Croom Helm, 1987) pp. 103–40, my emphasis.

28. T.J. Pempel, *Policy and Politics in Japan* (Philadelphia: Temple University Press, 1982) p. 101 and K. Yamaguchi, 'The Public Sector: Civil Servants', in T. Shirai (ed.), *Contemporary Industrial Relations in Japan* (Madison: University of California Press, 1973).

29. Watanuki, *Electoral Behavior in the 1983 Japanese Elections*, questions 61–1, 61–2, p. 166.

30. R. Parry, 'Britain: Stable Aggregates, Changing Composition', in Rose (ed.), *Public Employment* pp. 54–96.

31. M.P. Kelly, *White-Collar Proletariat. The Industrial Behaviour of British Civil Servants* (London: Routledge & Kegan Paul, 1980).

32. A.J. Taylor, 'The Politics of Non-Partisan Trade Unionism. The British Case', *Politics* 7(1) (April 1986) pp. 8–13.

33. *The Next Moves Forward*, Conservative Party Manifesto 1987, p. 5. See also, M. Moran, 'Industrial Relations', in, H. Drucker *et al.* (eds), *Developments in British Politics 2* (London: Macmillan, 1986) pp. 279–94 and J. MacInnes, *Thatcherism at Work* (Milton Keynes: Open University Press, 1987) pp. 136–59.

34. P. Basset, *Strike Free. New Industrial Relations in Britian* (London: Macmillan, 1987) pp. 44–64, and Taylor, *The Trade Unions and the Labour Party*, pp. 152–98.

35. *TUC Strategy* (London: TUC, 1984) para. 28, p. 10, para. 38, p. 13, and para. 45, p. 15.

36. R. Edwards and M. Podgursky, 'The Unravelling Accord: American Unions in Crisis', in R. Edwards, P. Garonna and F. Todtling (eds), *Unions in Crisis and Beyond: Perspective from Six Countries* (Dover, Mass.: Auburn House, 1986) pp. 14–160, and K. Moody, 'Reagan, the Business Agenda and the Collapse of Labour', *The Socialist Register 1986* (edited by R. Miliband and J. Saville. London: Merlin Press, 1986) pp. 133–76.

37. *NLRB 47th Annual Report 1982* (Washington: USGPO, 1986) pp. 1–15 provides an overview of the NLRB's operations, and *Department of Labor 70th Annual Report, 1982* (Washington: USGPO, 1982) pp. i, v.

38. 'Review Symposium: The Transformation of American Industrial Relations', *Industrial and Labor Relations Review*, 41 (April 1988) pp. 439–55.

39. *The Changing Situation of Workers and their Unions* (Washington: AFL–CIO 1985) pp. 14–116, and *Report of the AFL–CIO Executive Council 1985*, p. 75.

40. O. Jacobi, 'Economic Development and Trade Union Collective Bargaining Policy Since the Middle of the 1970s', in O. Jacobi *et al.* (eds), *Economic Crisis, Trade Unions and the State* (London: Croom Helm, 1986) pp. 213–14, and Jacobi, 'World Economic Changes and Industrial Relations in the Federal Republic of Germany', in H. Juris *et al.*, *Industrial Relations in a Decade of Change* (Industrial Relations Research Association Series: Madison: University of Wisconsin, 1985) p. 221.

41. Jacobi, 'World Economic Changes', p. 245.
42. A.S. Markovits, 'Introduction', in Markovits (ed.), *the Political Economy of West Germany* (New York: Praeger, 1986) p. 6.
43. A.S. Markovits, *The Politics of West German Trade Unions* (Cambridge: Cambridge University Press, 1986) pp. 413–14.
44. A. Schonfield, *Modern Capitalism* (London: Oxford University Press/RIIA, 1969) p. 205, my emphasis. This section depends heavily on K. Ahlen, 'Recent Trends in Swedish Collective Bargaining: The Collapse of the Swedish Model', *Current Sweden*, 358 (March 1988) and her, 'Recent Trends in Swedish Collective Bargaining: Heading Towards Negotiated Incomes Policy', *Current Sweden*, 359 (March 1988).
45. C. Goran-Kjellander, 'National Political Issues for 1984–1985 Session of the Riksdag', *Current Sweden*, 326 (October 1984) pp. 3–4, and M. Haag, 'The Swedish Economy in the Right Direction', *Current Sweden*, 333 (May 1986) p. 6.
46. 'The Swedish Collective Bargaining System in Transition', *Current Sweden*, 337 (August 1985) p. 6, my emphasis.
47. T. Ono, 'Low Growth Rates and the 1975 Spring Labor Offensive (I)', *Japan Labor Bulletin*, 14 (1 May 1975) pp. 7–10.
48. T. Ono, 'Low Growth Rates and the 1975 Spring Labor Offensive (II) The New Formula', *Japan Labor Bulletin*, 14 (1 July 1975) pp. 4–8.
49. K. Koshiro, 'Anti-Inflationary Wage Determination Under Free Collective Bargaining in Japan from 1974 to 1976', *Japan Labor Bulletin*, 15 (6 June 1976) pp. 5–7, 'The 1977 Spring Offensive: Symbolising a Shift in the Theories of the Japanese Labor Movement', *Japan Labor Bulletin*, 16 (5 July 1977) pp. 5–8 and, OECD, *Economic Survey of Japan* (Paris: OECD, 1986) p. 66.
50. OECD, *Economic Survey of Japan*, p. 90. Dispatched workers are workers surplus to a company's needs who are transferred to another company.

7 Unions, Power and Politics

1. G.K. Roberts, *What Is Comparative Politics?* (London: Macmillan, 1972), and A.C. MacIntyre, 'Is a science of comparative politics possible?', in P.G. Lewis, *et al.* (eds), *The Practice of Comparative Politics*, 2nd edn (London: Longman, 1978) pp. 266–84.
2. D.G. Garson, *Group Theories of Politics* (London: Sage, 1978) and P. Dunleavy and B. O'Leary, *Theories of the State: The Politics of Liberal Democracy* (London: Macmillan, 1987) Chapter 2.
3. G. Parry, *Political Elites* (London: Allen & Unwin, 1971) and Dunleavy and O'Leary, *Theories of the State*, Chapter 4.
4. Dunleavy and O'Leary, *Theories of the State*, Chapter 5, and R. Hyman, *Marxism and the Sociology of Trade Unionism* (London: Pluto Press, 1971).

5. A. Cawson, *Corporatism and Political Theory* (Oxford: Basil Blackwell, 1986), and W. Grant (ed.), *The Political Economy of Corporatism* (London: Macmillan, 1985) Chapters 1–3.

6. M. Olson, *The Logic of Collective Action* (Cambridge, Mass.: Harvard University Press, 1965), and C. Crouch, *Trade Unions. The Logic of Collective Action* (London: Fontana, 1982).

7. S. and B. Webb, *Industrial Democracy* (London: Longmans, 1978) p. 1, and M. Poole, *Theories of Trade Unionism. A Sociology of Industrial Relations*, rev. edn (London: Routledge & Kegan Paul, 1984). See also the classic article, P. Anderson, 'The Limits and Possibilities of Trade Union Action', in, R. Blackburn and C. Cockburn (eds), *The Incompatibles. Trade Union Militancy and the Consensus* (Harmondworth: Penguin, 1967), pp. 273–90.

8. W. Korpi, *The Working Class in Welfare Capitalism* (London: Routledge & Kegan Paul, 1978) Chapter 1, and J. Downing, 'Grave Diggers Difficulties: Ideology and Class Struggle in Advanced Capitalism', in R. Scase (ed.), *Industrial Society: Class Cleavage and Control* (London: Allen & Unwin, 1977) pp. 122–35.

9. F. Engels, *The Condition of the Working Class in England*, first published 1844 (London: Panther, 1969) p. 251. T. Clarke and L. Clements (eds), *Trade Unions Under Capitalism* (Glasgow: Fontana, 1977) contains a number of important articles. R. Hyman, *Marxism and the Sociology of Trade Unionism* (London: Pluto Press, 1971) and his *Industrial Relations. A Marxist Introduction* (London: Macmillan, 1975) examine these themes.

10. K. Marx, 'Wages, Prices and Profits', in K. Marx and F. Engels, *Selected Works in One Volume* (London: Lawrence & Wishart, 1970) p. 223.

11. Marx to E. Bolte (23 November 1871) in *Selected Works*, p. 673.

12. R. Dahrendorf, *Class and Class Conflict in an Industrial Society* (London: Routledge & Kegan Paul, 1959) pp. 267–79, and T. Nichols (ed.), *Capital and Labour* (Glasgow: Fontana 1980).

13. V.I. Lenin, *What Is To Be Done?* (Peking: Foreign Languages Publishing House, 1973) pp. 67, 75. See also, V.I. Lenin, *On Trade Unions* (Moscow: Progress Publishers, 1970) for a comprehensive picture of Lenin's writings on trade unions.

14. K. Marx, 'The Chartists', in *Surveys From Exile* (Harmondsworth: Penguin, 1973) p. 264.

15. V.I. Lenin, *British Labour and British Imperialism* (London: Lawrence & Wishart, 1969) p. 263.

16. A. Giddens, *The Class Structure of the Advanced Societies* (London: Hutchinson, 1973) p. 202, original emphasis.

17. M. Mann, *Consciousness and Action Amongst the Western Working Class* (London: Macmillan, 1973) p. 13.

18. Mann, *Consciousness and Action*, Chapter 6.

19. S. Lukes, *Power. A Radical View* (London: Macmillan, 1974) pp. 18, 20, 23–4, original emphasis. This section also uses B. Burkitt, 'Excessive trade union power: existing reality or contemporary

myth', *Industrial Relations Journal*, 12 (1981) pp. 65–71 which stresses the weakness of unions, and S.E. Finer, 'The Political Power of Organised Labour', *Government and Opposition*, 9 (1973) pp. 391–406.

20.   *Selections From the Prison Notebooks of Antonio Gramsci*, edited and translated by Q. Hoare and G. Nowell-Smith (London: Lawrence & Wishart, 1971) pp. 180–2, my emphasis, and R. Simon, *Gramsci's Political Thought* (London: Lawrence & Wishart, 1982) pp. 29–32, 67–77.

21.   D. Howell, 'Docile Diggers and Russian Reds: Contrasts in Working Class Politics', *Political Studies*, 29(3) (1981) p. 455–63, the quote is from p. 456, my emphasis.

22.   R. Brownstein, 'Labor Wants Respect', *National Journal*, 17(44) (2 November 1985) p. 44.

Index

223